The Thesis Writer's Handbook

A Complete One-Source Guide For Writers Of Research Papers

by
Joan I. Miller and Bruce J. Taylor

Alcove Publishing Company
West Linn, Oregon

Additional copies of this handbook may be obtained by mail.
Send check or money order for $10.95 plus $1.00 postage and
handling ($11.95 total) for each copy to Alcove Publishing
Company, P.O. Box 362, West Linn, Oregon 97068.

PRINTED IN THE UNITED STATES OF AMERICA

Library of Congress Cataloging-in-Publication Data

Miller, Joan I., 1958-
    The thesis writer's handbook.

    Includes index.
    1. Dissertations, Academic—Handbooks, manuals, etc.
2. Report writing—Handbooks, manuals, etc. 3. Research
—Handbooks, manuals, etc.   I. Taylor, Bruce J.,
1932-   . II. Title.
LB2369.M455 1987   808'.02   86-17290
ISBN 0-937473-12-X

To John Keefauver
Writer, journalist, poet,
and caretaker of the sunsets
at Carmel-by-the-Sea

The authors gratefully acknowledge the following individuals and institutions for their assistance during the writing of this handbook: For reading the text in manuscript and contributing valuable suggestions for its improvement; Thomas Gething, U. of Hawaii at Manoa and N. Joy Parton, Colorado State U., Fort Collins. *For reading the Punctuation Manual in manuscript and giving us the benefit of his expertise;* James P. Estes of Salem, Oregon. *For their generously given time and professional assistance;* Librarian Pam Williams and her staff at the West Linn Public Library. *For contributing style manuals for study during the research phase of this project, the graduate departments of the following schools;* U. of Alabama, U. of Arizona, Brigham Young U., Brown U., U. of California at Berkeley, U. of California at Chico, California State U. at Davis, U. of California at Irvine, Colorado State U., Columbia U., Cornell U., Florida State U., U. of Georgia, Harvard U., U. of Hawaii at Manoa, U. of Idaho, Indiana U., U. of Iowa, U. of Kansas, U. of Kentucky, U. of Maine at Orono, U. of Maryland, U. of Michigan, U. of Minnesota, Mississippi State U., U. of Southern Mississippi, Northwestern U., U. of North Carolina, Ohio State U., U. of Oklahoma, Old Dominion U., Oregon State U., U. of Oregon, Pennsylvania State U., Princeton U., Radford U., Rutgers U., SUNY at Stony Brook, U. of North Carolina, Texas A&M U., Texas Woman's U., Yale U.

CONTENTS

iv

LIST OF FIGURES

LIST OF FIGURES (cont.)

LIST OF TABLES

INTRODUCTION

A master's thesis is a formidable project for most graduate students; but it doesn't have to be. By the time you reach the graduate studies level, you have already acquired most of the knowledge and skills you will need to successfully write this important document. What you need now is to: (1) develop an understanding of the function of thesis writing, and determine how you, the thesis writer, must proceed within the academic system; (2) obtain detailed organizational and typing directions for the format of your thesis; and (3) acquire a clearly defined set of instructions to document your work in a manner acceptable to your university.

We have organized *The Thesis Writer's Handbook* around these three needs. The first eleven chapters will guide you through the procedural steps required to write a master's thesis.

Chapters 12 through 16 describe the typing format and page sequence specifications required by the majority of university style guides. These instructions should carry you through this phase of thesis writing with confidence, allowing you more opportunity to concentrate on the content of your project rather than on its physical form.

For documentation guidance, Chapters 17 and 18 contain detailed descriptions of the Chicago, MLA, and APA documentation styles, the three formats most often required by American universities. Chapter 19 contains an extensive compendium of footnote and bibliography entry examples you may use as models for your documentation listings. These chapters are designed to reduce the subject of documentation to what we feel it should be: an exercise in accurately recording the resources used for your writing, as opposed to a confusing challenge of interpretation presented by most texts on this subject.

The information in Chapters 12 through 19 is applicable to university term papers and doctoral dissertations as well as master's theses.

In *The Thesis Writer's Handbook*, the term "thesis" is used in its generic sense: as a position or proposition the writer advances, and offers to support by argument. This is the core of all term papers, master's theses, and doctoral dissertations. The purpose of these papers is to provide the student author with opportunities to learn and practice the skills required for organized research and documentation, analysis of information, and effective written communications. The use of these skills is not limited to the university: they are highly prized in the business community as well, and are usually required for advancement. "Thesis" writing, probably more than any other single type of course work at university level, prepares the student to successfully compete for work and for advancement after he or she leaves the university campus.

TERM PAPERS

The term paper is a student's first exposure to scholarly writing. It involves the same independent investigation, the same carefully organized taking of notes, evaluation, and reporting of information that is required for theses and dissertations. It also requires the use of documentation notes and a bibliography, and adherence to rigid typing and organizational controls. Mechanically, there is little real difference between term papers, theses, and doctoral dissertations.

But the comparison stops there. The subject of a term paper is often assigned by the instructor, or it is selected from a list provided to the class. The student may be the first to investigate his assigned or chosen subject, or one of many who submit almost identical papers to the same instructor every year. Limited time and resources dictate that term papers be short; usually ten to twenty pages. Though some writers may compare and weigh evidence and offer conclusions, most will simply report everything they could learn on their subject.

The audience for term papers is small. They are frequently seen only by the instructor, and sometimes by the writer's classmates. The term paper counts for but a fraction of the work in a course, and when the term is ended, it is usually forgotten.

MASTER'S THESES

A master's thesis differs considerably on these points, while at the same time retaining similarities of task organization, writing, documentation, and physical preparation. The graduate student brings with him the experience gained from writing term papers for undergraduate classes. He or she is expected to know how to conduct scholarly research, weigh evidence, and report conclusions. The scholarly conventions of documentation, typing formats, and information organization should be familiar skills when the student reaches this level.

The thesis subject ideally should be chosen and developed by the student. It should propose the investigation of a specific, limited problem or area of interest associated with his or her academic major. The student author must conduct a comprehensive search for information on the subject, which he must then sort and analyze. He will then write his report. In it he will explain his theme, describe his methods of research, the information discovered, and present his conclusions. This report will be his thesis, which he will present to a jury of scholars to be evaluated for its accuracy and accomplishment.

Successfully meeting the requirements for writing a thesis is an integral requirement for graduation when included in the program of a master's degree candidate. It is the first true test of scholarly writing, worth nine or more credits at most universities, and comprising about 25 percent of the graduate credits needed for the degree. Researching and writing a thesis is a large undertaking, frequently requiring more than a single academic year for completion, and averaging 100 to 200 pages of final manuscript. Each chapter in the thesis will be the equivalent, or more, of a term paper.

A thesis is more lasting than a term paper, and will be available to a larger audience for reading. When the final draft is approved by the faculty and given to the Graduate Department, it becomes the permanent property of the university, is bound, and shelved in the school's library. There, for all who wish to read it, is an enduring record of the student author's efforts, a representation of the level of accomplishment required by the university, and a reflection of the scholastic reputations of the faculty members who judged its quality. Some theses and thesis abstracts are published by University Microfilms International, making it possible for students or faculty from other campuses to borrow them through inter-library loan, widening the reading audience even more.

DOCTORAL DISSERTATIONS

A doctoral degree requires the accumulation of anywhere from 40 to more than 100 credits beyond the master's degree level, depending on the field of study and the university. The dissertation will account for 25 to 30 percent of the total. It is obvious from these figures that the work will be significantly greater than for a master's degree.

A dissertation writer is expected to conduct original research, and to contribute new information to his field of study. The work may extend over a period of years, with the final report usually consisting of hundreds of pages, frequently in more than one volume. Dissertations written in the United States are published and made available through the University Microfilms International Dissertation Publishing Program. Abstracts of these dissertations are obtainable world-wide. Because of this international audience, the quality of a dissertation may influence the academic or business world's perceptions of the writer for years.

As the master's thesis is the first real test of advanced scholarly writing, the doctoral dissertation is the candidate's demonstration that he or she is capable of the skills required for acceptance into the select world of advanced scholarship.

Writing a thesis takes time, hard work, and patience. Your aim is to complete the document on time for graduation, and to do a creditable job. *The Thesis Writer's Handbook* can be an important tool in this process. Look on it as a friend who is familiar with the labors of thesis writing, and use it to pilot you through the maze of procedures and around the ogres of academia.

We wish you success in your endeavors, and a peaceful world in which to live and prosper.

Joan Miller
Bruce Taylor
Barclay Street Cottage
West Linn, Oregon,

Chapter One

HOW TO CHOOSE YOUR THESIS TOPIC

The purpose of a thesis is to demonstrate your ability to: (1) select a topic of importance to your course of study; (2) research that topic; and (3) report the results of your research in both oral and written form.

If you are among the specially favored of this world, you will already have a thesis topic to work on. Alas, if you are like the rest of us, you will have to concentrate a portion of your scholastic energy toward discovering one. Your job will be to seek out a little-known but important subject in your field. You will then have to convince your thesis advisor that it meets his or her standards, and your school's requirements. Most important, you must make sure you are satisfied with your choice; you will be spending 24 hours a day with it over an extended period of time.

REQUIREMENTS FOR A THESIS TOPIC

As you consider thesis topics, compare what you know about them to the following list. If a subject meets the requirements described, it will probably qualify for presentation to your thesis advisor.

SUBJECT AREA — The topic must be related to your major field of study.

SUBJECT IMPORTANCE — A master's thesis is expected to contribute to the literature on the subject. The introduction of new knowledge is not required, but you should not simply repeat what has been already written. Your thesis should add to the available information on a subject; the object is to derive new perspectives from existing knowledge.

Three ways to accomplish this are to (1) present a new analysis of existing material; (2) reveal new conclusions arrived at by combining information from previously separate sources; and (3) writing about aspects of a subject that are not commonly or widely known in order to broaden the available information in those areas.

AVAILABILITY OF RESOURCES — Research material on your selected topic should be reasonably available. When evaluating, check as many potential sources as you can locate. Determine to your satisfaction that sufficient information to complete your thesis can be obtained within a practical time frame. If your thesis includes a project of some kind, be sure materials and facilities will be available for your work. An absence of any of these factors should make you carefully consider the practicality of your subject.

A BASIC COURSE OF ACTION

START EARLY. Begin thinking about possible thesis topics as soon as you enter graduate school. If you have your thesis in the back of your mind during your graduate course work, you can select prospective topics, and follow up on the most promising ones later.

Find out from your Graduate Department secretary where to obtain a schedule of thesis submission requirements. In most schools, your first draft will have to be handed in a specified number of days or weeks before your oral exam. Your final draft frequently must be in the Graduate Department office weeks before your graduation date. Knowing these requirements will help you plan for an orderly completion of your graduate work in keeping with your graduation schedule.

Take into consideration that preparing a thesis is an involved process. It is much like writing a book for publication. You will have to plan carefully to give yourself enough time to prepare, to gather information, to organize your data, do the writing, and produce the final document.

ENJOY YOURSELF. Look for potential thesis topics among your own interests. Explore ideas that excite you. Don't overlook obscure or little-known topics because they seem at first unclear or mysterious. Little-known incidents, persons, thought-processes, or a chain of events can make excellent thesis topics. You could end up as the quintessential expert on a subject — careers have been built on such as this!

Turn your search into a game; it's easy enough to discard themes that do not fit your standards while you are exploring. You will be spending a lot of time with your subject, so pick one you think you will enjoy.

SEARCH WIDE AND FAR. Your thesis topic may be gleaned from practically any source. A book you are reading, a film you have seen, a conversation with an instructor, or a course you are taking can spark an idea. In the beginning, you should keep your mind and your options open to all possibilities.

Record potential topics on index cards, along with the titles of books, articles or other sources of information associated with them. Add new information sources as you discover them.

FOLLOW UP. When time permits, check information sources for each potential topic. Use the resources of your university, county, and other local libraries. Look in card catalogs, the *Reader's Guide to Periodical Literature*, newspaper archives, the *Social Sciences Index*, the *Humanities Index*, and the Subject and Title indexes of *Books in Print* for information written on your subject. If your school library subscribes to a computer data bank service, it might be worth your while to pay for a literature search on your most promising topics. Record your findings for each subject on your index cards.

Check the availability of material you discover in your literature search. If you cannot readily locate information on a particular topic, you may want to discard that idea and go on to a more promising subject.

Scan the literature that is available to you. Evaluate its usefulness for the in-depth research you will conduct later. Check the bibliographies of books on the subjects that interest you. This will always lead you to additional sources of information, frequently in the form of monographs, articles, letters, diaries or microfilm that you may not find listed elsewhere. Check the availability of any new discoveries.

Discuss your topic ideas with people who are knowledgeable about each subject. Local business people, public agency employees, your academic advisors, and other members of your university's teaching and research staffs are available to provide you with a wealth of valuable insights if you seek them out and ask them. Use your imagination to find these people; ther's no richer source of information than a person who is asked about his special knowledge. Make notes of what you learn.

While you are in the library, take the time to look at recently completed theses from your department or related disciplines. Reviewing them will give you an idea of the kinds of topics others have chosen to research. You will also get a sense of writing styles and writing levels accepted by your school. Do not, however, use these theses as style guides. Typing and writing styles change: your Graduate Department's most recent style guide should be your only guide in this area.

ANALYZE YOUR FINDINGS. Compare possible subjects with the list of Requirements for Thesis Topics at the beginning of this chapter. Weed out topics that clearly do not fit your subject or resource availability needs. Review your remaining topics and rate them according to their potential. Take your top three favorites (if you have that many) and discuss them with your advisor.

GET YOUR TOPIC APPROVED. Your thesis advisor must approve your topic. Be aware that when you present potential thesis topics, you will be expected to justify (in academic language, "defend") your choices. Prepare yourself by formulating a statement for each topic describing what you intend to say in your thesis. Try to pinpoint exactly what it is about your subject that you intend to research: why did you choose the topic? why is it important? what is your hypothesis? what conclusions do you expect to reach? Keep in mind that your perspectives are subject to change as you conduct your research. Don't make your statement so rigid that it can't be modified as you progress. This preparation process will help you weed out unpromising topics as well as confirm the practicality of subjects with good potential.

Bring the lists of research material you have accumulated when you discuss projects with your advisor. Be prepared to describe how you will conduct your research, starting with the books, articles, pamphlets and other documents on your list.

The topic approval process is normally an informal one between you and your thesis advisor. However, some schools require that you write a formal proposal. In these cases, use the same information and procedures described above to present your written arguments.

Chapter Two

HOW TO CHOOSE
YOUR THESIS ADVISOR

One of the most important factors contributing to the success of your graduate program will be the faculty member who acts as your thesis advisor. This will be the person who approves your selection of topic, monitors your progress, provides guidance and advice, and acts as chairman of your thesis committee. It is crucial that you understand the functions of a thesis advisor, and your mutual responsibilities toward the completion of your project.

At some point in your graduate career, you will choose, or be assigned, an academic advisor. Some schools appoint an advisor immediately upon enrollment, others prefer that you attend a semester or two before an advisor is assigned or chosen by you. This faculty member provides assistance in planning your graduate program, and in choosing courses to accomplish your educational objectives.

Your thesis advisor may or may not be the same person you have as an academic advisor. The thesis advisor will, however, be a faculty member from your department, and should be knowledgeable in your area of study. Those schools that assign an advisor usually require that both the student and the faculty member approve of the appointment. The approval process leaves the student with some control over the final choice.

Your final selection of a thesis advisor should be the result of a careful process of interviewing and evaluating available candidates. Since your advisor will be a member of your department, and somewhat proficient in your major subject area, the number of potential candidates will be small. Some you will know from attending their classes, others by reputation. Your job will be to learn enough about faculty members available as advisors to choose one who will best serve your needs.

First, determine which faculty members qualify as a candidate for your thesis advisor. You should be able to obtain this information from your academic advisor, or from your department's head of graduate studies.

Make an appointment with each of the candidates to discuss your educational objectives and to express your ideas for thesis topics. Keep it informal; this is a preliminary conference. Ask each of them if he or she would be interested in serving as your thesis advisor. Don't commit yourself at this point, or force a commitment from them.

Talk to fellow graduate students. Ask them to share their experiences with the candidates on your list, both in the classroom and as thesis advisors. Talk to recent graduates from your department about their experiences with these faculty members as advisors. If the graduates live locally, you can obtain their addresses from the graduate office. Honor societies associated with your department and alumni associations are also potential sources of recent grad's addresses.

Look for specific traits during your first interview with candidates. First, your thesis advisor should be available on a long term basis. That is, he or she should not be planning a sabbatical, a leave of absence, or retirement during the period you will be working on your thesis. Take the health of your potential advisor into consideration; a lengthy illness could hamper your progress.

Accessibility is an important factor in working with your thesis advisor. Does he or she keep regular office hours? Are they available for appointments outside of regular office hours? Will they be willing to work with you over the phone when necessary? Are they too accessible? Will interruptions during your time with them be commonplace? Your best sources of information for evaluating accessibility will be your own experience with a particular instructor, and that of fellow students who have worked with the individual faculty members.

A potential advisor should exhibit the willingness and the ability to devote time to you and your project. Willingness stems from a desire to serve as an advisor. Ability, in this case, is related to the individual's time within his or her work schedule. If your candidate appears reluctant to take on the task, it may be because of a heavy class load or because he is advising as many graduate students as he has time for. You don't have to probe into reasons, just back off, thank him for his time, and go on to your next candidate.

A harmonious relationship with your thesis advisor, based on mutual respect and a shared responsibility for your project will contribute greatly to your success. Check out your feelings as you interview candidates. Are you comfortable in his or her presence? Is your conversation person-to-person or is he condescending? Is he open and expressive? Your association will be a long one; make certain you like each other.

Good advisors will have a working knowledge of your school's thesis requirements. When you have questions concerning procedures, style or deadlines, your advisor should be able to answer them, not just refer you to the graduate office.

In addition to being knowledgeable in your field of study, an interest by your advisor in your topic will promote a positive working atmosphere. Look for such an interest, or at least a curiosity about what you will produce.

As you write your thesis, you will need good, objective criticism, positive encouragement, and help staying on track. Criticism and encouragement go hand-in-hand. Your advisor should be able to evaluate your work for content, relevance, and style, and when needed, provide positive suggestions for editing and revision. Look out for the advisor who belittles students when he feels it necessary to criticize their work. Critical review of draft manuscripts is important, but should not be so harsh as to make you despair of ever getting it "right."

Staying on track means sticking to your topic, and not straying into interesting, but irrelevant, side issues. Unexpected data will undoubtedly surface in the course of your research. Being too close to a topic can sometimes cloud your vision and judgement, and you will be tempted to expand your thematic presentation. Your advisor should be able to question, when necessary, the direction of your work and caution you against such time- and energy-wasting side expeditions. Beware also, the advisor who takes too close an interest in associated areas of your topic, lest he lead you astray with suggestions for additional, but unprofitable, research and writing. Your best sources of information concerning these traits will be students who have worked with the instructors.

Keep in mind, there are no perfect thesis advisors, just as there are no perfect people. A professor has a plethora of concerns and obligations that occupy his time. In the press of his everyday responsibilities, you will not always occupy a prominent place in his mind.

It is important for you, as a master's degree candidate, to understand that the research, writing, and final completion of your thesis is entirely your responsibility. You will be relieved of many of the controls that guide undergraduate students through the system, and allowed a large measure of independence while working on your thesis project.

Your primary concerns during this period will be to maintain frequent contact with your advisor, informing him or her of your progress, periodically submitting portions of your work for critical review, and seeking advice when problems arise.

Your thesis advisor will be responsible for reviewing and advising you on the content, validity, and quality of your thesis, and for seeing that you follow procedures prescribed by your school. While he or she shares to some degree in your success or failure, the outcome of your efforts will be in your hands alone. It is up to you to succeed.

Chapter Three

HOW TO SELECT
YOUR THESIS COMMITTEE

Once you have begun officially working on your thesis project —
an act established in the eyes of most schools by your registration for
thesis credits — you will select a thesis committee, or one will be
selected for you. When your thesis is finished, it will be judged by this
committee. Its members, with your thesis advisor as chairman, will
also conduct your oral exam.

Your thesis committee will consist of three to five faculty
members, including your thesis advisor. A frequent requirement is
that the committee include at least two representatives from your
major field of study, and one from your minor. Often, a representa-
tive for the Graduate Office is appointed by the Dean of Graduate
Studies to sit on the committee. Thesis committee requirements will
differ between schools; ask your advisor what procedures apply in
your case.

In some schools, thesis committee members are appointed by the
Dean of Graduate Studies or by the head of your department. Most
often, however, you will be required to select your own thesis committee. The individuals you choose — usually selected in conjunction with
your thesis advisor — will normally be instructors from your department who have some knowledge of your subject, or of the general
topic area you are studying. You should be familiar with most of the
leading candidates from your efforts to select a thesis advisor.

When selecting committee members, you should look for individuals who know you and your work, who seem to have a genuine
regard for you, and appear interested in your project. This is especially important in schools that require you to work with your committee
almost as closely as with your thesis advisor.

Discuss tentative committee member choices with your thesis advisor; he will have insights on how well individual faculty members
will work together. Final approval of your thesis project is in the

hands of your committee members; their endorsement is required for graduation. Take the time to carefully select the most capable people you can.

Like your advisor, but on a lesser scale, your committee is responsible for seeing that what you write measures up to the level of quality for theses prescribed by your college or university. Your advisor and your committee together are your guides in the writing style, structure, and content of your thesis.

It is wise to initiate contact with your thesis committee members early, and advise them regularly on the direction of your work and its progress. The majority of faculty contact concerning your thesis will be with your advisor. However, it is usually beneficial to have committee members read completed sections, and offer suggestions. This will give you early warning of any problems, and you can make changes far in advance of submitting your final draft.

Copies of your final draft manuscript will be distributed to your committee members for evaluation and criticism prior to your oral exam. When the copies are returned, you will find out if you have satisfied their standards, or if you are faced with major rewriting.

The members of your thesis committee must approve of both your thesis and your performance in the oral exam before recommending that you receive your degree. Choosing the members carefully and attempting to work closely with them will go a long way toward putting friendly faces around the table when you sit down for your oral.

Chapter Four

RESEARCH: GETTING STARTED

To begin your research, you must formulate in your mind how you intend to express the statement you will make with your thesis. What you want to say about your topic should lead you to your initial information sources; your search will become more clearly defined as you accumulate material. The best place to begin your inquiries is in your university library.

All forms of scholarly research involve the use of primary and secondary information sources. Primary sources are the original words or direct findings of a writer. These can include poems, novels, public documents, original letters, manuscripts, diaries, surveys, and case studies. Secondary sources are those derived from primary writings. These are comments and observations about the original work and can include monographs, articles, texts, and histories.

Most schools require that original research, such as you will be conducting for your thesis, include a fair amount of material from primary sources. You should, therefore make every effort to locate and use references that fit in this category. As you conduct your research, make a list of your information sources, separating them into primary and secondary divisions. This list will later be used to make up your thesis bibliography, so be sure to record full bibliographic information (see Chapter 18).

In your initial research efforts, it will be useful to examine as large a selection of information sources as possible. Your objective will be to ferret out data that relates to your subject, and supports or substantiates what you feel is the statement you are making in your thesis. You can return later to the most valuable references on your list for in-depth study.

As a first step in your research, you may want to examine the *Subject Guide to Books in Print* which lists all books currently available in the United States by subject. Another is *Books in Print*, which comes in two sets of volumes; one listing titles alphabetically, the second listing authors. It has been published since 1948; older editions are valuable for listings of books no longer in print.

Look also in the *Cumulative Book Index*, an author, subject, and title index of all books published in English, dating from 1898 to the present. Check the subject headings of the card catalog to see which books the library has on hand. If the books you want are not at your own library or one close by, ask your librarian about the possibility of interlibrary loan.

Book reviews can help you evaluate the book titles you find. There are a number of book review indexes; the most widely used is the *Book Review Digest*, which contains listings of reviews from 1905 to the present.

There are a large number of specialized encyclopedias available as research aids. Among these are, *Encyclopedia of American History*, *Encyclopedia of the Biological Sciences*, *Encyclopedia of Education*, *Encyclopedia of Psychology*, and *Encyclopedia of Banking and Finance*.

The *Reader's Guide to Periodical Literature* lists general interest articles in popular magazines on nearly every subject. You should be able to find a number of articles, past and present, that address your topic. *Poole's Index to Periodical Literature* is an index of early articles, dating from 1802 to 1906.

For more specialized, scholarly reading, you may want to investigate the *Humanities Index*, *Social Sciences Index*, or the *Applied Science and Technology Index*. These three indexes list carefully documented articles contained in specialized journals topically related to the disciplines described. The references accompanying the articles could be as valuable to you as the articles themselves.

Additionally, nearly every discipline has its own specialized index or abstract directory which contains information sources important to that specific field of study, and in the case of abstracts, provides comments on the books and articles it lists. If your area of interest is history, you would want to look in *Historical Abstracts*, or the *International Bibliography of Historical Sciences*. If economics is your field, you should look in the *Index of Economic Articles*. Business majors should examine the *Business Index*; chemists, *Chemical Abstracts*; philosophers, the *Bibliography of Philosopy* or the *Philosopher's Index*.

Other specialized indexes include: *Accountant's Index*; *Architectural Periodical's Index*; *Engineering Index*; *Film Literature Index*; *Nuclear Science Abstracts*; and *Television News Index and Abstracts*.

For newspaper coverage of your subject, you would be best advised to look in the *New York Times Index*. Most university libraries contain a microfilmed file of the *New York Times*; the index will give you the data you need to pinpoint information on your subject contained in a specific issue. Other helpful newspaper indexes include the *Christian Science Monitor Index*, the *Official Index to the London Times*, and the *Wall Street Journal Index*.

Small, local papers may not have been indexed, but chances are good that the state historical society or one of the larger county libraries in the paper's circulation area will have a back issue file, or microfilmed copies of prior issues. You can sometimes look in one of the major newspaper indexes to get the date your subject was in the news, then look it up in other papers published on the same date.

Copies of all government publications are required to be distributed to regional depositories to make them available for public use. As of June, 1984, there were 1385 designated federal depository libraries in the United States, many of them located within major public and university libraries. Some federal depositories carry all publications available from the Government Printing Office; others carry a limited selection of the most asked-for texts. This vast array of published information may be a valuable source of information for you.

There may also be a U.S. Government bookstore near you where you can purchase government publications, or order them through catalogs. The government issues two monthly catalogs listing available publications. The *Monthly Catalog of United States Government Publications* can usually be found in the documents section of university and large regional libraries; it contains thousands of titles. The second, *Selected U.S. Government Publications*, lists about 200 of the most popular texts. This catalog can be obtained free by writing the Superintendent of Documents, U.S. Government Printing Office, P.O. Box 1821, Washington, D.C. 20402.

You can find out the location of federal depositories or book stores near you by phoning the Federal Information Center listed under Government Offices in your phone directory, or by writing to the Superintendent of Documents at the address above.

Most government and military publications are accessible to anyone, or are covered by the Freedom of Information Act. Write to the appropriate government agency for information, or for specific material that you feel you want to examine.

If the information you are looking for originated from a government office, but is not current, it may have found its way into the

National Archives in Washington, D.C. This formidable repository of the nation's papers holds a prodigious array of government and government-related documents and records.

Two helpful publications listing a portion of the National Archive's holdings are *A Select List of Publications of the National Archives and Records Service*, and the *Catalog of National Archives Microfilm Publications*. Both can be obtained free by writing to the Publications Sales Branch (NEPS), General Services Administration, Washington, D.C. 20408.

The National Archives also has a number of research facilities open to the public in areas throughout the U.S. These are the six Presidential Libraries and eleven Archives Branches of the Federal Archives Records Centers that hold primarily regional materials. Check to see if any of these establishments are accessible to you, and visit them if you feel it would aid your research.

Some university libraries offer literature search services that make use of a number of commercially available databases accessed by computer. These database files are similar to indexes and directories, but because they are computerized, the search is quicker, more complete, and the information is recovered faster. Find out if this service is available at your library, how you may use it, and what it costs.

Sometimes your research requires you to travel to your sources of information. But don't underestimate local materials or the power of letter writing; you may be surrounded by a wealth of information and not realize it. If your college or university is small, there is a good chance that a large university with a more extensive library is within 200 to 250 miles of you. It may be to your advantage to examine their resources before planning longer trips.

Finally, the abundance of information can sometimes overwhelm you. It is difficult to know how much data to collect and when to stop. Although it is better in the long run to collect too much information rather than too little, in most cases it's impossible to read everything written on your subject. Most of the time, not all that you do read can be incorporated in your thesis.

Remember that your focus may change a number of times in the course of your research, leaving you with collected information that no longer has any bearing on what you are writing. Take good notes, and maintain a file on the data you collect. This will help you to select the useful from the superfluous.

Chapter Five

TAKING NOTES:
ORGANIZING AND STORING YOUR DATA

Good note taking is the key to successful thesis writing. When you get to the writing stage of your project, a well-organized set of notes will help keep you on track, and within the scope of your subject. Remember, you can read everything ever written on your topic, but if you don't compile a set of usable notes, it's a wasted effort.

You will find it invaluable if, at the beginning of your research, you make up a rough outline of what you intend to include in your thesis. The outline should be sufficient to guide your note-taking, and to differentiate between what has a bearing on your paper, and what does not. It should help you answer the questions: what kinds of data are you looking for? and what kinds of subsections do you feel your thesis will be divided into? You will be filling in and developing a more complete outline of your thesis as you progress. For now, it will be sufficient if this rough draft gives you direction.

Most authorities suggest putting your notes on 3x5 or 4x6 index cards; this keeps them manageable. Write the complete bibliographic information for each source you investigate on a separate card. For books, this is the author's name, the title of the work, place of publication, the publisher, and the year published. For magazine and journal articles, the author's name, the title of the article, the name of the journal, volume number, series number (if applicable), date of publication, and page numbers. For newspapers, list the title of the article, if any, the author, if given, the name of the paper, the date, and page. After the bibliographic data, write the information you wish to keep.

When your notes require more than one card for a single source, abbreviate the bibliographic information on the additional cards and number them in sequence in case they become separated. Also note somewhere on your cards where the source is located, whether a library, a historical society, or your own bookshelf.

15

If you don't feel comfortable filing your notes on index cards, you can devise your own system. Just be sure to keep accurate bibliographic and location records of your information sources, so you can find them again.

Make certain that the notes you take are self-explanatory. There's nothing worse than looking at your cards a few weeks or months later, and not being able to understand what you wrote down, or why. Write down the page numbers where your information is located. Use your rough outline to keep you on track, but do not try to force your notes to fit your outline. Nothing is etched in stone at this point — keep your options open.

Make photocopies of important articles or pages from books. If your research involves the use of microfilm, you might want to have key pages enlarged and printed for easier reading; most university libraries will provide this service for a fee.

Since note taking is a vital part of the thesis writing process, it is here that you should be aware of plagiarism, what it is, and how to avoid it. To plagiarize is to take someone else's words and/or ideas and put them into your writing as though they were your own. It usually occurs in student's research papers through carelessness or ignorance. All schools have regulations against plagiarism, with severe penalties for offenders.

A clear form of plagiarism, and one that should be obvious to any writer, is the verbatim copying of a source without acknowledging that it is someone else's work. Changing a few words in a passage or rearranging the order of the words or sentences still does not make the work yours.

To avoid plagiarism, you must acknowledge borrowed ideas, statements and facts as well as direct quotations. When using direct statements, put quotation marks around them. When paraphrasing or summarizing another writer's ideas or statements, give the writer credit by name. Credit the source of any material or ideas that cannot be considered general knowledge. Note the source of any charts, graphs, tables, or other data originated by others. And finally, provide a footnote or endnote in the text for each source in the categories described above.

Organize your notes as you go along. Classify them by topic, chronologically, by type, by the problems you will deal with, by theme, by the results of experiments, or any other method that suits your purpose. Once you have organized the information in your notes, you are ready to begin writing.

Chapter Six

WRITING YOUR FIRST DRAFT

The goal of your written thesis is to report the results of your research. As you compile your notes, you should be forming ideas of how you will organize your information into book format, with chapters for each of your main points.

GETTING ORGANIZED

It is useful to think of a thesis as containing four major parts: (1) a statement of what you intend to say about your subject; (2) a discussion of information revealed by your research; (3) arguments based on the researched information, for and against the points you wish to make; and (4) your conclusions. Using this basic structure, your first task is to refine your outline.

Begin with a cursory review of your notes. Compare the information accumulated with the rough outline you maintained during note-taking. Make whatever changes you feel are necessary in the rough outline to achieve a logical arrangement of data to fit the basic structure above.

Take some time out. Take a long walk; talk to friends; go to a movie; sleep on it for a couple of days. Let your subconscious mind work on further organization of the material.

Go back to your outline and begin filling in the details of each chapter. List all the points you want to cover in each chapter by heading and by subhead. Write a paragraph under each subdivision outlining what you expect to write concerning that subject. Check to see that your information flows logically; look for inconsistencies, and for repetition.

Your outline serves as your basic writing plan. It gives direction and clarifies your organization. It should show clearly, on paper, what you need to write. The time you spend improving your outline will be well invested.

Most important, your detailed outline makes your thesis real — a visible, tangible representation of the task ahead; a pathway to completion.

FORMULATE A WRITING PLAN

Step back from your work at this point and make some specific plans for the writing task ahead. The first thing you want to take into consideration is the size of the project. Writing a thesis is equivalent to writing a book. In most schools, you will be expected to have an average of between 90 and 150 pages in your thesis. Each chapter will be the size of a term paper.

While it is important to understand the size of the project you are starting, it is just as important that you don't let it overwhelm you. Talk to your advisor about the average length of theses written in your department. Your school library is another place to examine completed theses for length. The purpose here is for you to develop a perspective from which to plan your work.

Keep in mind as you organize your writing tasks, that it is the content that counts, more than the volume of pages or information. Some subjects can be adequately covered with fewer pages than others. You will be judged more on the quality of your research and writing, than on the size of the book you submit.

A thesis is like any other book; it has a beginning and an end. In between, information flows in a clear and reasonable sequence from chapter to chapter. The fundamental premise of a thesis is to present an argument or prove a proposition. For this reason, most theses use the statement, discussion, argument, and conclusion structure — outlined at the beginning of this chapter — as a logical presentation of information. Within the thesis, each chapter uses the same structure to present specific points.

When planning your thesis, you should visualize the book as a whole. When writing individual chapters, treat each one as a separate building block. If you write your thesis a chapter at a time, instead of trying to write the entire book at once, you will find it a much easier task.

The strategy here, is to break the job into manageable pieces. Plan each chapter as you would a term paper. Make it as complete as you would if you were handing it in as an individual assignment. When finished chapters are placed in sequence, the information flow should match that required by the overall book structure. Complete enough chapters, and you will have completed your thesis; it's as simple as that.

FIND A PLACE TO WORK

We all know people who seem to be able to study and write anywhere. Some individuals thrive on an environment teeming with activity and sound. Most of us, however, need a relatively quiet place to work.

Good thesis writing habits will be easier to maintain once you identify a specific location as your workplace. Make it clear to your family and friends that you are not to be interrupted when working on your thesis.

ESTABLISH A REGULAR WORK PATTERN. Consistent association with your thesis is vital, whether you are actually writing, going through your notes, or simply waiting for inspiration. Going to the place where you are creating your thesis and keeping regularly scheduled hours puts your mind into "thesis gear" and stimulates ideas, whether you believe it at the time or not.

Spend some time with your thesis each day. It is more productive in the long run to work two to three hours a day, five days a week, than to try and squeeze it all into weekends. If you work sporadically, the infrequent work sessions will result in time lost while you reacquaint yourself with your material.

START WRITING

You do not have to start writing your thesis at page one. In fact, it is frequently easier to start somewhere in the middle. Since each chapter should be relatively self-contained, it is possible for you to begin writing at any point in your book. Most writers find it convenient to start with the chapter they find most interesting, or feel the most comfortable with. Your outline will keep you on track, and ensure a logical sequence of information.

The Chinese are credited with the maxim that "a trip of a thousand miles begins with the first step." In the same manner, completion of a 150-page thesis begins with the first word. It is a rule you will have to remind yourself of every day.

When creativity eludes you, write freestyle. Ask yourself what it is you want to say, then express it any way that comes to you. It is not uncommon to discover the "right" words for what you want to communicate in the third or fourth paragraph.

Just sit down and write the first word. Follow it with another. You will have to throw away some of your "getting started" copy, but the writing practice will help to develop your skills. Putting words on paper will give you a good feeling, and at this early stage, getting the words out is the important thing.

REWARD YOURSELF. Writing is a lonely business. When you are enrolled in regular classes, your performance is consistently evaluated by your instructors. Aside from periodic conferences with your advisor, you will have to provide your own progress evaluations of your thesis, and give out your own gold stars.

Be conscious of the little victories. Think of your thesis in terms of chapters you have finished, rather than those you have yet to complete. View each written page as a personal success. Watch the pages pile up; they are your production gauge, the measure of your accomplishment. You will be amazed at how quickly the pages accumulate.

OBTAIN A UNIVERSITY STYLE MANUAL

Various style manuals are available describing the requirements of page format, and the documentation procedures for footnotes, endnotes, and bibliographies. Some areas of study require that you follow specific methods when preparing academic papers. The graduate departments of most schools publish a thesis style manual for your guidance. When they are required, special discipline style manuals are usually available through the departments that use them. Check with your thesis advisor for your specific needs. Familiarize yourself with the style required by your department, and follow that style consistently throughout your thesis.

IDENTIFYING SOURCE DATA

Writing a research paper requires the collection, sifting, and evaluation of a large amount of data. From this effort, you will select ideas, statements, facts, or quotations to support your interpretations and conclusions. In all probability, most of the data you use will come from the printed works of other authors. You will be required, both as a courtesy and as a demonstration of your willingness to have your information sources checked for accuracy, to acknowledge the use of these materials. To use the ideas or words of another without crediting the source is plagiarism, an act that can result in severe academic penalties and, in some cases, civil penalties as well. The following information on plagiarism is adapted from style guide material contributed by The University of Alabama, University, Alabama; and Portland State University, Portland, Oregon.

Plagiarism in its purest form involves the copying of entire passages either verbatim or nearly verbatim, with no direct acknowledgement of the source. Another form of plagiarism occurs when, instead of quoting a passage directly, a writer attempts to avoid the necessity of using quotation marks by making a few superficial changes in the text. But by far the most common (and unconscious) form of plagiarism is when a direct quotation is simply paraphrased. *Paraphrasing does not relieve you of the obligation to provide proper identification of source data.*

The best way to avoid plagiarism is to accurately list all the information you will need for the footnote and bibliographic listings of your information sources, and make sure all quotes, ideas, or conclusions not your own are given proper acknowledgement in your text. See Chapter 17, "What You Need To Know About Footnotes, Endnotes, And Other Documentation Styles," and Chapter 18, "What You Need To Know About Bibliographies And Reference Lists" for information on how to acknowledge your source material. The following points should be kept in mind as you write your thesis:

(1) When material is quoted, it must be quoted exactly as it appears in the original, mistakes and all; any additions, deletions, or alterations must be clearly signaled by brackets or ellipsis dots as indicated in the punctuation manual. Quotations serve a purpose that would not be served by paraphrase; they include a technical definition, an authoritative or controversial opinion, an important distinction, a noteworthy phrase, or some other quality that makes them interesting or important enough for the reader to see in the original form.

(2) Paraphrasing is more appropriate than quoting when the researcher is summarizing an entire document or a lengthy part of it. Generally, if you have to rely so heavily on a particular passage that you must have a copy of it in front of you as you write, you should quote the passage verbatim. The acknowledgement of material that is quoted or paraphrased from a single passage in the original must include the page number or numbers on which the original appeared.

(3) Data that is not commonly available should never be cited without a clear indication of its source.

(4) Terminology or phraseology that is not common in the literature should never be copied without proper acknowledgement.

CONFER WITH YOUR ADVISOR

The success of your thesis depends partly on your ability to seek out editorial suggestions and accept criticism. It is your responsibility to set up conferences with your thesis advisor while you are working on your manuscript. Your advisor has an obligation to review your work, but he will not come looking for you. You will benefit the most by scheduling regular meetings with him.

Where it is appropriate, you may find it valuable to arrange periodic sessions to review your work with individual thesis committee members in addition to the meetings with your advisor. Though you may encounter conflicting advice, you can use it to your advantage to develop new insights to your work. When you submit your thesis for reading and criticism, it could be a valuable asset to have your committee members feel they contributed to your efforts.

Be firm about what you are writing, and be clear about the course of your topic. Avoid over-editing in response to recommendations from your advisor and committee members. It is too easy to get hung up attempting to find every suggested source, read every suggested author, and change the wording in a paragraph over and over again. Too much criticism can kill your inclination to write; you cannot react to every recommendation. Worrying about perfection in your manuscript at this point will not help you to maintain steady progress.

KEEP BACKUP COPIES

The storage and protection of your data and your manuscript is a serious matter. While writing your thesis, you should keep an updated copy of your work in a separate and protected place.

If you are using a computer to write your thesis, copy frequently over onto your disk as you write. Make certain you have backup copies of all of your disks, in addition to a current printed copy. Computer disks are very fragile and can be easily damaged through mishandling. Smoke, extreme heat, dust, food, and writing on the protective jacket of the disk can hurt its recording surface. Placing magnets or paper clips on your disks, leaving the disk on your computer cabinet, or close to your telephone receiver will expose the disk to magnetic fields that can erase or scramble recorded data.

Computer disks should be kept in their special plastic file boxes. Cardboard boxes produce dust that can injure the disk surface when it is used. Backup copies of your floppy disks should be kept separate from your working disks, preferably in a metal file cabinet, or in a heavy safe inside the home. Don't, however, store them in standard fire-proof safes. These safes are constructed with insulating material that emits moisture when it gets hot. The moisture can harm your disks. There are special safes designed to protect magnetic recording media (like computer disks) but these are very expensive. You can get details of how these safes are constructed, and their costs, from a local lock and safe company. Look for them in your yellow pages.

The most recommended method for safe storage of copy disks is to place them in a bank safety deposit box, and update them on a regular basis. Keep one backup copy current in your work room, for example, and exchange it with a second backup copy at the bank on a weekly basis. Update the bank copy at your next work session, and keep it as your work room copy until it is again time to exchange it with the one left in the safety deposit box.

If you are typing or writing longhand, make photocopies of your manuscript on a regular basis. Keep printed copies of your manuscript in some disaster-proof container; your refrigerator or freezer will do if you don't have a fire-proof safe. Make certain you place it in a moisture-proof wrapping. Protecting your thesis and making updated copies not only preserves what you write, but preserves your sanity as well.

Chapter Seven

EDITING YOUR MANUSCRIPT

A writer is much like a builder, and must be prepared to smooth out rough edges and fill in the cracks as a project progresses. Also like a builder, you, the thesis writer, will have to see that your creation passes certain requirements, and fulfills certain specifications. This is the purpose of editing: to evaluate, and where necessary, to change what you write to improve the effectiveness of your product.

Before editing your manuscript, it is a good idea to step away from your work for a time, and let your thoughts cool. It is easy to overlook mistakes when reading something you have written, simply because you are so familiar with your subject and the words you have put down. The mind can correct errors internally so quickly, that your eyes are deceived and made to believe that no mistake existed in the first place. Put some distance between you and your paper. You will return to your thesis with clear eyes and a fresh perspective.

THE EDITING PROCESS

The best way to begin editing is to read your work through completely — red pen in hand — as if you had never seen it before. Note and change the obvious punctuation, spelling, and typographical errors. Make notes where you stumble over words, where passages seem unclear and you have to reread to get the correct meaning. Make minor changes as you go, and mark the places where you feel major revisions will have to be made. Don't make these revisions immediately. Continue your examination of the thesis and get an overall sense of how it reads.

Next, read your thesis out loud, and listen to how it sounds. This will give you a different feeling for what is actually written on each page. Reading out loud is a good method for catching mistakes that may not be immediately clear when reading silently.

Let someone else proofread what you have written. An outside evaluator (not necessarily an academic) is more likely to catch errors you have missed. The reader may not be familiar with the subject, but he or she can still comment on what reads well and what does not. Since reading for errors and clarity will take time and care, you will probably want a volunteer rather than someone you simply saddle with the task. An individual who reads your thesis haphazardly will not be of any help to you in this editing phase.

Now go back and work on the sections you or your proofreader have marked for revision. You want to rewrite to improve readability, to fill in gaps, and to insure continuity of information. There may be some reorganization involved. Many authors resort to the cut and paste method to test and improve sequence. This is where you literally cut paragraphs or sections from your manuscript, rearrange them, and paste them back together — with cellophane tape — in the order you want them. Using a computer to write your thesis can be very helpful at this stage. Most computer writing programs allow blocks of text to be moved, erased, or added to with ease.

Once your paper has been reassembled, repeat the editing process. Read through it again, looking for mistakes and making changes in the manner described above. Do this four or five times until you feel you have a relatively error-free copy that reads smoothly, and satisfactorily expresses what you want to say. Don't cheat on this procedure; it involves the most valuable work you will do on your thesis. Be hard on yourself. Continue to make changes until you are completely satisfied. Remember to take time off between editing sessions to let your subconscious mind consider problems and sort out solutions; too much concentration can lead to burnout.

ABOUT STYLE

Good style is an integral part of good writing, and must be part of any discussion of editing. While writing your thesis, you will encounter the term "style" used three ways: (1) as an individual way of expressing yourself in writing; (2) as a set of rules determining the use of punctuation, the placement of footnotes, the listing of bibliographies, and other mechanics of writing; and (3) as a set of rules, usually dictated by your Graduate Department, concerning such things as margins, page number placement, title page and chapter heading form associated with formatting the completed document. This third interpretation of style will be discussed in Chapter 13, "The Mechanics of Thesis Production."

WRITING STYLE. Style in writing is the way you employ your individual background, vocabulary, knowledge, and thinking processes to express yourself through the written word. The tone of your personal writing style will vary for different types of writing. A letter to a friend, for example, is deliberately less formal than a college paper. A business letter and a resume are written from different perspectives; distinctions reflected by changes in your writing style.

A thesis is meant to be a scholarly work that presents the results of your research. The writing style should be clear, concise, and should reflect mature thinking and critical judgement. Don't try to be too formal, but strive for a clear, straightforward, natural style. What you write will be all the more convincing if it reflects you rather than your imitation of someone else. Above all, work for consistency in the structure of your writing, your use of words and phrases, and the perspective from which you approach your material.

PUNCTUATION. What you don't know about punctuation can hurt your thesis. When you speak, you use pauses, intonation, speed, and gestures to mark your speech and indicate certain meanings to your listener. Punctuation serves the same purpose in writing; it helps the reader understand your train of thought and controls the rhythm, the emphasis, and the meaning of what you write. Failure to use proper punctuation implies ignorance, or simply an unwillingness to learn the correct rules. Either case is enough to guarantee you a large amount of extra work when your thesis is reviewed by your advisor and your thesis committee. It is far better to employ good punctuation habits as you write, rather than have your mistakes pointed out by one of your professors after your draft is complete.

Guard against punctuation mistakes by familiarizing yourself with the punctuation style section of this handbook. Refer to it often, until you automatically incorporate proper punctuation into your writing style. Be aware, though, that there is some disagreement on the rules of punctuation. Some of these rules have undergone changes over time. You may encounter faculty members, and others, who adhere to the older forms of punctuation, initiating a kind of "generational clash" between themselves and the student whose work they are editing. Conflict over punctuation may also arise from the differences between two diverse schools of thought, represented by their various "authoritative" works. The punctuation styles presented in this handbook are a compilation of the foremost texts available as of the most recent printing.

GENERAL ORGANIZATION

After you have noted and made the most obvious of your revisions, it is time to shift gears, step back, and look at the overall effectiveness of your thesis. In order for it to be effective, all of its parts must interlock and its progress must be both logical and convincing. It is your task as a thesis writer to get a specific message across to the reader. Is that message there? Is the purpose of your thesis understandable? Your thesis statement should be clearly worded, developed cleanly through the sequence of chapters, and supported by tight organization.

Good organization is vital to the effectiveness of your thesis. To gauge development and organization, skim through your thesis and sort of *feel* what you have written. Look closely to make certain that your chapter divisions are logical and your chapter titles descriptive and relevant. Try to insure that each chapter progresses in ideas and development to the next without unnecessary repetition or extraneous information. Do not be afraid to excise anything that is out of place or detracts from the unity of your overall presentation.

Examine individual paragraphs. Make certain that your paragraph-to-paragraph transitions flow smoothly and tie your information together. Each paragraph should contain enough information to develop the ideas expressed. Make certain each has a topic sentence or main concept. Include plenty of details, examples, descriptions, explanations, statistics, and/or analyses to clarify and highlight your points. Though very short paragraphs, even one-liners, are sometimes justified, you should strive for writing that fully investigates and expresses your ideas, and captures the attention and interest of your readers.

Your sentences should employ emphasis, variety, and appropriate language. Vague or ambiguous words should be replaced with specific and concrete terms. Above all, avoid excessive repetition of words, expressions, and sentence patterns. Vary your presentation. Improve your ability to write "word pictures" to convey your information. Make sure each sentence is a complete statement. Avoid long or wordy sentences.

THE COMPLETED FIRST DRAFT

The final edited version of your first draft is the one you will submit to your advisor and committee to read before your oral exam. You want it to be as perfect as possible. The more time and care you take with your final draft, the more your examining committee will see it as a serious effort.

It is inevitable that your thesis committee will ask you to do some editing and rewriting. It is a function of your committee to seek out errors or weaknesses in your manuscript. You should prepare yourself for this type of criticism, and anticipate requests for changes. This method of giving advice and criticism is often seen as an adversary procedure. It is. Just remember, it is not a challenge to your personality, but a test of your abilities; an effort to bring out the best in you and your work. If you have conscientiously edited your thesis, you have readied yourself and your paper in the best way possible.

Chapter Eight

HOW TO OVERCOME WRITER'S BLOCK

Unlike your previous scholastic work, thesis writing is truly a solitary experience. The interaction between students all working toward the same goals in undergraduate classes contrasts significantly with researching and writing on your own. The experience can be both lonely and traumatic.

PLAN AHEAD

A thesis project can, and usually does, promote fear and anxiety. It is usually done alone, and frequently in isolation. This can lead to writer's block, depression, and feelings of guilt when you are not writing.

When things are at their worst, and when you cannot think of the next word, let alone the next sentence, you will find that everything else in your life will begin to take precedence over writing. Cleaning out your closet, washing your car, or running errands will seem vital, and the need immediate. If you give in, these distractions will take you away from your thesis, which is exactly what your subconscious mind is trying to do.

Being unable to write another word and becoming blank-minded at the thought of writing anything is common enough for most writers. Depression and doubt about your work should be expected. No one ever said it was going to be easy, so it's okay to have bad and wordless days. The best writers have them. *It is all a part of the writing process.*

Once you've accepted the fact that you will experience thesis-inspired writer's block and depression, it's time to look around and see what you can do about it.

CREATE A WORKING ATMOSPHERE

Writing a thesis is like being self-employed. Most people are tied to a 9-to-5 routine where they are obligated to be on the job because they're working for someone else. Not putting their time in on a regular basis will result in their unemployment. You, on the other hand, are working for yourself. Nobody is going to make you work. In fact, no one cares whether you work or not. You are in charge, and it is up to you to designate what needs to be done, and when to do it.

Make out a work schedule for yourself and stick to it. Write down the hours you will devote yourself to your thesis, and the hours that will be occupied with other pursuits. When working on your thesis, make certain you include time for breaks and meals. We are all creatures of habit, and we have been trained to follow direction. Having a schedule you can see lends authority to your task, and helps you stay at it even when you don't seem to be producing. The very act of placing yourself among your books and notes for a specific time each day helps to get by the rough spots.

Make your writing manageable by breaking it into small segments. Concentrate on single paragraphs or pages at a time. Go for the little victories. If you write a page or even a line that sounds good and that you are happy with, celebrate it. Give yourself credit for what you produce. Don't worry about quantity — that comes from stringing paragraphs together. If you are positive with yourself, each line and each paragraph you produce will encourage you to do more. And the more you get on paper, the easier it will be to come out of writer's block and depression periods when they happen.

BUILD A SUPPORT GROUP

Next, learn to be your own best friend, and gather a support group around you.

We tend to take the support we get in our early years in school for granted. Family, friends, and colleagues all seem to be able to get behind time spent acquiring a bachelor's degree, or going for a law, medical, or other professional degree. But the reasons behind a Master's degree are sometimes harder to define, and thus harder for friends and family to understand.

You can expect to spend six months to a year of concentrated work writing your thesis. For some it will be even longer. It is important during this period that you interact with people who understand your commitment and the discipline it will take for you to complete your task.

What you will need is positive people with whom you can discuss your work, your frustrations, and your successes; people who wish you well. Stay away from those who are not willing to try to understand what you are doing; those who wonder "why you are still in school." Look out for people who keep asking: "are you still working on that?" Or: "when are you going to get a job?"

You *are working*. Your *job* during this period is thesis writing. Learn to prize those who reinforce your commitment.

Within your circle of family and friends is one of the best places to develop your support group. Though many of them may not understand what you are doing, they know you best, and are more willing to try to comprehend your objectives.

Fellow students, especially those who are also working on a thesis, can be good sources of feedback and support. They will be experiencing the same ups and downs as you, and with them, you will share a commonality of purpose.

You may find individuals from your school's teaching staff, in or out of your department, willing to give valuable encouragement and help. They, after all, have been through the process and survived. There is nothing like helpful advice from battle-scarred veterans.

What you need are sympathetic listeners willing to share the frustrations and joys of your work. They should be willing to help you find ways to handle your problems without indulging in amateur psychoanalysis at your expense. And they should respect you enough to tell you when you are indulging yourself in complaining, instead of defining obstacles that must be overcome. You will need encouragement, not pampering, to write your thesis.

Since the responsibility for your thesis is yours alone, you have to develop a strong sense of the importance of what you are doing and a strong desire to complete it. Faith in yourself and self-reliance are the key elements to your success. In the final analysis, only you can sustain yourself when you are down. Liking yourself, and learning to be your own best friend will go a long way toward building a strong foundation under the support system you develop.

TAKE TIME OFF

It is important, when you are concentrating hard on a project, to relieve the strain by taking time off. We all need periods of rest and relief, that, like sleep, renew our strength and freshen our outlook. Writing your thesis will never be far from your mind, but it is essential that you physically separate yourself from it from time to time and do something different.

Take a couple of days off once in a while. Go for frequent drives or walks. Work in your yard or garden. Go to the movies, a concert, or a party. Build something — a model airplane or a bookshelf, for example.

Too much concentration can lead to burnout. Learn to pace yourself, and to give your mind and your body frequent respites from the strain of your efforts.

Chapter Nine

WRITING YOUR THESIS ABSTRACT

Most universities require an abstract to accompany the submission of a Master's thesis. The abstract is a summary of the entire thesis. It should describe, in short, concise language, your statement of purpose, methods of investigation, and conclusions reached.

ABSTRACT CONTENT

The abstract should begin with a clear statement of the problem or problems you are researching. Ask yourself what the purpose of your paper is, and what you are trying to prove or discover. Try to express these points in the fewest words possible.

Describe briefly your methods of investigation, and where and how you obtained your information. Relate how you used the materials and data you found to study your problem and make your points. Outline your system of analysis.

Finally, state your conclusions, and how they relate to the original problem.

FORM AND LENGTH

Each graduate school has a set of requirements regarding the form and length of abstracts. Most schools set limits for the number of words that can be used. A few have no limits. Check with the Graduate Office or your department to ascertain the abstract length desired by your college or university.

If you wish, you can have your thesis abstract published through University Microfilms International. For a fee, they will microfilm your thesis, and publish the abstract in their quarterly journal, *Master's Abstracts*. The journal is distributed internationally, and readers, if they are interested, may order a copy of your thesis from the microfilm files of UMI. Most universities require that all doctoral dissertations be published through UMI.

To take advantage of this service, you must limit the thesis abstract submitted to UMI to 150 words or less (350 words for dissertations), no matter what your school may require. Since most schools allow longer abstracts, the easiest way to meet this requirement is to write a supplementary abstract to go with your submittal. Information on UMI and its services should be available through your Graduate Office.

ABSTRACT IMPORTANCE

The abstract may or may not be required at your final examination. Your committee may not even read it. On the other hand, it may be the one part of your thesis that they read with the most intensity. To play it safe, your abstract should be written with as much care as your thesis.

Your thesis will be deposited in your college or university library and made available to the academic and local community. The abstract is bound with it, usually in the front of the book, and serves the same purpose as the published abstract. It is used by potential readers to determine the content of your thesis, and decide whether or not to read the entire publication. To encourage others to benefit from your work, it is vital that your abstract contain a precise and well-written summary of your thesis.

Chapter Ten

HOW TO PREPARE
FOR YOUR ORAL EXAM

The oral examination is nothing more than a question and answer period. Your committee members will ask the questions, and you will answer them to the best of your ability. Unfortunately, through the processes of institutionalized education, it sometimes seems to be a hostile event: you against them. It is an alarming prospect for most graduate students, partly because of its reputation, partly from the aura of ominous mystery that surrounds it. You can ameliorate your position and stave off anxiety by finding out what to expect at your oral exam, and by adequately preparing yourself for it.

STAY IN TOUCH

From the beginning, you and your thesis committee know that your thesis is being written by you to be judged by them. Once you begin writing, however, it is easy to simply disappear from your department, and from the minds of your committee members. Guidelines are often vague on how often you should meet with your advisor during this period, and it may never even be suggested that you meet with your committee members. As a result, many students fail to take advantage of services available from their advisor and committee during their project.

While you are writing your thesis, you should meet with your advisor at regularly scheduled intervals to report on your progress, have your work reviewed, and obtain advice. The actual schedule will depend on your working pace, the problems you encounter, and your advisor's requirements. Make use of your advisor and his or her expertise; that's what an advisor is for. Your thesis advisor has the background to help you overcome barriers, improve your work, and generally help you get through, what for most students, is a very tough writing project.

It is also a good idea to routinely review your work with members of your committee. These encounters will allow them to observe how you work, and to offer suggestions. You, in turn, will have an opportunity to get to know them on a one-to-one basis, and to better understand what attitudes and questions they might bring with them to your oral exam.

Working with all the members of your committee will give each of them an opportunity to contribute to your thesis. This can be an important factor, since it gives them a stake, however small, in your success. This sense of contribution will be especially important with your thesis advisor, since he will be the person working with you the most, and will be the one most familiar with your material. He will have a strong, personal interest in seeing you pass; no one wants to be known as the advisor whose student *did not* make it.

Your committee members also provide you with a safety valve against failing your oral exam. When you work with them regularly, you will have a good idea of how your work is being received. They are not likely to encourage you to take the exam if you are not prepared, or are certain to be unsuccessful in the attempt. If you get the message that your thesis is not ready, you should wait and improve your manuscript before taking the oral exam.

FOREWARNED IS FOREARMED

During the final stages of writing your thesis, you will set a date for your oral examination. At the same time, you should find out what to expect during the exam. Your advisor will chair the examination committee, will direct the questions, and will have some influence on the question areas. Go to him or her, and ask how your exam will be conducted. Ask what kinds of questions you can anticipate, from both your advisor and the other committee members.

THE QUESTIONS. Your advisor will act as the presiding officer, or moderator, during your oral exam. His job is to make certain the event runs smoothly. He watches that no one abuses you, yells, interrupts, or monopolizes the time. He will usually ask the first question. The remaining committee members will follow with questions of their own in an orderly fashion.

Two questions you should prepare for are: "Why did you choose this topic"; and "How does this topic contribute to your field of study?" Remember, the oral exam is considered a "defense" of your thesis. Be certain you know the value of your thesis and the research you conducted. And be ready, as your own chief advocate, to champion the reasons behind your work. Your committee will want to be convinced that you know what you are talking about.

You will probably be challenged on your findings or conclusions. "Why do you say this?" "What proof do you have of this?" "Is this source reliable?" "Is this date correct?" are common questions you may encounter. You never know when a section of your thesis may generate in-depth questions from one of your committee members. Your only defense is to be prepared substantively on everything.

Expect bibliographic questions about your sources. Questions like: "Which sources were the most helpful?"; "Why did you use X's book instead of Y's book?"; and "Which book did you find the most useful for this chapter?" Your committee members will be trying to determine how well you know your reference material, and why you chose specific works.

Your sources must be sound. If you have packed your bibliography, this may be where you are found out. Know your sources, especially those you quoted from the most. Know where your information came from, and how you used it in your thesis.

There may be queries concerning grammar and punctuation. Every professor seems to have his own writing style. Following a style manual (such as this one) will protect you only so much. If you don't use commas, or consistently misspell words or names of central figures in your thesis, you will be in trouble. Do not oppose differences in style between you and your committee members too strongly during your exam. Discuss them later with your advisor, and decide together which suggestions to adopt or ignore in the final draft of your thesis.

You may also be asked about your choice of words. A committee member, for example, may consider some of your selections too strong, not strong enough, or not sufficiently descriptive. There are no rules to cover this situation, and differences of opinion are common. Use good English when writing your thesis, and be ready to defend your selection of language.

Although the oral exam is considered primarily a defense of your thesis, you may be questioned about coursework in your major or minor fields. In some departments, this final exam is expressly designed to test the student's ability to answer questions drawn from the thesis, graduate coursework, and the written examination. You will be well advised to go over all your graduate work class notes prior to your exam date.

Keep in mind that your committee members may have only read through your entire thesis manuscript once before your oral exam. They will be looking at your thesis as a whole — what you are trying to prove, and whether or not they think you have succeeded. The questions they will ask, and the comments they will make will reflect what *they* feel is important.

You will be the only expert on your material in the room during your oral exam. Your committee members can't possibly match the detailed knowledge you will have of your subject. So act like an expert. State your answers in a positive manner directly to the questioner. Look confident, whether you are or not — it makes your answers more authoritative. Answer directly, without straying from the question or falling into the trap of explaining. Let your committee know by the way you conduct yourself that you are prepared, and are proficient in your material.

PRE-EXAM PREPARATION

There are various ways you can combat pre-exam jitters. One of the most effective is to find out from your department's secretary where your oral exam will be held, and familiarize yourself with the room and its setting.

Most exams are conducted in conference rooms, furnished with a long conference table with chairs placed around it. There may be a blackboard on one or two of the walls. Go to the room when it is vacant. Sit in different chairs around the table to find the one most comfortable for you. Get used to the feel of the room. If you can, spend some of your pre-exam study time in it. At the very least spend two or more thirty minute sessions in the room just before your exam date. It is important that you are at ease and in control of yourself in this particular setting; the more time you spend in it, the more comfortable you will be during your exam.

The seating arrangements during oral exams usually fall into one of three patterns: (1) the candidate on one side of the conference table and the committee on the other; (2) the candidate at the head of the table and the committee on two sides facing him or her; (3) the candidate at one end of the table and the committee grouped around the other end. Obviously, patterns one and three offer the strongest adversarial positions. The third pattern can, in fact, be very intimidating.

Check out the orientation of the room. Where are the windows in relation to the table? Will the sun shine in anyone's eyes if they face the windows during the time of day your exam is to take place? Where are the blackboards? Will you be at an advantage if you sit with one directly behind you so you can use it? If you have graphic displays to be placed on an easel, or attached to a wall, where in the room will they be best displayed? Where would you sit in relation to such a display?

The purpose of evaluating the exam room orientation is to allow you maximum control over the environment. Determine what you think will be the most advantageous seating arrangement for you and your committee. Arrive early for your exam and arrange the room the way you want it. Draw sun shades, arrange the table and chairs. Set up any displays you may want to use. When your committee arrives, suggest your seating arrangements to them.

There is nothing wrong with handicapping your exam environment in your favor, as long as you don't shout to the world that you are taking over. Everyone admires an efficient meeting coordinator, just stay cool about it. Get as much control as you can without stepping on anyone's toes. You can emphasize your preferred seating arrangements, for example, if you place yellow note pads and pencils at the places where you wish your committee to sit, and your papers at your place. The traditions of our organized society are so strong, your committee, in all likelyhood, will go directly to the places you have designated for them. If they question it, just point out that you thought the exam could be most efficiently conducted with this particular seating plan.

Rehearse your performance. Sit in the conference table position you choose for yourself, and talk about your thesis. Take both sides of the exam; make up questions, then prepare answers to them. Ask yourself the questions out loud, then answer them the same way. Get used to your voice. Listen to how you sound in the room. Work on diction, expression, and voice projection. If you can, make up a list of exam questions and have a friend quiz you. During your rehearsals, you will think of new questions; add them to your list. Knowing your material and talking about it are two different things. Take the time to thoroughly train yourself to discuss your thesis by asking and answering questions out loud in the exam room.

Above all, prepare yourself by rereading your thesis. Recheck your bibliography; make sure you know what information you obtained from each source and where you used it. Review your class notes; you never know what the committee will ask. Do not, under any circumstances, study right up to the last minute. Allow yourself a full day before your exam to rest and let your mind relax. When exam time comes, don't march as if going to your own hanging. Walk tall, take charge, and go in there and break a leg!

AFTER THE ORAL EXAM

The oral examination traditionally lasts for two hours. After the last question has been asked and the exam is concluded, your advisor will ask you to wait outside while the committee confers and decides whether or not you have passed. Waiting is done either in a daze because you are still in shock from the exam, or in a mood of extreme panic because you're worried about all the questions you think you answered wrong, or all the things you forgot to say, or wished you had said.

Whatever your state of mind, waiting is hard. Keep in mind that no one expects you to answer every question correctly. No matter how sadistic they may appear to you at the time, your committee members are aware of the pressures involved for the student taking the oral exam. They will make allowances.

A majority vote of the committee is required for a pass. Some schools require a unanimous vote. However, the verdict of the committee is rarely a question of a simple pass or fail. The oral exam is not an arena of absolutes, where you will either be loved or hated. Instead, its elements are those of compromise and qualification, of criticism and praise, and finally, of conditions.

A complete rejection of your thesis is not likely if you have kept your committee advised on your writing, and the conclusions of your research. On the other hand, passing the exam is almost always subject to the condition that the student make some revisions before a degree will be granted. The revisions are subject to review by your advisor, and sometimes by other members of your committee.

If you fail the exam, your department usually has the option of disqualifying you completely from the program, or permitting you to retake the exam after a specific waiting period — three months, for example. Taking the exam again will require certain major revisions and rewriting, since failing indicates deep-rooted problems in the basic structure of your thesis.

Give yourself the best possible chance. Keep in contact with your advisor. Make your thesis available for periodic review. Pay attention to detail in your final draft, in both appearance and content. Find out about the oral exam, how it is conducted and the kinds of questions that are asked. Control the exam environment as much as possible by familiarizing yourself with the room setting, and arranging it to your satisfaction before the event. Don't let fear undermine you and your performance. Be conscious of your knowledge of your thesis. What you know is your greatest asset.

Chapter Eleven

POST-EXAMINATION EDITING

Passing your oral exam is a major step toward completing your graduate studies. But your thesis is not finished yet. You will still have some editing ahead; important modifications that will turn your final draft into a finished work ready to take its place on a university library shelf. You should begin this post-oral editing immediately. The oral exam may be over, but you still need the final edition of your thesis accepted by the Graduate School before you can qualify for graduation.

Each member of your examining committee will make critical comments and suggestions on how they think you can improve your thesis. Some will write out their observations and questions on separate sheets of paper. Others will make notes directly on their draft copy.

Comments by your committee may include remarks on grammar, punctuation, spelling errors, or awkward or inappropriate words or phrases. It may be suggested that sections of your text be rewritten to eliminate confusion. Weak points in your analysis or unconvincing arguments may be pinpointed for change. You may be asked to correct repetitive or wordy parts of your manuscript, or to condense portions to improve readability. Areas of major criticism will have been discussed with you during your exam.

Whatever the specific comments on your thesis, you should accept them gracefully. No matter how much you disagree at the time, or feel hurt by the criticisms, your committee members will be doing you a favor by meticulously critiquing your thesis and pointing out the weak spots. Examine and consider each member's comments carefully, and record their suggestions on a master copy of your thesis.

Corrections will generally be straightforward for spelling, grammar, and typographical errors. But questions can arise over other demands by the committee. It is not unusual for committee members (who are just as human as the rest of us) to bring their personal quirks with them when reading a thesis.

Because of inherent human differences, each professor has his own sense of what is important, and what should or should not be included in a particular thesis. You can change an offending word or phrase to please one person, but if no one else on your committee recommended changes at that point, should you alter your words because of one individual's particular bias? The dilemma is obvious: when should you accept changes, when should you negotiate, and when should you hold out and insist that your work remain unchanged?

In most schools, your advisor will be the final arbiter on post-oral revision of your thesis. Negotiate with him or her on what you find contradictory or unacceptable in your committee's requests. Work out between the two of you how to handle conflicting suggestions from professors on your committee. Do not chase after committee members for clarification of comments unless your advisor suggests it. Keep the confusion down by letting him or her be your ambassador to the rest of the committee. Try to be objective; your thesis will be your proudest possession at this point. It will be difficult not to be prejudiced in favor of every word you wrote. A diplomatic demeanor, in-depth knowledge of your material, and a lot of patience will be of immeasurable value to you during this period.

When you and your advisor have agreed on the corrections and alterations to be made, and you have entered them on your master copy, begin reorganizing and rewriting. Read through your manuscript again and again and again. Change anything that does not sound right or seems awkward. You are striving for smoothness and clarity in your text. The theme of your thesis should be clear, your arguments strong, and your conclusions sound.

When you are satisfied with your revisions, it is time to read for spelling, punctuation, and typographical errors. This takes a different kind of reading. Instead of absorbing information, you must concentrate on the text a word at a time. You have to "see" each letter and punctuation mark, and ignore meaning entirely. If possible, have someone who has not read the text examine it for copy errors. They will be less likely to pass over mistakes because of familiarity with the information.

Your advisor will read through your thesis after you have completed your editing. He will be evaluating the changes you made, and will also be checking for misspelled words and incorrect grammar and punctuation. You may be required to make additional changes after your advisor is through with your thesis.

Depending on your program, you may be required to submit your thesis to a graduate coordinator within your department. The graduate coordinator will look at format rather than content. He or she will make certain that margins, spacing, pagination, and form are correct before final copies of the thesis are made and submitted to the Graduate Office. A Graduate Office reader will probably also go through your thesis and make a final check for mistakes in form. Once it is accepted, your thesis will be bound and placed in your school's library for future generations of students to read and to marvel over.

Now you can go out and celebrate.

Chapter Twelve

WHAT YOU NEED TO KNOW
ABOUT THE COPYRIGHT LAW

The subject of Copyright Law involves two major concerns: protection of your work from unauthorized use, and protection for the material created by others that you use in your thesis or dissertation.

The decision whether or not to copyright your thesis should be made with care, and with the knowledge that when your Graduate Department delivers copies to your university library for display and these copies are made available to the scholastic community, *your thesis may, for legal purposes, be considered published.*

Also, aside from the scholastic integrity involved, you should be aware of the general guidelines governing "fair use" of material taken from other writings and incorporated into your thesis. Infringing on someone's copyright by using their material without permission can be the basis of legal action against you; it can also delay graduation if you use such material without obtaining written permission to do so.

The following information is taken from The 1976 Copyright Act (17 USC, effective January 1, 1978), various analyses written about the Act, and subsequent court decisions. *The authors of this manual are not qualified to give legal advice; the contents of this chapter are intended only as an overview on the subject of Copyright Law.* For specific legal advice on copyright law, consult an attorney.

THE COPYRIGHT LAW AND YOUR THESIS

Your thesis becomes "published" when you distribute copies "to the public by sale or other transfer of ownership, or by rental, lease, or lending," or if there has been an "offering to distribute copies or phonorecords to a group of persons for purposes of further distribution, public performance, or public display" (The 1976 Copyright Act, Sec. 101). Thus, when you give archival copies, which will eventually be available to the public through your university library, to your Graduate Department, you are "publishing" your manuscript.

43

If you have not placed a copyright notice on it, you may be placing it in the "public domain." Being in the public domain means that anyone can copy it, sell it, or otherwise make use of it without having to ask your permission or pay you for the privilege.

The copyright law reserves to the author of literary, musical, dramatic, audiovisual, and other creative works, and sound recordings, the exclusive rights to:

(1) reproduce;
(2) prepare derivative works from;
(3) sell or otherwise transfer ownership;
(4) perform publicly; and
(5) display publicly

the copyrighted work. *If you think you will want to publish your work commercially, write articles derived from its contents, or otherwise try to profit from it, you should obtain a copyright registration.* Just keep in mind that receipt of a copyright certificate from the Copyright Office does not mean that the federal government will step in and punish anyone who infringes on your copyright. They only register your claim, recording the fact that you are the first claimant for the work you submit. This simply provides you with a basis to sue anyone who misuses your work.

If you publish your work without placing the copyright notice on it and later decide that you want copyright protection, you may under certain circumstances, register your copyright up to five years after publication. To do this, you must follow the procedures outlined in The 1976 Copyright Act, Sec. 405. There are, however, limitations on the recovery of damages or payment of court costs if you decide to sue anyone for unauthorized use of your work during the time your copyright was not registered. The copyright law provides a "safe harbor" for anyone who copies a copyrighted work in reliance on the absence of notice. These people are known as "innocent infringers," and may not be liable for damages.

Under The 1976 Copyright Act, your unpublished thesis or dissertation is protected from the time you commit it to paper until it is published. But the protection is of little practical value because very few people are aware of this provision in the law. If someone makes unauthorized use of your work, your only recourse is to take them to court, which can be an expensive process. The best way to protect your unpublished work is to place a copyright notice on every copy. This way, others are notified of your intention to protect your rights.

It is not necessary to register unpublished works with the Copyright Office, though you may do so if you wish.

To indicate that your work is copyrighted, you must follow the form prescribed in the copyright law. The copyright notice form is described in U.S. Copyright Office Form TX, which is used to apply for copyright protection:

The Copyright Notice: For published works, the law provides that a copyright notice in a specified form "shall be placed on all publicly distributed copies from which the work can be visually perceived." Use of the copyright notice is the responsibility of the copyright owner and does not require advance permission from the Copyright Office. The required form of the notice for copies generally consists of three elements: (1) the symbol "©" [the letter "c" in a circle — ed.], or the word "Copyright," or the abbreviation "Copr."; (2) the year of first publication; and (3) the name of the owner of copyright. For example: "© 1981 Constance Porter." The notice is to be affixed to the copies "in such a manner and location as to give reasonable notice of the claim of copyright."

For further information about copyright registration, notice, or special questions relating to copyright problems, write:

> Information and Publications section LM-455
> Copyright Office
> Library of Congress
> Washington D.C. 20559

To obtain a registration of your copyright, fill out Form TX, obtainable from the Copyright Office address above, and return it, along with $10 for the registration fee and two copies of your thesis. If you submit the registration form and fee only, you will be required to send two copies of your registered work to the Copyright Office within three months of publication. Copyright protection is not lost if you do not send the copies, but fairly heavy monetary fines can be imposed if the Copyright Office requests copies and you fail to send them.

In some cases, an exemption from the copy submittal rule can be obtained. Two reasons for exemption or an alternative form of deposit are: financial hardship (imposed on the author), and the publication of less than five copies of the work (The 1976 Copyright Act Sec. 407). Write to the Copyright Office for details on how to obtain an exemption. Special rules apply to creative works other than written publications; write to the Copyright Office or consult an attorney for specific advice in your case.

THE COPYRIGHT LAW
AND THE USE OF OTHER PEOPLE'S WORK

You do not need to obtain permission to use works in the public domain, i.e., works on which copyright never existed and those on which the copyright has expired. Academic integrity, however, dictates strict identification of all source material used in your thesis, including material that is not protected by copyright, or is unpublished.

Material contained in your thesis that is protected by copyright must not only be properly acknowledged, but, unless its use comes within the doctrine of "fair use," may be included only with the written permission of the copyright owner.

Fair use, according to Section 107 of the 1976 Copyright Act, is defined as follows:

> "The fair use of a copyrighted work, including such use by reproduction in copies or phonorecords or by any other means specified [in Sec. 106] for purposes such as criticism, comment, news reporting, teaching (including multiple copies for classroom use), scholarship, or research, is not an infringement of copyright. In determining whether the use made of a work in any particular case is a fair use the factors to be considered shall include:
>
> (1) the purpose and character of the use, including whether such use is of a commercial nature or is for nonprofit educational uses;
>
> (2) the nature of the copyrighted work;
>
> (3) the amount and substantiality of the portion used in relation to the copyrighted work as a whole; and
>
> (4) the effect of the use upon the potential market for or value of the copyrighted work."

As you can see, the rules for fair use are not precisely defined. Most of the university guidelines we studied listed the inclusion in theses of excerpts of up to 150 words, provided they do not constitute a major portion of the original work, as acceptable within the fair use doctrine. Check with your Graduate Department for specific guidelines applying to you.

If you think the material you are borrowing qualifies under fair use, you may use it without written permission. However, you must credit the source for the borrowed material by including specific page numbers in a footnote reference, and listing the source in the bibliography.

If a large portion of another author's work or an entire creation (such as a photograph, a cartoon, or a completed form, for example) is to be used, you must obtain written permission.

Only two of the university style guides consulted during the writing of this manual contained forms for requesting permission to use copyrighted material. Figure 1 illustrates the form used by The Florida State University, Tallahassee, which the authors feel is the better of the two. Check with your Graduate Department to see if they have a form they prefer over this one. To request permission, type out the form, fill in all the blanks except the signature line and send it to the copyright owner through the publisher. If the copyright owner is other than an individual, fill in the name listed on the copyright notice. Publisher's addresses are listed in the back of the last volume of *Books In Print* (published by R.R. Bowker Company), which is available in the reference section of most libraries.

Most universities will not accept a thesis containing material that requires written permission for its use from the copyright owner that is not accompanied by that permission. This could delay your graduation. Obtaining permission can take weeks or months, so mail your request forms as early as you possibly can.

PHOTOCOPYING COPYRIGHTED MATERIAL. Under certain circumstances, libraries can make copies of portions of copyrighted works for the use of individual researchers. In addition, the Fair Use doctrine appears in its language, to allow portions of copyrighted works to be copied by researchers for their personal use. Such copies, however, are "not to be used for any purpose other than private study, scholarship, or research" (Copyright Office Circular R21, pg. 24).

The authors were unable to locate specific guidelines governing photocopying by individuals, so do not take the sentence above on what the Fair Use doctrine language "appears" to allow as a permissive statement. Ask your attorney or your librarian for more specific information on how to avoid liability for copyright infringement when making photocopies. Guidelines for libraries and for teachers who wish to photocopy copyrighted material for classroom use are available in Copyright Office Circular R21, *Reproduction of Copyrighted Works by Educators and Librarians*. This publication may be obtained by writing or phoning the Copyright Office and requesting it by number.

```
PERMISSION TO QUOTE/REPRODUCE COPYRIGHTED MATERIAL

I (We,)_____, owner(s)

of the copyright to the work known as

_____

hereby authorize _____

to use the following material as a part of his/her

master's thesis/doctoral dissertation  [use one or the

other]  to be submitted to the  (name of your

university).

               Inclusive      Beginning & ending words
Page           line numbers   or other identification




I (We) further extend this authorization to University
Microfilms International, Ann Arbor, Michigan, for the
purposes of reproducing and distributing microformed
copies of the thesis/dissertation  [use one or the
other].


                        _____
                        Signature
```

Figure 1. Permission form for the use of copyright material.

Chapter Thirteen

THE MECHANICS
OF THESIS PRODUCTION

As you work on your thesis, it will progress through a number of stages. The most important of these will be: (1) the creation of rough drafts from your notes; (2) producing a final draft for your committee; and (3) making archival copies of your thesis for the Graduate Department. Each of these stages require that you set words to paper. How you approach this requirement — writing by hand, using a typewriter, or using a word processing program on a computer — will influence how efficiently you work, and the quality of your product.

Your final draft should be prepared with care, and with special attention to neatness. The archival copies you must submit before graduating will be required to meet your school's requirements for page format, image quality, and the type of paper used. Some advanced planning on your part will smooth your way to successful completion of your thesis.

PUTTING WORDS ONTO PAPER

It is said that F. Scott Fitzgerald wrote his manuscripts in longhand. But Fitzgerald had a typist who cleaned up his work before it was sent to his publisher, a luxury few of us can afford. Most colleges and universities require that papers be typewritten, or have a typewriter-like appearance. During undergraduate studies, individual professors sometimes relax this rule, but most graduate schools are more demanding, and require all papers to be typed before they are handed in. Rarely, if ever, is a hand-written thesis manuscript acceptable. Your choices, then, revolve around what kind of machine you will use to obtain typewritten copy.

MANUAL AND ELECTRIC TYPEWRITERS. A manual typewriter will serve most of your needs, and is usually less expensive than an electric. Electric typewriters, however, do a better job in a number of areas: They allow you to type faster by eliminating the necessity of having your fingers supply the force to move the typing keys. Constant letter impact pressure and more exact engineering employed in manufacturing electric typewriters results in straighter and more evenly spaced lines of type than is possible with most mechanical machines. And carbon ribbons, available for higher-priced electrics, make a cleaner, sharper letter image on paper.

In addition, corrections are made easily and neatly with the self-correcting ribbons available for some electric typewriters.

TYPING ON A COMPUTER. The practice of typing on a computer has become relatively commonplace with the increased availability of personal computers. Many word processing programs are available that allow you to type your manuscript on a computer's electronic screen, then print it on paper at a later time. Computer keyboards are almost identical to those on standard typewriters. The main difference is that computer keyboards contain extra keys that provide special functions.

As you type on a computer keyboard, your copy appears letter-by-letter on the computer's video screen. Most word processing programs have features that allow you to stop typing and go back into your text and make corrections on the screen. You can change words, sentences, or whole paragraphs, entering the new copy and erasing the old. Entire blocks of text, from paragraphs to pages, can be moved to new locations in the text, or erased in one operation. These "editing" features make personal computers the first choice for writing long papers and thesis manuscripts.

When you want to stop, you can file your work onto a storage disk, where it will reside in the form of electromagnetic patterns until you again call it up on the video screen for review or editing. When you want a hard copy of your work printed on paper, you can connect a printer to your computer and have your manuscript printed out by typing the appropriate commands (from your instruction manual).

The most valuable advantages of computer word processing over typewriting are the ability to make changes without having to retype pages, and the ability to print your work as often as you wish, knowing it will be an accurate copy each time.

IMAGE QUALITY. The sharpness, and the density (blackness) of the letters printed by your typewriter or computer printer will have a strong influence on the readability of your copy. There is a wide range of letter designs available to choose from, and a number of methods used to transfer the letter forms onto paper. The following suggestions will help you select the combination that will provide you with the highest quality available.

Letter Size. Two letter sizes are traditionally available on typewriters: elite and pica. Elite is generally equivalent to ten-point (12- or 15-pitch) type on computer printers; pica to 12-point (10-pitch) type.

Pica, or 12-point size type is overwhelmingly preferred for manuscripts, though most schools will accept elite. Pica types produce six lines of copy per vertical inch; elite types, eight lines per inch. Larger type sizes are available on some computer printers, but it is wise to stay with tradition when typing your thesis. In short, use pica-size type.

Letter Design. Older typewriters use what is known to typesetters as a typewriter-face, or square-serif design. It consists of letters drawn with lines of all the same thickness, and utilizes serifs (the small cross-lines at the foot of some letters, and at the ends of the top line on the capital "T").

Most modern typewriters employ a modified Roman type face design, originally derived from the carvings on Roman monuments, and long a favorite of book publishers. The most noticeable feature of Roman letters is that they are drawn with lines of variable thickness to emphasize curvature. They also employ serifs. Tests show that Roman type designs have the highest readability of all the typefaces.

A third type face design you may find on modern typewriters is known as sans-serif. As you might guess from the name, the small cross, or serif, lines have been eliminated; the lines are of a single thickness. This type design has a high recognition factor, and is used for chapter and subject headings in printed publications. It is, however, difficult to read in large blocks. For this reason, you should not use it for any manuscript copy you intend to have read by faculty members. In many schools, sans-serif type is not acceptable on papers.

Italic or script faces are frequently available on typewriters and computer printers. Next to Old English, these are the most difficult type faces to read. They will seldom be acceptable for papers, so do not use them.

A Roman-style type face will be your best choice. If you have to use an older typewriter, the square-serif type will be acceptable in most circumstances. Use pica, or 12-point, type. The larger-size type face will read better, and conform to most Graduate Department requirements.

The Printed Image. In addition to type face design, typewriters and computer printers use two basic methods to transfer letters from the keys onto paper. The first is by impacting a molded letter against a cloth or polyester ribbon carrying a thin film of ink or carbon black on the surface facing the paper. The pressure of the molded letter hitting the ribbon causes the ink or carbon black to transfer to the paper, depositing an image of the selected letter. Molded letters, whether from traditional typewriter elements, typing balls, rotating thimbles, or daisy wheels, all leave a solid line image known as "letter quality."

Many computer printers and some "electronic" typewriters use a print head containing a matrix of small pins to print letters on paper. When an electronic keyboard letter is struck, it sends coded pulses to internal circuitry, which in turn causes a combination of pins in the print head to strike the ribbon and paper, leaving an image of the selected letter made up of small dots. These are known as "dot matrix" printers. The dots may be low density, as in a 4x7-dot matrix, or high density, as in a 24x24-dot matrix. Some printers allow selection of high or low density printing by the operator. Besides the different appearance, low density print speeds are faster on most machines.

One of the most debated questions in Graduate Departments across the country concerns what quality of printing may be acceptable for thesis manuscripts printed on dot matrix printers. At this point, low density dot matrix print is generally not acceptable. High density printing, called "near letter quality" by the manufacturers, has been approved by some schools.

If you intend to use a dot matrix printer, our advice is to first check with your advisor. In many cases, even low-density dot matrix printing is acceptable in the final draft for your committee. Next, take samples of printed pages from the printer you intend to use to your Graduate Department, and ask if they are acceptable for your archival copies. Do this early. If you are turned down, you will have time to make other plans.

The dot matrix printers discussed above use actual pins, driven by electromagnets to impact their letter images. A new standard of very high density dot matrix printing became available with the marketing of Apple Computer's Laserwriter and the Hewlett-Packard Laser printers. These machines, and others using the same or similar technology, employ a laser beam and photocopy machine techniques to print letters from a 300x300-dot matrix that is difficult to distinguish from letter-quality printing. If you intend to use one of these printers, be sure to obtain prior approval from your Graduate Department.

The purpose of submitting letter quality, error-free copies of your thesis to your Graduate Department is two-fold. First, your school will bind two or three copies, and make them available through the school's library to the academic community. And second, some theses, and almost all dissertations, are microfilmed for publication and distribution. It is imperative that the letters of the text be photo-reproducible both in their form and in their density.

In addition, your school, by accepting your thesis and awarding your degree, places its academic reputation on the line. The quality of your thesis argument is judged by your committee. The quality of your thesis product, in the form of a book, is ensured by the Graduate Department imposing requirements for type quality and margin standardization. See figure 2 for examples of typewritten and printed text copy.

Print Image Transfer. An inked cloth, or polyethylene carbon-black surfaced ribbon is required for all the image transfer methods discussed except the laser printers. The selection of ribbons will strongly affect the quality of your image.

If you are using a cloth ribbon, specify nylon or silk, with a high density black ink. When the letters begin to fade, or gray-out, replace the ribbon immediately to maintain uniform density on your typed pages. Do not, however, change a ribbon in the middle of a page. This would result in two densities of type on the same sheet. Do not use standard cloth typewriter ribbons on dot matrix printers. Use the special ribbons sold in computer stores for these machines. They look the same, but the special ribbons carry an oil-based ink that lubricates the impact pins. Using standard typewriter ribbons can result in damage to dot matrix printers because they lack the required lubricant.

Cloth ribbons are available for some electric typewriters and computer printers. However, they do not make as sharp an image as carbon ribbons, so we do not recommend their use except for rough draft copies.

Carbon ribbons come in two styles: single-strike correctable, and multi-strike. When you use a typewriter with the correctable feature, you will need to use a correctable ribbon. Always buy the highest quality ribbons available. The nature of correctable carbon ribbon is that the image can be lifted from the paper fairly easily. Portions of letters typed with poor quality ribbons will sometimes not stick to the paper, or may flake off later.

Multi-strike ribbons carry a carbon surface that sticks more permanently to the paper when transferred. They are called multi-strike because some computer printers pass them through the machine more than once. Watch for image fade or gray-out if you use a multi-strike ribbon. Replace the worn-out ribbon immediately.

Draft-quality dot matrix printers
like this one are good for fast
printouts and are frequently
acceptable for committee copies of
the finished thesis.

Near-letter-quality dot matrix
printers form more readable text and
are accepted by a few schools for
final text.

Manual typewriters print solid
letters, which are preferred for
final thesis copies,

As do electric typewriters, which,
with their carbon ribbons, are
still the standard for office use.

Letter-quality computer printers,
though, are gaining on electric
typewriters because of their
association with word-processing
programs.

The latest development in computer
printers is the "laser" printer,
which produces high-density
(300x300) dot matrix characters.

Figure 2. Samples of typewritten and printed text copy

SPECIAL CHARACTERS AND SYMBOLS

English is one of the few languages that does not require special marks or symbols under normal use. If you utilize foreign words or phrases, however, you may encounter a need for accent marks (as in Spanish and French), umlauts (as in German and some Scandinavian languages), or other diacritical marks. Typewriter or printer fonts containing these marks can be obtained for some machines with changeable typefaces. When they are not available, or you need special mathematical or other symbols, individual characters can be inserted neatly in the manuscript by hand using a pen and permanent black ink. India ink and a fine-line graphic arts pen are preferred; do not use a ballpoint pen or a water-based felt tip pen to make insertions in your archival copies.

CORRECTIONS

All corrections must be made with the same typeface used to print your thesis manuscript. Strikeovers, crossed-out words or lines, and words inserted between printed lines are not acceptable.

When submitting original copies, do not use liquid correction fluids, white strike-over carbon, or any type of paste-on correction tape. In short, type a perfect copy, or use only self-correcting ribbons to make corrections. These requirements may be relaxed by your advisor for final draft copies submitted to your committee; check with him or her for what is allowable.

If you are submitting photocopies made from your original (the preferred method), you may make corrections in any manner you desire, as long they are not visible on the archival copies.

PAPER

Standard white, 8-½x11-inch, 20-lb bond paper is satisfactory for your rough drafts and for the copies you submit to your committee. Most universities, however, insist that the final copies of your thesis be prepared on cotton-rag content paper with a watermark that specifies the rag content. The rag content requirement will vary, depending on the school, from 25 percent to 100 percent.

Rag content papers contain fewer of the impurities found in lesser quality sulfite papers which are sold as standard bonds. Papers containing these impurities tend to dry out and become brittle with time, or sometimes fade or turn color. Using a high quality paper assures the school that your thesis will be readable for many years.

Some schools allow the replacement of rag content paper with specially manufactured archival paper that has no rag or wood fiber content. These papers are usually less expensive than rag papers. Find out from your Graduate Department whether or not you can use this archival paper, then check on to see if it is available through your campus book store or paper dealers in your area.

In general, most schools will not accept erasable bond paper, onionskin, or any other paper with a chemically treated surface. All of the paper in your archival copies must be of the same color, weight and texture. Lined, punched, stapled, or any paper that is not white (including ivory) is not acceptable. The paper surface must not have smudges, an embossed texture, or manufacturing defects. Type or print on one side only.

Continuous-form computer paper is usually acceptable for copies submitted to your committee. But check whether your Graduate Department will accept the perforated edges on your archival copies; you will probably be required to use clean-cut paper, and feed your printer one sheet at a time.

Some universities require, or recommend, that your manuscript be produced on special thesis paper that outlines the correct margins in blue, called, of course, "blue-line paper." This paper can usually be purchased at the university book store.

MAKING COPIES

First, determine how many final draft copies will be required for your committee, then find out how many final copies you must submit to the Graduate Department. Your school's style manual or your thesis advisor should provide you with this information.

A real born-in-the-woods-masochist will make copies with carbon paper. With photocopy machines so readily available, this is a terrible waste of time.

Concentrate on making your original copy as clean and as free from mistakes as possible. When you have done this, take it to the nearest copy shop and run off the number of copies you need for your committee. Check out the photocopy machine carefully. Make sure it produces good black copies, with no toner in the background. If it doesn't, ask the shop operator to service the machine until it does, or look for another shop and another machine.

"Original and three copies," is the terminology used in most Graduate Department style manuals for the number of archival copies they require. Where the process is understood, four photocopies can be substituted. University archival librarians have told us that when properly done, photocopy manuscripts are preferred over originals, or carbon copies. Electrostatic photocopiers, they tell us, duplicate the type on your original with a wax-content toner containing graphite.

The image is then baked into the paper by a thermal process, and is more permanent than most typewriter or computer printer-produced text.

If you plan to photocopy your thesis for submission, prepare the original with extreme care. Carefully inspect each final page for broken type or other problems. Corrections, as outlined above, can be made with self-correcting tape, correction liquids, or paste-on tapes. When your original is ready, run off a "master" copy; this will be used as an original for the archival copies you will submit.

Use liquid correction fluid (make sure it is formulated for photocopy) to white-out smudges, unwanted typing marks, outlines of correction tape, and imperfections in the paper surface. When you have an absolutely clean master copy, you are ready to duplicate your archival copies.

The advantages of submitting photocopies to the Graduate Department are a significant savings in time and cost, and a superior product. You can use standard bond paper for your typed original and your "master" copies, then run off your archival copies on whatever special paper is required. The alternatives are to type, or to have someone else type, all the copies required, or to print as many originals as necessary on your computer printer. The greatest hazard in typing each copy separately, is the number of mistakes that can be made each time the manuscript is retyped. The drawback to multiple computer printouts is the time and concentration required for the job.

The most important factor in photocopying archival copies is that you must use a top-of-the line electrostatic photocopy machine to obtain the required quality. The copy machines available in drug and hardware stores will not make the quality copies you need. Test the image permanency of any machine you intend to use by giving it five minutes to "set," then rubbing your finger across the type on a copied page. If the ink smears or comes off, one of three things may be wrong: (1) the machine's thermosetting process is not working; (2) the machine does not use a thermosetting process; (3) the paper you are using is not compatible with the machine's thermosetting process. Consult the copy shop operator to work out a solution.

In some cases, operation of the better quality copy machines is restricted to copy shop personnel, so you will have to hand the work over to them. Some on- or near-campus copy shops offer thesis copy services. You just hand them your original; they make the "master" and run off the required number of copies. Many times, they also stock the special kinds of paper required for the job. Check with your department or graduate department for thesis copy services available to you locally. They should also be able to tell you where to purchase any special paper stock required. If not, check with your campus book store, or with local paper dealers (not retail outlets).

All papers have a "grain" direction, either top to bottom, or side to side. The paper sheet will curl in the direction opposite the grain. For this reason, you want top-to-bottom, or long-grain paper, so any curl will be in line with the binding edge.

When you purchase paper a ream (500 sheets) at a time, the label on the package will usually indicate whether it is long or short grain. If you don't have the original wrapper, fold a sheet length-wise, then across the short dimension. The fold made in the grain direction will be smoother than across it. Another check is to tear a sheet, from top to bottom, then side-to-side. The edges will be smoother along the tear made in the direction of the grain.

Beware of paper purchased in campus book stores; most paper supplied to retail outlets is short-grained. If your duplicating service provides the paper, be sure you specify long-grain paper when you order your copies.

TIPS ON HIRING A TYPIST

You may do your own typing on the final draft of your thesis, you may hire a professional typist, or you may have an accommodating friend type the final draft for you. Whichever option you choose, remember that the ultimate responsibility for accuracy, for both content and form, is yours alone.

If you have someone else do your typing, it should not be an inexperienced or inefficient typist. Skill is required if the manuscript is to be accurate, consistent in style, acceptable in form, and neat and attractive in appearance. Your manuscript should be proofread carefully before and after submission to the typist. Regardless of a particular typist's skill, he is only responsible for copying exactly the material that he has been given.

Finding a competent thesis typist can save you money and heartache. Your department, advisor, or fellow graduate students may be able to suggest qualified candidates; many Graduate Departments maintain a list of thesis typists. Ideally, the person chosen should have experience in typing theses for your university, and should be familiar with the required format guidelines. Ask prospective typists for references. Go to the library and use the reference list to locate and check copies of theses your prospect typed for other students. A sloppy typing job depreciates the well-written thesis. In contrast, the work of a professional typist will appear sharp and clean, and can only add to the quality of a manuscript.

As important as selecting a good typist is reaching a good business understanding with the person you choose. Disagreements over deadlines or extent of services can unnecessarily complicate the submission process and may delay your graduation. In general, you and your typist should agree (in writing) on the following points:

1. **Form of your original.** Will the typist accept hand-written drafts or pasted together copies: How much more will the typist charge to type a draft that is in less than ideal condition (hand-written notes in the margins, extensive corrections).

2. **Materials.** A clear understanding should exist about who will provide paper, ribbons, and any other special material (e.g. special type or symbols).

3. **Typewriter.** The typewriter should conform to the required type face and size. The typist should have access to the same typewriter if later corrections or additions are necessary.

4. **Proofreading.** Are you or the typist the final proofreader? Responsibility for performing this important function should be clearly assigned.

5. **Corrections.** Who's responsibility are they? How much will they cost? Do certain kinds cost more than others? Will they be scheduled so as to meet your submission deadlines?

6. **Revisions** (after your oral exam). Will the same typist still be available? How much will the revisions cost?

7. **Deadlines.** Can you agree on deadlines? Will the typist be able to comply with the schedule? Are there to be monetary or other penalties assessed if the typist fails to meet deadlines?

8. **Quality.** Who will be responsible for judging the final quality of the work? What recourse will be available if the quality is not adequate?

9. **Rates.** Both the candidate and the typist should understand whether the charges are to be by the hour, the page, or the job. Extra charges for difficult work should be agreed upon in advance.

In short, make your arrangements as clear and explicit as possible. Keep in mind that a thesis typist is NOT:

1. **A mind reader.** Give the typist a neat draft (preferably typed) to type from, with any corrections typed or neatly printed, and inserted in appropriate places in the text.

2. **An Editor.** Do not expect the typist to edit your work for you. Proofread your manuscript before giving it to the typist and check the spelling and dates of all references. Proofread the work again after it has been typed.

3. **An errand person.** Do not expect the typist to do any legwork for your thesis unless you have made special arrangements, and are willing to pay for extra chores.

Chapter Fourteen

STANDARDIZING YOUR
PAGE AND TEXT FORMATS

Nearly all graduate schools publish their own style manual or style guide containing page and text format specifications for theses and dissertations. The purpose behind these specifications is to achieve a uniform and professional appearance within an individual school's library system, and with the academic community.

Page format requirements consist of the descriptions of margin allowances and the placement of text on pages. This involves front material pages, the first page in each chapter, regular text pages, and back material pages. Front material pages include the approval page, the abstract, the title and copyright pages, the foreword, introduction, and contents. Back material pages include endnotes, the bibliography, appendices, and the index. Placement of page numbers is also described under page formatting.

Text formatting involves spacing between headings and the text, and between lines of text. Indentations and footnote placement are also covered under text formatting.

The formatting suggestions in this chapter are the result of a study of thesis style guides obtained from universities across the country, and information from book design professionals. The specifications adopted reflect the requirements of a majority of the universities, as well as advice contributed by the consulted book designers. Not all of the school style guides agree with these specifications — but very few differ significantly. The universities contributing to this study are listed on the acknowledgement page in the front of this handbook.

Your department or graduate school may have special requirements that vary from those discussed in this chapter. Be sure you obtain a copy of your school's style guide. If differences exist, your university's style guide will supersede this one. You may wish to write your university's particular specifications, if any, into this handbook, in order to work from a single reference.

PAGE FORMAT

Page formatting requires that you place the typed copy for each particular kind of page (title, foreword, contents, text, etc.) within a set of margins, and space it according to specific directions. To accommodate this requirement, and to provide you with an easy reference guide, each type of page used in a thesis is represented in the illustrations at the end of Chapter 15, and are presented in the order they would appear in a completed thesis.

The following format specifications should remain constant throughout your thesis.

GENERAL TYPING RULE. The first rule in typing theses and dissertations is to type on one side of the page only. The single exception to this rule is when there is no room for the title on a full-page illustration. In this case, the title is placed on the back side of the previous page, facing the illustration. See Chapter 16, "How to Prepare Illustrations, Tables, and Special Material" for additional information.

GENERAL PAGE MARGINS. All pages will have a top, bottom, and right margin of one inch from the edge. The left margin will be 1-½ inches; the additional space is for binding. All copy *must* remain inside these margins, with a single exception: page numbers placed at the upper right-hand corner of the page (see figure 6). If you intend to photocopy your thesis to make archival copies, you should take into account that copy machines will enlarge the text two to three percent. Keep the text well within the allowed typing space.

PAGE NUMBER PLACEMENT. On front matter pages and the first page of each chapter or section, the page number will be placed in the center of the text at the bottom of the page, with the bottom of the number resting on the one-inch margin.

On all other pages, the page number will be placed at the top of the page, one inch from the right side, so the bottom of the number rests on the top one-inch margin.

Page numbers must stand alone: do not use periods, hyphens or other decorative marks with page numbers.

Inserted pages carrying number-letter combinations (3a, 3b, 27a, etc.) are not acceptable.

PAGE NUMBER SEQUENCE. All front matter pages are numbered in lower-case roman numerals (ii, iii, iv, etc.). The title page is counted as the first page, but does not carry a number. The copyright page, if used, is not counted, and does not carry a number. The first page of front matter carrying a number, is numbered "ii."

All text pages following front matter carry arabic numbers, beginning with "1" on the first page of text and continuing to the end of the book. All text pages must be accounted for in the numbering sequence.

When a thesis is bound in more than one volume, each volume will contain front matter and text pages. The lower-case Roman numeral series for front matter pages is started over in each succeeding volume. The arabic numeral series for text pages continues in each volume, with the first page of narrative text carrying the number following the last page of the previous volume.

Abstracts, when they precede the title page, are not considered part of the thesis, and are numbered with a separate sequence of arabic numbers. When the abstract is included in the front matter sequence, it is numbered with the front matter series of Roman numerals.

Official forms preceding the title page are not numbered.

TITLE SPACING. The first line on any page carrying a title (title page, front matter pages, and the first pages of chapters and major sections) will rest on a line two-inches from the top of the page.

TEXT SPACING. On title pages, the first line of text will begin three spaces below the last line in the title. The last line of text will be two spaces above the page number.

On all other pages, the first line of text will begin two spaces below the page number. The last line of text will be on or above the bottom one-inch margin.

COPYRIGHT PAGE. The first line of the copyright notice will rest on a line four-inches from the top of the page.

TEXT FORMAT

The visual appearance of any text strongly affects its readability. Commercial book designers take great care in matching type styles, margins, line spacing, and subject heading organization to minimize eye strain and promote easy reading. The basis for thesis design is derived from a long history of using the typewriter for manuscripts submitted for publication, and for assigned scholastic papers. Its final form is a cross between the two: page and text spacing is standardized for readability, and organized in logical parts and subparts, and room is left for editing or correcting. The following specifications are a compilation of the most desirable features for a thesis from a design perspective, taken from our study of university style guides and from advice contributed by book designers.

TEXT HEADING ORGANIZATION. Most theses are organized in book form. They are divided into chapters or sections, with each division covering a portion of the thesis topic. The divisions are arranged in a sequence that presents a logical flow of information, from an introduction of the thesis subject to the writer's final conclusions. There may be as many divisions as is necessary to clearly present the desired information to the reader.

Chapter or section divisions are further divided into subdivisions to present information in a logical sequence. The first-level subdivisions usually progress from an overview to the more focused information of the chapter or section topic, followed by additional sub-level divisions offering progressively more detailed information.

Book designers separate the text into subdivisions by selecting distinctive type faces, and by the physical arrangement of headings on the page. Theses are divided in the same way, utilizing heading placement, capital and lower case letter combinations, and underlining. A standard typewriter can be used for either of the following title organization schemes. See figures 3 and 4 for examples of heading organization. Most theses will not require the number of subdivisions illustrated; use only what you need to make your presentation clear.

Some scholastic departments or Graduate Offices will require specific heading organization for theses. Check with your advisor to determine what form you should employ.

```
                       CHAPTER IV

                 CHAPTER OR SECTION HEADINGS
              ARE IN ALL CAPITAL LETTERS, CENTERED,
                   AND CARRY A ROMAN NUMERAL,

SECOND-ORDER HEADS

      Are typed in capital letters, flush against the left
margin, on a separate line.

      THIRD-ORDER HEADS. Are in all capital letters,
underlined, indented, and in line with the text.

      Fourth-Order Heads. Are in capital and lower-case
letters, underlined, and in line with the text.
```

Figure 3. General-purpose heading organization.

```
                        CHAPTER 5

       CHAPTER OR SECTION HEADINGS ARE CAPITALIZED,
           CENTERED, AND CARRY ARABIC NUMERALS

5.1 SECOND-ORDER HEADS
     5.1.1 Are numbered according to placement in the chapter
or section, are typed in capital letters, flush with the left
margin, and on a separate line.
     5.1.2 Paragraphs are numbered sequentially by adding a
digit, then advancing the last digit in the paragraph number
(5.1.3, 5.1.4, 5.1.5). Every paragraph must be numbered.
     5.1.2.1 THIRD-ORDER HEADS. Are numbered according
to placement under second order heads. The title is typed in
capital letters, underlined, indented, and in line with the
text.
     5.1.2.2 Paragraph numbering is the same as for second-
order heads.
     5.1.2.2.1 Fourth-Order Heads. Are numbered according to
placement under third order heads. The title is typed in
capital and lower-case letters, underlined, indented, and in
line with the text.
     5.1.2.2.2 Paragraph numbering is the same as for second-
order heads.
```

Figure 4. Numbered sequence heading organization.

A second form of numbered sequence heading organization uses Arabic numerals only for the first- and second-order heads. Paragraphs under these heads are not numbered, but use the third- and fourth-order typed style headings illustrated in figure 3.

CHAPTER TITLES. Chapter titles are typed in all capital letters, and centered between the page copy margins two spaces below the chapter number heading. They may consist of more than one line, with the lines single-spaced. The lines need not be of the same length. Each new chapter begins on a separate new page.

GENERAL TEXT. The main body of the thesis text is double-spaced, and begins three spaces below the chapter heading. The first line of each paragraph begins six spaces in from the left margin.

A minimum of two lines of text must appear at the bottom of the page when dividing a paragraph or beginning a new subdivision. If the natural page break leaves fewer than two lines, end the page sooner. The bottom one-inch margin is the minimum space to be left on the page; it may be larger. When the text does not continue to the bottom of the page, bottom page numbers are still to rest on the bottom one-inch margin line.

Hyphenated Words. Hyphenated words at the end of sentences are to be kept to a minimum of three per page. The right-hand one-inch margin is the minimum space to be left on the page; it may be larger. Carry long words falling at the end of lines to the next line rather than risk intruding on the margin. Never hyphenate the last word on a page.

Underlining Words in the Text. (1) Underline the titles of books, periodicals, pamphlets, plays, movies, long poems, musical compositions, works of art, and the names of ships, trains, aircraft, and spacecraft when used in text.

(2) Underline foreign words or phrases not commonly used in the English language. (Foreign expressions in common use are usually found in the body of collegiate dictionaries. Additional familiar foreign expressions are listed in the "Foreign Words and Phrases" section at the back of the dictionary.)

(3) Underline letters, words, or numbers when they are used in a sentence for other than their commonly accepted meaning. (The ph in physics is pronounced as if it were an "f.")

See the Appendix, *The Punctuation Handbook* for additional information on underlining.

Long Quotes. Quotes of four lines or more are typed in "block" form, single-spaced, indented four spaces from the normal right and left margins, and are not enclosed in quotation marks. The first line of each paragraph is indented two additional spaces, so the line begins six spaces in from the left margin. Block-typed long quotes begin three spaces below the general text, and are separated from subsequent text by three spaces. Quotes of less than four lines are enclosed in quotation marks and typed within the general text. (See figure 18.)

Long Poems. Poems of four lines or more are typed in "block" form, with a left and right margin four spaces in from the general text margins. Line spacing of the poem will depend upon its importance to the text. The general text resumes two spaces after single-spaced poems. Poems of less than four lines are typed within the general text, enclosed in quotation marks, with a virgule (/) separating the lines of the poem.

Footnote Documentation. Footnotes or endnotes documenting the text correspond to an arabic numeral placed at the end of a sentence, phrase, or statement that the author wishes to support with authoritative and substantial information. The reference number may be typed superscript, one-half space above the line[26], or be enclosed in parentheses (26). The first reference in the thesis is numbered "1," and the numbering sequence continues to the end of the thesis.

FOOTNOTES. Footnotes should be typed at the bottom of the page where they are cited. They are divided from the text by a line made by a typed underline 20 spaces long, two lines below the general text. The footnote entries begin two spaces below this line.

Each footnote entry begins by repeating the reference number used in the text. If superscript reference numbers are used in the text, they should be superscript in the footnote. If they are enclosed in parentheses in the text, the matching footnote number should be typed without parentheses, and followed by a period. The first line begins six spaces in from the left margin. The second, and additional lines, are flush with the left-hand margin. (See figure 18.) Footnote entries are separated from each other by a line space. When a page contains three or more footnote references, and the references are short, the entries may be typed in-line, with two spaces separating the end of one entry and the reference number of the next.

Space for typing footnotes at the bottom of a page must be planned carefully; the last line must conform with the general margin rules, and not intrude on the bottom one-inch margin. Very long footnotes may be continued to the next page, but this practice is discouraged. See Chapter 17, "What You Need To Know About Footnotes and Endnotes" for information on the content and form of footnotes.

ENDNOTES. Endnotes are cited in the same manner as footnotes; by placing a number in the text where the author wishes to make the reference. Instead of typing the references at the bottom of the page where they occur, however, they are listed at the end of each chapter, or at the end of the general text. In-text reference numbers are typed superscript[26], or enclosed in parentheses (26). The numbering sequence begins with "1," and continues sequentually to the end of the thesis.

The first page of a listing of endnotes is titled "ENDNOTES," or "NOTES" in all-capital letters, on a line two inches from the top of the page. Endnote entries begin three spaces below this title.

Endnotes are listed by the chapter in which they appear, so the first entry under the page title is "Chapter 1," on a line by itself. Skip one line and type the first endnote entry. Skip two lines between the last entry for a chapter and the next chapter heading, and repeat the listing format. See figure 19 for a listing format example. The page number is entered at the bottom of the page, centered, and rests on the bottom one-inch margin line.

Subsequent endnote listing pages are numbered in the upper-right corner, in line with the one-inch right margin, and resting on the one-inch top margin. Endnote entries begin two spaces below the number. When less than two lines of an entry are left on a page, carry the entire entry over to the next page.

Each endnote entry begins with the reference number, followed by a period (26.). The first line is indented six spaces. The second, and additional lines, are flush with the left-hand margin. Entries are separated from each other by a line space. (See figure 19.) The contents and form for endnotes is described in Chapter 17, "What You Need to Know About Footnotes, Endnotes, and Other Documentation Styles."

BIBLIOGRAPHY. The first page of a bibliography listing is titled "BIBLIOGRAPHY," "A SELECTED BIBLIOGRAPHY," "REFERENCES," "SELECTED REFERENCES," "LIST OF WORKS CONSULTED," or "LITERATURE CITED" (see Chapter 18, "What You Need To Know About Bibliographies and Reference Lists" for the differences in title selection) in all-capital letters on a line two inches from the top of the page. Bibliography entries begin three spaces below this title. The page number is entered at the bottom of the page, centered, and rests on the bottom one-inch margin line.

Subsequent bibliography pages are numbered in the upper-right corner, in line with the one-inch right margin, and resting on the one-inch top margin. When less than two lines of an entry are left on a page, carry the entire entry over to the next page.

Each bibliographic entry is flush with the left-hand margin. The second, and additional lines, begin six spaces in from the left margin. Entries are separated from each other by a line space. (See Figure 20.)

When bibliographic entries are classified into separate sections (primary and secondary sources, letters, diaries, newspapers, etc.), the section headings are centered between the page margins, three spaces below the preceding entry. Section headings of more than one line are single-spaced. Bibliographic entries resume two line spaces under the section heading. When less than two lines of the first entry under a section heading are left on a page, end the page short, and carry the heading and the entry over to the next page.

APPENDICES. Appendices may be composed of standard text, newspaper clippings, photocopies of letters, photographs, graphs, maps, charts, or any other form necessary to present information to the reader. Each appendix, however, should begin with a title page in the same format as the first page of a chapter or main section. When no explanatory text is required, the page will contain only the appendix letter or number designation and the title. When text is included, it should comply with the general text format requirements. When presenting other than standard textual material, consult with your thesis advisor and your Graduate Department to determine a suitable format.

The sequence of page numbers in the main text is continued in the appendices. Separate numbering sequences for appendices (i.e., A1, A2, A3, etc.,) are not acceptable.

GLOSSARY. The first page of a glossary should comply with the format of the first page of chapters or main sections. Succeeding pages should comply with the general text format.

Glossary entries should begin flush with the left margin. Second and additional lines should be indented six spaces. Entries should be single-spaced, with two spaces between entries.

INDEX. The first page of an index should comply with the format of the first page of chapters or main sections. Subsequent pages should comply with the general text format.

Index entries should begin flush with the left margin. Second and additional lines should be indented three spaces. Entries should be single-spaced, with a single space between entries. Leader dots (period-space-period) should extend from the last line of each entry to the entry page number. The dots should be vertically in line with each other.

Chapter Fifteen

ORGANIZING YOUR THESIS
FOR PRESENTATION

The basic arrangement of theses' contents is dictated by the long-standing practices of book publishers, with a few elements added to satisfy the needs of academia. Most non-fiction books, including theses and dissertations, contain title and copyright pages, and a table of contents. They may also contain a dedication, acknowledgements, a foreword, a preface, and an introduction by someone other than the author. Together these are known as "front matter," that is, in front of the text. All front matter pages, both in commercial and academic books, are sequentially numbered with lower-case Roman numerals.

Next is the narrative text, or body of the book. This is followed, according to choices made by the author and the publisher, by end-notes, a bibliography, appendices, a glossary, an index, and an author profile. The sections following the text are collectively known as — you guessed it — "back matter." Academia's contributions to this list of pages are the abstract, official forms, such as the Thesis Committee Approval Page, and the author's Vita, which takes the place of the commercial publisher's author profile. In academic books, all text and back pages are sequentially numbered with Arabic numbers. Commercial books sometimes use separate letter-number sequences for their appendices.

Assembling your thesis into its final form is more complex than writing and handing in a term paper. Such a paper would probably represent no more than one chapter of your thesis. Once your main text is written, you must formulate a check-off list of front and back pages that will be needed, then type and assemble these pages according to the formats required by your Graduate Department.

Each university lists required page formats and a preferred order of pages in their thesis style guide. Most schools follow standard publishing practices; the major differences between schools are the placement of the abstract and the official forms employed by the

Graduate Department. Figure 5 lists an order of pages reflecting the preferences in most of the university thesis and dissertation style guides studied while writing this handbook, and the general practices of most commercial book publishers. Figures 6 through 20 illustrate the page formats; they are presented in the same order they are listed in figure 5. Be sure you check your Graduate Department style guide; where your school's requirements differ from this list, the school list takes priority.

Front Flyleaf (blank page)
Abstract (when submitted separately)
Title Page
Copyright Page (if used)
Thesis Committee Approval Page
Dedication Page (optional)
Acknowledgement Page (optional)
Biography/Vita (2nd choice placement)
Epigraph or Frontispiece (optional)
Abstract (when bound with thesis)
Introduction (optional)
Table of Contents
List of Tables
List of Figures or Illustrations
List of Abbreviations Used
List of Symbols Used
Preface or Foreword (optional)
Text (main body of the thesis)
Appendices
Endnotes (if compiled at the end of the text)
Bibliography, Selected References, or Literature Cited
Glossary
Index
Biography/Vita (1st choice placement)
Back Flyleaf (blank page)

Figure 5. Page sequence organization for theses and dissertations.

PAGE CONTENT DESCRIPTIONS

Following are descriptions of page format and content requirements for the most often used of those pages listed in figure 5:

FRONT AND BACK FLYLEAF PAGES. These are blank sheets of the same paper used for the thesis text. They serve as protective pages when the thesis is bound; they are not numbered.

ABSTRACT. The abstract may consist of one or more pages. The first page is formatted the same as a first chapter page; subsequent pages are formatted the same as general text pages. Two possible locations are listed in figure 5 for the abstract: one for schools that consider it a document separate from the thesis and bind it in front of the title page; and one for schools that consider it a part of the thesis and bind it where a commercial publisher would place the foreword to a text, just in front of the contents pages.

The abstract should provide an accurate account of the thesis contents, and should succinctly summarize the thesis. It should provide enough information for the reader to decide if the text is of interest to him, and serve as a critical introduction to the whole thesis. See Chapter 9, "Writing Your Thesis Abstract," for additional guidelines.

TITLE PAGE. The title page bears the title of the thesis, the name of your scholastic studies department, the institution granting the degree, the degree to be awarded, the year the degree will be granted, and the writer's name, *exactly* as it appears in the records of the school Registrar. The title page is considered page "i" in the front matter Roman numeral sequence, but is left unnumbered. Some schools include the copyright notice on the title page. (See the Copyright Page listing below for information on copyright form.)

The first line of the thesis title is typed in the center of the general page margins in all-capital letters on a line two inches from the top of the page. The remaining title page copy will be typed centered, as illustrated in figure 8, and spaced vertically to present an optical balance on the page. Titles of more than one line should break in a logical place for easy reading. For example:

ANIMALISM AND HUMOR
IN THE WORKS OF JOHN STEINBECK

not;

ANIMALISM AND HUMOR IN THE WORKS
OF JOHN STEINBECK

Some schools require multi-line titles to be typed in inverted pyramid style (like the second title above). The authors feel that the arrangement that best communicates the thesis contents to the reader should supercede such concerns as the length of lines or the preference of formats.

With an increasing reliance on computer listings and electronic information retrieval, it is important that writers take great care in selecting a thesis or doctoral dissertation title that will allow others to locate their work. "Catchy" titles should be avoided. A thesis concerning "The Purchasing Power of Unwed Teenage Mothers," for example, would be difficult to locate if titled "Suzie Needs A New Wardrobe." *Your title should clearly describe your thesis contents, and should facilitate its location on a subject index through the use of key words.*

Avoid the use of phrases such as "A Study of," "Effect of," "Laboratory Study of," and other such introductory phrases in your title. It is not only bad form, but uses an unnecessary number of words. Abbreviations in titles are unacceptable unless they are recognized acronyms in the study field. Symbols should not be used in your title.

COPYRIGHT PAGE. Commercial publishers place their copyright notice on the back of the title page. Since thesis and dissertation pages are typed on only one side, a special page is inserted following the title page to carry the copyright notice. The notice is centered between page margins, with the first line resting on a line four inches from the top of the page. (See figure 9.) The Copyright Page is not counted in the numbering sequence, and carries no number.

The copyright notice consists of the word "Copyright," followed by the year of publication and the copyright owner's name. For example:

Copyright 1985 James P. Verrica
All Rights Reserved

You may wish to modify your copyright notice to include international protection. The Universal Copyright Convention (UCC) specifies that the international copyright symbol, the letter "c" in a circle (©), be used in place of the word copyright. You may use the symbol only, or both forms, and still satisfy U.S. requirements. The United States is not a signatory to the UCC, but most European countries are. Some of them will recognize U.S. copyrights when they carry the proper notice.

The Buenos Aires Convention, to which the U.S. is signatory, requires inclusion of the statement "all rights reserved" in the copyright notice. The Buenos Aires Convention covers most Central and South American countries as well as the United States.

Anything else added to your copyright notice (i.e., "No part of this book may be reproduced in any form . . .," and other such notices) is just extra fluff to scare the would-be infringer. It does not provide you with extra legal protection, so don't depend on it for such.

When you do not copyright your thesis or dissertation, common practice is to insert a blank page after the title page. The only reason we can assign for this, is that under certain circumstances copyright protection can be obtained for uncopyrighted work up to five years after publication. If this option is exercised, the page will be available on which to place the copyright notice.

This short discussion on copyright is intended for information only. For legal advice on this subject, consult an attorney. For additional information, and a discussion on whether or not to copyright your thesis, see Chapter 12, "What You Need To Know About The Copyright Law."

THESIS COMMITTEE APPROVAL PAGE. The Approval Page is your official receipt that your thesis has been sanctioned. By signing the Approval Page, the members of your committee, the head of your department, and the Dean of Graduate Studies attest to the fact that they have inspected and accepted your work. The signed form is bound into the archival copies.

The first line of the Approval Page rests on a line two inches from the top of the page, and is flush with the left margin. The second line begins six spaces in from the left margin. (See figure 10.) Four spaces separate the first signature line (typed as a solid underline) from the last line of the approval statement, and each subsequent signature line from the name above it. Names of the members of your thesis committee are typed one space below the signature lines.

The word "APPROVED" at the bottom of the page is typed flush with the left margin, 27 lines below the first signature line (measuring from the first line allows insertion of additional committee signature lines if required). The first signature line below that is four spaces, and the last signature line is four spaces below the name above it. Your department head and the Dean of the Graduate School sign on these lines.

The number of copies requiring original signatures varies with different schools; check with your Graduate Department. All signatures *must be in black ink*. You should provide your own pen, one that writes smoothly without skips, so the signatures will all be the same color and density. *No one may sign for another person on your Approval Page*, so check the availability of your signers carefully to be sure you can get the signatures you need, and still meet the Graduate Department's schedule for submission and graduation.

DEDICATION PAGE. The Dedication Page provides you with an opportunity to give special tribute to persons, organizations, or others who provided extraordinary encouragement to you in your scholastic career. It is an optional page, and used for very special recognition only.

The Dedication Page does not require a title in the usual sense. The dedication is expressed in the first line of text, which rests on a line four inches from the top of the page. Copy is flush left, six spaces in from the left page margin and single-spaced. The right margin is moved in six spaces from the right page margin. (See figure 11.)

ACKNOWLEDGEMENT PAGE. Acknowledgements recognize the persons to whom you are indebted for guidance and assistance, those to whom you are grateful for any special non-routine aid, and any grant fund support you may have received for your work. The Acknowledgement Page is optional.

The Acknowledgement Page is formatted in the same manner as first chapter pages, with the word "ACKNOWLEDGEMENTS" resting on a line two inches from the top of the page, and text beginning three spaces below. Margins, line spacing, and paragraph indentations are the same as for general text. (see figure 12.)

BIOGRAPHY/VITA. The Vita, Curriculum Vita, Biography, or Autobiographic Statement is a summary of the writer's educational and professional background, usually contained on one page. A Vita section is required for most dissertations, and is usually optional for theses. The information should include

1. Date and place of birth. Citizenship should be added if not indicated by place of birth;

2. Educational institutions attended and degrees awarded;

3. Professional positions held; and

4. Scholastic publications.

The Vita should not contain personal information. Two possible locations are listed in figure 5 for the Vita; check with your Graduate Department for your school's preference. When included, the Vita carries a page number (Roman when placed in front of the book, Arabic when in the back) but is not listed in the Table of Contents.

The Vita Page is formatted the same as the first page of a chapter, with the title resting on a line two inches from the top of the page. See figure 13 for a suggested format.

EPIGRAPH OR FRONTISPIECE. This page is optional for those authors who wish to include a pertinent quotation as an epigraph or an illustration as a frontispiece to the entire thesis or dissertation.

When a quote is used, it should be short and to the point. The first line of copy rests on a line four inches from the top of the page. All lines of text are flush left, six spaces in from the left margin and single-spaced. The right margin is moved in six spaces from the right page margin. (See figure 14.)

When an illustration is used, with or without a title at the bottom, it is placed centered on the page margins and optically balanced between the top and bottom of the page.

INTRODUCTION. When it appears before the Table of Contents, the introduction is not considered a part of the thesis, and is usually written by someone other than the author. Most often it serves as an endorsement by a person well known to the potential reading audience, and outlines why he thinks the text deserves attention. When the title "Introduction" is used for the first chapter of the text, it is an essential part of the thesis, contains the author's opening remarks about the thesis subject, and describes the scope of the completed work.

The Introduction is formatted the same as the first page of a chapter. Subsequent pages are formatted the same as general text pages.

TABLE OF CONTENTS. This is essentially a topic outline of your thesis. It may be broad, listing only major (chapter) headings, or it may be detailed, listing all subdivisions. The title of each Table of Contents entry *must* correspond exactly to the title listed in the text. If you list some second- or third-order subheads, list *all* subheads of the same order. Each listing must specify a page number where it can be found.

Table of Contents pages will vary according to the type of subject and the level of detail in the listings. In general, the first page is formatted like a first page of a chapter, with the title on a line two inches from the top of the page, and the first entry three spaces below that. All copy must be kept within the general page margins. Subsequent pages are formatted the same as general text pages. See figure 15 for a recommended listing format and spacing.

LIST OF TABLES. The first page is formatted the same as a first page in a chapter; subsequent pages are formatted the same as general text pages. List each item number, caption or title, and page number as it appears in the text. Include all items, including those appearing in appendices.

The listed title should match that used in the text; however, if a title or caption is lengthy, a shortened form may be substituted. The shortened form may be truncated, but do not change the order of words. If a table extends beyond one page, only the first page number is entered.

Tables may be numbered consecutively throughout the manuscript, (Table 1, Table 2, Table 10) or by chapter (Table 1.1, Table 1.2 for Chapter One; Table 2.1, Table 2.2, for Chapter Two; Table 10.3 for Chapter Ten), depending on the major section format you employ. See figure 16 for a suggested format and spacing.

LIST OF FIGURES OR ILLUSTRATIONS. Format the same as for the List of Tables.

LIST OF ABBREVIATIONS USED. Format the same as for the List of Tables.

LIST OF SYMBOLS USED. Format the same as for the List of Tables.

PREFACE, OR FOREWORD. The Preface, which is optional, is a short discourse meant to either put the reader in the right frame of mind for the understanding or appreciation of what he is about to read, or to supply him with information that may be necessary to his proper understanding or use of the information to come. It may also contain qualifying statements covering the thesis as a whole. It differs from the first chapter of the text, which may or may not be titled "Introduction," in that the author speaks directly to the reader, departing from the principles of scholarly writing. It leads into the material rather than tells what is in it.

The Preface is formatted the same as the first page of a chapter. Subsequent pages are formatted the same as general text pages.

TEXT. The text is the main body of the thesis, and contains the author's narrative argument on the subject being written about. It is divided into major divisions (usually chapters), each presenting a main point in the argument; with each division containing subdivisions that will aid in understanding the given information. See figures 17 and 18 for text page examples.

The formatting of text pages is described in Chapter 14, "Standardizing Your Thesis Page and Text Formats."

APPENDICES. Material in Appendices is intended to contribute, by way of illustration, amplification, or the citation of documents,to the narrative text of the thesis. Additional illustrative material such as forms and documents, long or complex tables, charts, computer print-outs, and amplifying technical notes are examples of information that might be placed in an appendix. (See Chapter 16, "How To Prepare Illustrations, Tables, and Special Material" for suggestions on how to process non-conforming material for inclusion in your thesis.)

A small collection of material can be grouped together and simply titled "APPENDIX." If, on the other hand, the amount of material is extensive, it should be classified into categories with each grouping constituting a separate appendix. When more than one appendix is used, each must be designated by a letter (Appendix A, Appendix B, . . . Appendix F), as well as by a title.

If a cover sheet is used, the Appendix designation (APPENDIX A, for example) should appear centered between the page margins, on a line four inches down from the top of the page, and typed in all capital letters. The title, if one is used, should be centered and begin two spaces below the Appendix designation. If the title is more than one line, it should be single-spaced. If the title appears on a page with Appendix material, its placement should be consistent with chapter headings.

ENDNOTES. References cited in the narrative text may be placed at the bottom of the page where the citations occur, listed at the end of each chapter, or combined into a single list at the end of the text. When they are listed at the end of each chapter or at the end of the text, they are termed "Endnotes" (see figure 19).

For a description of the Endnote format, see Chapter 14, "Standardizing Your Thesis Page And Text Formats." For a discussion of Footnote and Endnote differences, and the numbering and author-date systems for citing references and sample pages, see Chapter 17, "What You Need To Know About Footnotes, Endnotes, and Other Documentation Styles." For examples of Endnote entries, see Chapter 18, "Footnote, Endnote, and Bibliography Examples."

BIBLIOGRAPHY. Every thesis or dissertation that makes use of other sources either by direct quotation or by reference must list those sources at the end of the manuscript. Each listed source must be accurate and complete enough for the reader to find in the library. References to unpublished sources must clearly indicate where the material may be found.

The title "Bibliography" is usually reserved for a list of all the sources you consulted that are relevant to the topic of your paper, whether actually cited in the text or not. "Selected References," "Literature Cited," or some other equivalent title is used for a list that contains only those items that you actually referenced in the text. See figure 20 for sample bibliography pages.

For a description of the Bibliography format, see Chapter 14, "Standardizing Your Thesis Page And Text Formats." For a discussion of Bibliographic forms and uses and sample pages, see Chapter 18, "What You Need To Know About Bibliographies and Reference Lists." For examples of Bibliography entries, see Chapter 19, "Footnote, Endnote, and Bibliography Examples."

GLOSSARY. A Glossary is an alphabetized list of uncommon or specialized words used in the text, and their definitions. It is an optional (and rarely used) section in a thesis or dissertation.

The first page of a Glossary is formatted the same as a first page of a chapter; additional pages comply with the general text format.

INDEX. An Index is an alphabetized list of key words representing information to be found in the text, and the page number(s) where it may be found. It is an optional and little used (unless the document is unusually long or complex) section in a thesis or dissertation.

The first page of an Index is formatted the same as a first page of a chapter; additional pages comply with the general text format.

TABLE 1. A SUMMARY OF PAGE AND TEXT FORMAT SPECIFICATIONS

Page Margins

Top, right, and bottom.	1 inch
Left.	1-1/2 inch

Page Numbers

Title pages.	Center, on a line one inch from the bottom edge.
All other pages.	Upper-right corner, on a line one inch from the top, and one inch from the right edge.

Title Placement

Title page, front matter pages, and the first pages of chapters and sections.	On a line two inches from the top edge of the page. Titles are single-spaced.

Text Spacing

On title pages.	Begins three spaces below the last line in the title. Ends two spaces above the page number.
All other pages.	Begins two spaces below the number. Ends on or above the bottom one-inch margin line.
	All text is double-space.
Paragraphs.	Begin six spaces in from the left margin.
Long quotes and long poems.	First line begins six spaces in from the left margin, and ends four spaces before the right margin. subsequent lines begin four spaces in from the left margin and end four spaces from the right margin for "block" typing form.

TABLE 1. CONTINUED.

Long quotes (cont.)

	All lines are single-spaced when typing in "block" form.

Footnotes

In-text reference numbers.	May be typed superscript[6] one-half space above the line of text, or enclosed in parentheses (6). There are no spaces between superscript reference numbers and the words they follow.
Typed at the bottom of pages where they are referenced.	Separated from text by a line made by a typed underline 20 spaces long, two spaces below the text. Entries begin two spaces below this line.
	Footnote entries begin with the reference number, superscript if typed that way in the text; number only followed by a period if not typed superscript.
	First line begins six spaces in from the left margin. Subsequent lines are flush with the left margin.

Endnotes

In-text reference numbers.	May be typed superscript[6] one-half space above the line of text, or enclosed in parentheses (6). There are no spaces between superscript reference numbers and the words they follow.
Page format.	See Chapter 14 for a detailed description.
Bibliography, Appendices, Glossary, Index	See Chapter 14 for a detailed description.

SAMPLE MANUSCRIPT PAGES

The following pages contain illustrations of pages representing various parts of the thesis. Typing formats for each of these pages are described in Chapter 14. Contents of the pages are described in Chapter 15. Keep in mind that these illustrations represent the formats described in this handbook; where the requirements of your Graduate Department differ, their specifications take precedence.

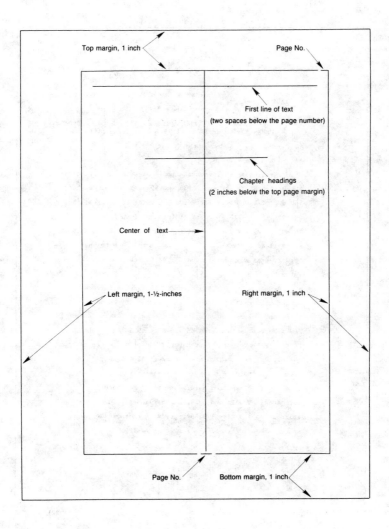

Figure 6. General layout of page margins.

ABSTRACT OF THESIS

SPIES IN AMERICA
GERMAN ESPIONAGE IN THE UNITED STATES 1935-1945

by Ronald P. Urquart

This thesis addresses the topic of German espionage in the United States between 1935 and 1945. It examines what the expectations were for Germany's spies in America, their activities, and the success or failure of their operations. In addition, the reaction of the American public to these spies is also studied, as well as the response to what was perceived as a threat to the United States from Nazi Germany.

Research on this subject reveals that there were a number of German espionage agents involved in several different spy rings operating in the United States before Pearl Harbor. Information obtained by these individuals primarily concerned the transportation of war materials to the Allies, and America's industrial and military production. Much of the information sent to Germany was not of a highly classified nature and could be found in technical journals and publications, and through verbal affirmation and visual sightings. Most of these German spies were arrested in the summer of 1941

1

Figure 7. Abstract page.

SPIES IN AMERICA

GERMAN ESPIONAGE IN THE UNITED STATES 1935-1945

by

RONALD P. URQUART

A thesis submitted to the Department of History
and the Graduate School of Portland State University
in partial fulfillment of the requirements
for the degree of

MASTER OF ARTS
in
HISTORY

Portland, Oregon
1984

Figure 8. Title page.

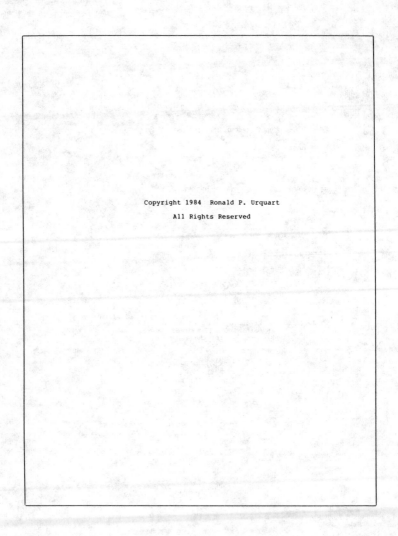

Copyright 1984   Ronald P. Urquart

All Rights Reserved

Figure 9. Copyright page.

TO THE OFFICE OF GRADUATE STUDIES AND RESEARCH:

The members of the Committee approve the thesis of
Ronald P. Urquart presented on October 26, 1984.

_____
George C. Clagborne, Chairman

_____
Jerald M. Spencer

_____
Dorthea S. James

_____
William B. West

APPROVED:

_____
Vernon T. Charles, Head, Department of History

_____
James F. Healy, Dean of Graduate Studies and Research

Figure 10. Thesis committee approval form.

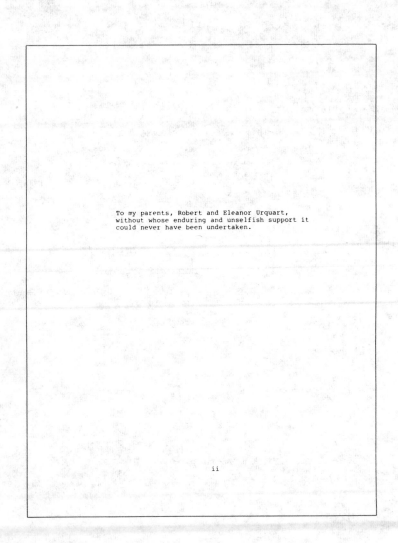

To my parents, Robert and Eleanor Urquart,
without whose enduring and unselfish support it
could never have been undertaken.

ii

Figure 11. Dedication page.

ACKNOWLEDGEMENTS

The author wishes to express sincere appreciation to
professors Spencer and James for their assistance in
preparing this manuscript. Special thanks are due to Mr.
Hugh Danzer of the United States National Archives for his
help in locating original documents of the German Abwehr
and to Mr. Thomas Karlile of the Federal Bureau of
Investigation for suggestions relating to the location of
official reports of the trials of German saboteurs.

iii

Figure 12. Acknowledgement page.

```
                              VITA

NAME OF AUTHOR:   Ronald P. Urquart

PLACE OF BIRTH:   Portland, Oregon

DATE OF BIRTH:    January 14, 1958


GRADUATE AND UNDERGRADUATE SCHOOLS ATTENDED:

        Portland State University, Portland, Oregon
        University of the Pacific, Stockton, California


DEGREES AWARDED

        Master of Arts in History, 1984, Portland State
        Bachelor of Arts, 1980, University of the Pacific


AREAS OF SPECIAL INTEREST:

        Modern Germany, 1860-1945


PROFESSIONAL EXPERIENCE:

        Teaching Assistant, Department of History,
           Portland State, 1983


AWARDS AND HONORS:

        Who's Who Among Students in American Universities
           and Colleges, 1978
        Member, Phi Alpha Theta, Portland State Chapter, 1983


PUBLICATIONS:

        Article on German espionage in the United States
           accepted for publication by American History
           Illustrated


                              iv
```

Figure 13. Biography/Vita Page.

Figure 14. Frontispiece (left) or epigraph (right) page.

TABLE OF CONTENTS

vi

Figure 15. Table of contents page.

LIST OF TABLES

vii

Figure 16. List of tables page.

CHAPTER 11

THE STRUCTURE OF THE AMT/AUSLAND ABWEHR

The German military intelligence system, which had operated since the days of Frederick the Great, was dismantled after Germany's defeat in World War I. However, it was almost immediately resurrected. The purpose of this intelligence service was ostensibly to combat leftist extremism and revolution within the new and unsteady Weimar Republic, and to counter attempts of foreign interference in German governmental operations. The clandestine aim of this revived intelligence group was to aid Germany in circumventing portions of the Versailles Treaty restricting foreign intelligence operations. The title of the new intelligence and reconnaisance service was "Abwehr" from the verb "abwehren," which means literally "to ward off or defend," a designation intended to camouflage the real purpose of the Abwehr--to spy for Germany.

Captain Wilhelm Canaris became the head of the Abwehr on January 1, 1935. Canaris was forty-eight years old when he took over the Abwehr. A career Navy man, he entered the Imperial Naval Academy in 1905. He served on the light cruiser "Dresden" in World War I, until the ship was scuttled near Chile in 1915. Canaris first became involved

5

Figure 17. Text page, first page of chapter,

115

containment of Soviet Expansion. In 1942, the eight
saboteurs had been "the enemy." in 1948, Burger and Dasch
were merely extra baggage left over from an incident that
had lost much of its significance; who were remembered only
to be released, deported, and forgotten.

The Abwehr learned of the dissolution of Operation
Pastorius when J. Edgar hoover announced the arrests of the
eight German agents. General Lahousen, the head of the
Abwehr's sabotage division wrote:

> . . . we have been receiving Reuter reports of
> American radio transmission announcing the arrest of all
> participants in Operation Pastorius, some in New York
> and some in Chicago. The reports give the correct
> location of the landings in the United States and of the
> targets for the planned sabotage operations.[71]

The failure of Operation Pastorius, coming no more than a
year after the Abwehr had suffered the humiliating Sebold
affair, hurt the status of the Abwehr in Germany. The
inefficiency of Admiral Canaris' intelligence organization
had become more apparent, and it was clear it had blundered
particularly in its choice of agents.

In 1941, William Sebold had double-crossed the Abwehr
and an entire network was uncovered by the FBI. Now a year
later the Abwehr had been stung by treachery again, this
time in the person of George Dasch, who ambitiously sought

---

[71]Charles Wighton and Gunter Peis, _Hitler's Spies
and Saboteurs_ (New York: Henry Holt and Co., 1958), 71.

Figure 18. Text page, with indented quotation and footnote.

ENDNOTES

CHAPTER 1

1. David Kahn, <u>Hitler's Spies</u> (New York: Macmillan Co., 1978), 226-229.

2. Stanley E. Hilton, <u>Hitler's Secret War in South America</u> (Baton Rouge, Louisiana: Louisiana State University Press, 1981), 16; Kahn, <u>Hitler's Spies</u>, 238.

3. Karl Abshagen, <u>Canaris</u>, trans. Alan Broderick (London: Hutchinson and Co., 1956), 93.

4. Ibid., 95; Heinz Höhne, <u>Canaris</u>, trans. J. Maxwell Brownjown (New York: Doubleday and Co. 1979), 197.

5. Höhne, <u>Canaris</u>, 196.

6. United States Navy Department, Office of Naval Intelligence, <u>Espionage-Sabotage-Conspiracy: German and Russian Operations 1940 to 1945</u> (Washington, D.C.: Office of Naval Intelligence, 1947), Appendix III/I; National Archives and Records Service, <u>Guides To German Records Microfilmed at Alexandria, Virginia., No. 80. Records of the German Armed Forces High Command, Part VI, Amt Ausland/Abwehr</u> (Washington, D.C.: National Archives and Records Service, 1982), xv; Hilton, <u>Hitler's Secret War</u>, 17.

CHAPTER 2

7. Kahn, <u>Hitler's Spies</u>, 47; National Archives and Records Service, No. 80, x.

8. Höhne, <u>Canaris</u>, 303.

9. United States Navy Department, Office of Naval Intelligence, OP 32-E, <u>German Naval Intelligence</u> (Washington, D.C.: Office of Naval Intelligence, 1946), 10.

10. U.S. Navy, <u>Espionage-Sabotage-Conspiracy</u>, 9.

11. U.S. Navy, <u>German Naval Intelligence</u>, 10.

160

Figure 19. Endnotes, first page of listing.

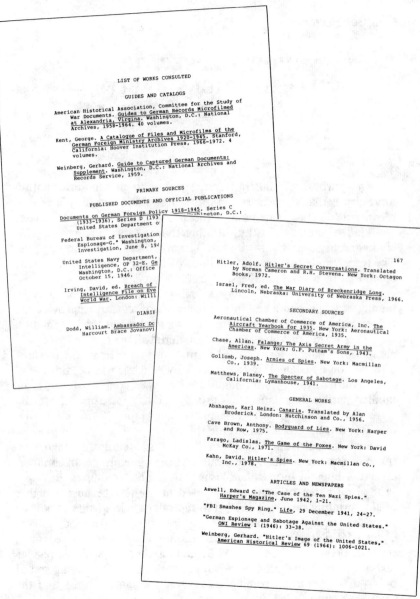

LIST OF WORKS CONSULTED

GUIDES AND CATALOGS

American Historical Association, Committee for the Study of War Documents. Guides to German Records Microfilmed at Alexandria, Virgina. Washington, D.C.: National Archives, 1958-1964. 40 volumes.

Kent, George. A Catalogue of Files and Microfilms of the German Foreign Ministry Archives 1920-1945. Stanford, California: Hoover Institution Press, 1966-1972. 4 volumes.

Weinberg, Gerhard. Guide to Captured German Documents: Supplement. Washington, D.C.: National Archives and Records Service, 1959.

PRIMARY SOURCES

PUBLISHED DOCUMENTS AND OFFICIAL PUBLICATIONS

Documents on German Foreign Policy 1918-1945. Series C (1933-1936), Series D (193⸺ ⸺shington, D.C.: United States Department o⸺

Federal Bureau of Investigation⸺ Espionage-G." Washington,⸺ Investigation, June 8, 194⸺

United States Navy Department, Intelligence, OP 32-E. Ge⸺ Washington, D.C.: Office October 15, 1946.

Irving, David, ed. Breach of⸺ Intelligence File on Eve⸺ World War. London: Willi⸺

DIARIE⸺

Dodd, William. Ambassador Do⸺ Harcourt Brace Jovanovi⸺

Hitler, Adolf. Hitler's Secret Conversations. Translated by Norman Cameron and R.H. Stevens. New York: Octagon Books, 1972.

Israel, Fred, ed. The War Diary of Breckenridge Long. Lincoln, Nebraska: University of Nebraska Press, 1966.

SECONDARY SOURCES

Aeronautical Chamber of Commerce of America, Inc. The Aircraft Yearbook for 1935. New York: Aeronautical Chamber of Commerce of America, 1935.

Chase, Allan. Falange; The Axis Secret Army in the Americas. New York: G.P. Putnam's Sons, 1943.

Gollomb, Joseph. Armies of Spies. New York: Macmillan Co., 1939.

Matthews, Blaney. The Specter of Sabotage. Los Angeles, California: Lymanhouse, 1941.

GENERAL WORKS

Abshagen, Karl Heinz. Canaris. Translated by Alan Broderick. London: Hutchinson and Co., 1956.

Cave Brown, Anthony. Bodyguard of Lies. New York: Harper and Row, 1975.

Farago, Ladislas. The Game of the Foxes. New York: David McKay Co., 1971.

Kahn, David. Hitler's Spies. New York: Macmillan Co., Inc., 1978.

ARTICLES AND NEWSPAPERS

Aswell, Edward C. "The Case of the Ten Nazi Spies." Harper's Magazine, June 1942, 1-21.

"FBI Smashes Spy Ring." Life, 29 December 1941, 24-27.

"German Espionage and Sabotage Against the United States." ONI Review 1 (1946): 33-38.

Weinberg, Gerhard. "Hitler's Image of the United States." American Historical Review 69 (1964): 1006-1021.

167

Figure 20. Bibliography, first and second pages of section.

Chapter Sixteen

HOW TO PREPARE
ILLUSTRATIONS, TABLES,
AND SPECIAL MATERIAL

The purpose of illustrative material is to present information more clearly than it can be stated with words alone. For the purpose of identifying illustrative material in theses, the term "figure" designates any kind of graphic illustration other than a table. Figures may include graphs, charts, drawings, diagrams, maps, and photographs. The term "table" designates columns of information, which may be composed of words, numbers, or both.

Figures are predominately visual presentations used to communicate details contained in an idea or a concept, or to provide the reader with pictorial evidence for his own analysis of the information the writer wishes to convey. Tabular material allows the reader to view comparative data in a structured format, or to determine the merit of information by evaluating the process by which it was obtained.

A third catagory, Special Material, may consist of visual or tabular matter. Its uniqueness is usually tied to its size or to the media on which it is prepared (slides, microfiche, tapes, films, etc.), that makes it difficult to bind into the thesis.

Some schools still use the term "plate" to identify full-page illustrations, and assign them a separate numbering sequence. In commercial publishing the term "plate" is usually applied to illustration pages printed on paper other than that used in the text because a higher quality printing surface is needed to reproduce high quality photos or color drawings. At one time, it was necessary to prepare individually engraved "plates" for such illustrations. They were printed on a separate press run, then inserted by hand and bound with the regular text pages. With the technical advancement of photo engraving and of photo-offset printing, commercial use of the plate process and the term have almost died out.

Unless your school or your scholastic department requires separate designation of "plates," we suggest that all graphic illustrations be included in a single numbering sequence designated by the term "figure." If you do use "plates" in your thesis, it will be necessary to prepare a separate List of Plates for the front matter.

GENERAL REQUIREMENTS

The following specifications apply to all illustrative material:

1. All illustrative material must appear as soon as possible, consistent with page layout, following reference to it in the text.

2. All images, *including their titles*, presented on 8-½x11-inch format must be contained within the 6x9-inch area allowed by the standard page margins of one-inch from from the top, right, and bottom edges, and 1-½ inch from the left edge of the page.

3. The bottom of illustrative images placed parallel to the 11-inch edge of the page must be along the right, or outer, margin. Titles to illustrations mounted broadside must appear at the top of the image for tables; at the bottom for figures; not the top or bottom of the page.

4. All titles and page numbers must be in the same type face as the body of the text, and be full-size, regardless of any reductions made of the original illustration image.

5. All information within an image must be typed or set in the same type face. The type face may be the same as that used in the text, or one set by a typesetter or with rub-on art type, but it must be consistent. Every effort must be made to use the same type face for information in all illustrations in the thesis.

6. When an image is optically reduced to fit on a page, to preserve readability in the original, 12-point (pica) type should not be reduced more than 50 percent, and 10-point (elite) type not more than 30 percent. Some schools may have even more stringent requirements for theses and dissertations that will be microfilmed. Check with your Graduate Department for specific limitations applying to you.

7. All images to be bound into the thesis must be printed, drawn, photocopied, or mounted on the same paper used for the body of the thesis text unless special permission has been granted from your advisor or the Graduate Department to use an alternate kind of paper.

8. Every effort must be made to render illustrative images in black and white. This is especially important for theses and dissertations that will be microfilmed. The microfilming process cannot separate

colors, but renders them as grays, frequently indistinguishable from each other.

9. Images, other than tables, occupying more than one-half of a page must be placed on individual pages by themselves.

10. Images, including tables, occupying less than half a page may be interwoven with text, or appear two or more to a page. In this event, the image must be separated from the text by three spaces before and/or after it. Images on the same page must be separated from each other by three spaces.

11. Titles for images that fill the 6x9-inch space allowance may appear on the back of the preceding page, centered on the page, and oriented to read in the same direction as the image. The front of such a page should be blank, except for the page number. The page carrying the image is not assigned a number. This option should be exercised *only* if special circumstances restrict optical reduction of the image sufficiently to place the title on the same page. (See "Oversize Tables and Figures" below.)

TABLES

1. Titles should appear at the top of tables, with the bottom line of the title two spaces above the first line of the table.

2. Titles should begin with the word "Table," followed by a number, and a period. Tables may be numbered with an Arabic (1, 2, 3) or a Roman (I, II, III) series of numbers. The numbering sequence may be from the beginning of the thesis to the end, including any appendices, or by chapter.

The title proper may be in all capital letters, or with capital letters used only for the first letter of main words. The form adopted must be used consistently throughout the thesis. Titles of more than one line are typed flush-left with the first word in the first line. The two basic styles for titles of tables are as follows:

TABLE 133. ENDOWMENT FUNDS OF THE 100 INSTITUTIONS OF HIGHER EDUCATION WITH THE LARGEST AMOUNTS: UNITED STATES, FISCAL YEAR 1981.

Table 133. Endowment Funds of the 100 Institutions of Higher Education With the Largest Amounts: United States, Fiscal Year 1981.

Some schools specify that the last line in a multi-line title be centered; consult with your advisor or your Graduate Department to see if this applies to you.

3. The first and last lines in all tablular matter should be solid lines. (see figure 21.)

4. Footnotes for tables are listed at the bottom of the table, not at the bottom of the page. To reduce the possibility of confusion with text references, footnotes are referenced by lower-case letters (a, b, c) in tables. The alphabet series is started anew in each table.

5. When a table is too long to fit onto one page, it may be continued to the next page. In this event, the portion on the first page must not end with a solid line. The first line on the second page will read: "Table 6, continued." The table will resume two spaces below this line. (See figure 22.)

6. Optically reduced tables are treated the same as graphic and photo illustrations for page placement. (See figure 23, and items 9 and 10, General Requirements, above.)

FIGURES

1. Titles should appear at the bottom of graphic illustrations, with the first line of the title two spaces below the image.

2. Titles should begin with the word "Figure," followed by a number and a period. Graphic illustrations are numbered with Arabic numbers (1, 2, 3). The numbering sequence may be from the beginning of the thesis to the end, including any appendices, or by chapter.

3. The title proper should use capital letters for the first letter of main words in the title. Titles of more than one line are typed flush-left with the first word in the first line. Some schools specify that the last line in a multi-line title be centered. Consult with your advisor or your Graduate Department to see if this applies to you.

4. Unless color is an integral part of the presentation, every effort should be made to render graphs, charts, drawings, and the like, as black and white illustrations. More often than not, color illustrations are not acceptable for inclusion in theses. Differentiation between portions of an illustration can be indicated by dot or line patterns. Commercially available drafting tapes and artist's press-on sheets are available for this purpose, or the patterns can be drawn by hand. (See figures 24 and 25.)

5. Photographic prints in color and photographic slides are usually not acceptable for inclusion in theses except under special circumstances; every effort should be made to have black-and-white prints made. Most photo service stores can make black-and-white prints from color negatives and slides. If a color negative is not available for

114

TABLE 7. COMPARABLE RANKS OF SS, U.S. ARMY,
AND GERMAN ARMY OFFICERS.

SS	GERMAN ARMY	U.S. ARMY
Reichsführer	Generalfeldmarschal	General of the Army
Oberstgruppenführer (from 1942 only)	Generaloberst	General
Obergruppenführer	General (der Infanterie etc.)	Lieutenant General
Gruppenführer	Generalleutnant	Major General
Brigadeführer	Generalmajor	Brigadier General
Oberführer	. . . . . . no such rank	
Standartenführer	Oberst	Colonel
Obersturmbannführer	Oberstleutnant	Lieutenant Colonel
Sturmbannführer	Major	Major
Hauptsturmführer	Hauptmann	Captain
Obersturmführer	Oberleutnant	First Lieutenant
Untersturmführer	Leutnant	Second Lieutenant

Figure 21. Illustration of full-page table.

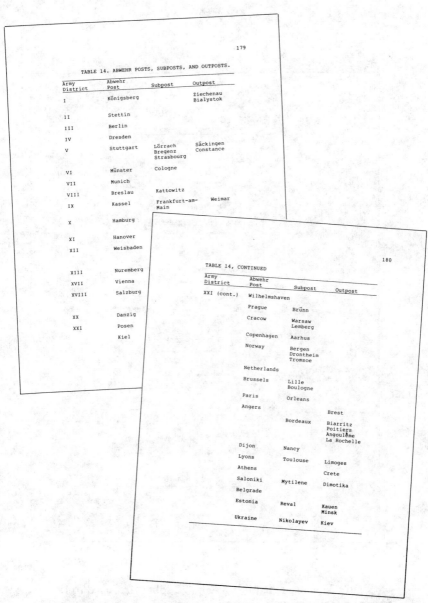

Figure 22. Illustration of table on two pages.

179

TABLE 14. ABWEHR POSTS, SUBPOSTS, AND OUTPOSTS.

Army District	Abwehr Post	Subpost	Outpost
I	Königsberg		Ziechenau Bialystok
II	Stettin		
III	Berlin		
IV	Dresden		
V	Stuttgart	Lörrach Bregenz Strasbourg	Säckingen Constance
VI	Münster	Cologne	
VII	Munich		
VIII	Breslau	Kattowitz	
IX	Kassel	Frankfurt-am-Main	Weimar
X	Hamburg	Bremen Flensburg	
XI	Hanover		
XII	Weisbaden	Metz	Kaiserslautern Saarbrücken Luxembourg
XIII	Nuremberg		
XVII	Vienna		
XVIII	Salzburg		Graz Klagenfurt Innsbruck
XX	Danzig		Bromberg
XXI	Posen		Litzmannstadt
	Wilhelmshaven		
	Kiel	Swinemünde	
	Prague	Brünn	
	Cracow	Warsaw Lemberg	
	Copenhagen	Aarhus	
	Norway	Bergen Drontheim Tromsoe	
	Netherlands		
	Brussels	Lille Boulogne	
	Paris	Orleans	
	Angers		Brest
		Bordeaux	Biarritz Poitiers Angoulême La Rochelle
	Dijon	Nancy	
	Lyons	Toulouse	Limoges
	Athens		Crete
	Saloniki	Mytilene	Dimotika
	Belgrade		
	Estonia	Reval	Kauen Minsk
	Ukraine	Mikolayev	Kiev

Figure 23. The same table as Fig. 22, photo-reduced to fit on one page.

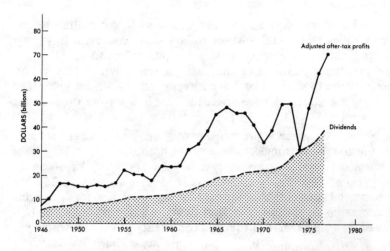

Figure 24. Illustration enhanced with commercial rub-on dot pattern.

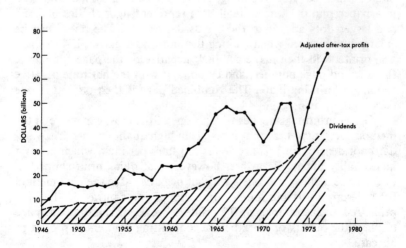

Figure 25. Illustration enhanced with hand-drawn pattern.

a print, the print can be rephotographed, using a close-up lense and black-and-white film, or this service can be obtained through a local photo store.

6. Photographic images should contain sufficient contrast to adequately illustrate the information to be visually conveyed. It is better to err slightly on the contrasty side in a photo than to have too little contrast and a gray-looking image. If you rephotograph color prints, make extra exposures at least one lens stop higher and one lower than the reading indicated, then select the best image from the resulting prints.

7. Photocopying unprocessed photographs onto paper for inclusion in the thesis is unacceptable. The photocopying process cannot accurately reproduce grays, and renders them as "dirty" areas on the copy print, frequently making details illegible (see figure 26). We recommend one of the four following methods for preparing photographs for inclusion in your thesis. All photos should be processed by a single method to retain consistency in your presentation.

a. *Offset printing.* Your local full-service print shop can print your photo(s) on thesis paper. You will need to prepare each page to be printed with a figure title and page number where they will appear on the final print, and indicate on the page where you wish the photo(s) to appear. The printer will make a halftone negative of the photo, which converts the image into a dot pattern similar to that in newspaper photos, where small dots represent light shades of grey, and larger dots appear to the eye as dark areas. The photo can be enlarged or reduced when making the halftone negative, if you wish. The printer will then make a "line" negative of the page containing the title and page number, and combine it with the halftone negative to make a printing plate. The combined page is then printed in one pass on the press.

Offset printing using negatives is one of the most expensive of the methods presented here, but it results in high quality prints. The standard dot density for this process is 133-lines per inch, which prints a high quality image. Be aware, however, that quick-print shops frequently use a cheaper process without negatives (see the next method for a description), and are notorious for losing contrast in the final print. Ask to see samples of the printer's work, or run only one page to judge the quality of work before committing your entire project to his care.

b. *Make a PMT halftone print from the photo, then have it printed or photocopy it onto thesis paper.* The term "PMT" is taken

Figure 26. Unprocessed photograph copied on a photocopy machine (top) compared to an 85-line halftoned photo (bottom) copied on the same machine.

from Kodak's Photo-Mechanical-Transfer process, which uses light-sensitive paper to make black-and-white copies without a negative. The photo image may be reduced or enlarged when the copy is made. Aside from the quick-copy shops, this conversion service is offered by most printers and blueprint and graphic services. They may use a different manufacturer's paper, but they will always know what you are talking about if you ask for a "PMT."

The halftone print(s) can be pasted or taped in position on a page containing the figure title(s) and page number. This page can be taken to a quick-copy shop or to a full-service printer, where they will make an inexpensive printing plate and print the entire image onto thesis paper. An alternative is for you to make photocopies of the page containing the PMT on thesis paper with a high-quality copying machine.

Two factors must be taken into consideration when using PMT halftone prints for reproduction: the halftone dot density must not be more than 100-lines per inch to retain image quality (you may even prefer 85-line — see figure 27), and the person making the PMT must know how to hold contrast in the copy. You may specify 100-line or 85-line halftone prints from your photos; these are standard densities. Ask to see samples of halftone PMT prints to check the shop's ability to retain contrast. If no samples are available, be wary of the service. Have them process only one of your photos, and check the quality of their work before committing your entire project. If the print contains significantly less contrast than your original, shop around for another service to make your PMTs.

The use of PMTs results in a slightly lower quality reproduction than the printing process using a halftone negative, but it will probably be less expensive. The difference between a reproduction by a quick-copy shop and a high-quality photocopy should not be noticable. (See figure 28.)

c. *Mount photographic prints directly onto thesis paper.* Most universities will accept this method of including photos in your thesis. They differ, however, in the stringency of their mounting requirements. The majority of the university style guides we studied recommended dry-mounting as the preferred method for permanently attaching photos to thesis paper. Scotch Photo-Mount, 3-M Mounting Adhesive Sheets, Falcon Perma-Mount, or Photo-Mount material were specifically recommended in many of the guides.

Non-rubber-based spray photo adhesives and 3-M Double-Backed "Transfer Tape" were also recommended by a small number of schools. Every school made a point that adhesives must be used on the entire backs of photos to be mounted, and that edges must be firmly attached.

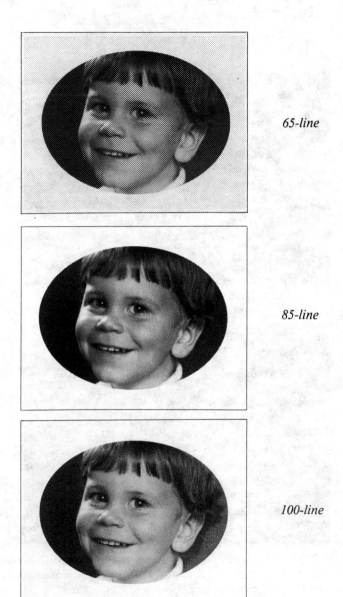

65-line

85-line

100-line

Figure 27. Examples of halftone dot patterns.

Figure 28. Halftoned photo (100-line) photographed and printed as a line shot from a PMT (top) compared to a 133-line halftone processed for offset printing (bottom).

Rubber cement and library paste, though accepted by a few, were condemned by most universities for mounting photos. Picture corners, cellophane or other clear tapes, mucilage, household glue, and staples were ruled out by everyone. These products (other than the staples) dry out, and the photographs will fall off the page.

Our advice is to check with your school's style guide, *and* with your Graduate Department for guidelines to mounting photographs in your thesis.

Label the backs of photographs to be mounted so they can be returned to their proper place in the text if they become detached. Information written on the back should include the author's name, the thesis or dissertation title in short form, and the page on which the figure is mounted.

Some schools require that photographs to be included in theses be processed according to archival standards. In general, this means careful and complete washing of the prints to remove all chemical residues left from the developing process. Check with your Graduate Department for instructions if this is a requirement at your school.

d. *Bind photos printed on full page-size photo paper into your thesis*. Full page-size means 8-½x11 inches, not a full-page image on standard 8x10-inch photo paper. The image on such a page, including the title, must not exceed the 6x9 area allowed by the standard margins.

The first problem you are going to encounter with this method is obtaining page-size photo printing paper. Your best bet is to purchase 11x14-inch sheets, which are standard, and cut them to the required measurements. Kodak Type A/single weight Polyfiber is the preferred paper for this use, but it has to be special ordered from most dealers in boxes of 50 sheets. If you shop around, you may be able to find a custom photo lab in your area that stocks type A Polyfiber paper and can print your photos for you. Alternative papers are: Kodak Rapid Contrast II RC, and Polyprint RC. Both are available on medium weight paper stock and are available at most photo dealers in packages of 10 or 25 sheets. Other brand papers may also be used. Medium weight and heavier papers, however, may be difficult to bind into your thesis.

Your second problem will be to find someone to print your photos so that they meet thesis format requirements. It will require special care to print the images the right size, and to make sure they are placed correctly within the page margins.

Your third problem will be to find a way to print or type titles and page numbers on the photographic print so they will be permanent.

One way, is to prepare the area you will type on by rubbing it with a soft rubber eraser to remove surface gloss. Type your information, then spray it with artist's fixitive spray (available at art suppy stores) to make it permanent. An alternative is to place the title on the back of the facing page (see Item 11 under "General Requirements," above).

It is not our intention to make this method sound too difficult, but there are some obvious problems to overcome in order to use it to process photos for inclusion in your thesis. The quality of your images will be the highest of all the methods described, but you will have to weigh this benefit against the costs. You can easily spend more time and money having enlarged custom prints made of your photographs than for any of the previously described procedures. Discuss the use of full photographic pages in your thesis with your advisor and with the Graduate Office. They may know of some shortcuts or local services that will help you, or have some alternative suggestions.

OVERSIZE TABLES AND FIGURES

You may need to include tables or figures in your thesis that you obtain from other sources. It is not unusual for such material to be too large to fit within the 6x9-inch space allowed by the general page margins, or to be unreadable when reduced to this size. You have three possible choices for handling such material: reduce it optically to fit on a page; prepare an oversize page to be bound into your thesis; or enclose it in an envelope or special pocket attached to the thesis cover.

OPTICAL REDUCTION. Shrinking the size of large tables or figures to fit onto a standard thesis page is the preferred method of handling oversize material. Tabular material and figures consisting of drawn lines are the easiest to handle, because they can be duplicated with any line copying process. When a desired image size is within the reduction range offered on standard photocopy machines, the material can simply be optically reduced, pasted in place on a thesis page containing the title and page number, and copied again for the final product.

Sometimes a two-step process can be used to reduce the image a second time to bring it to the required size. Keep in mind that 12-point (pica) type should not be reduced more than 50 percent of the original; 10-point (elite) type not more than 30 percent, or you may lose readability. There may be additional limitations if your document is going to be microfilmed. Ask at your Graduate Department.

Large photographs and other illustrations containing tonal values can be optically reduced onto PMT paper (see Item 7b under "Figures," above), pasted in place on a thesis page containing the title and page number, and copied again for the final product.

Large color photographs (and any other large tables or illustrations) can be rephotographed on black-and-white film, from which a print can be made, and processed by one of the methods described in Item 7 under "Figures," above.

OVERSIZE PAGE PREPARATION. Sometimes it is not possible to reduce oversize material to standard page size. One method for handling such information is to reproduce it on an oversize page and bind it with the rest of the thesis. You should check with your Graduate Department, however, since not all universities will accept oversize pages. Some specify a maximum size for oversize sheets. In the event your university allows insertion of large pages, the following guidelines should be closely followed.

1. Oversize sheets should not measure larger than 17x22 inches, and should be the same or lighter weight than the regular thesis paper. The use of other than thesis paper will probably require special permission from your Graduate Department.

2. The general margin requirements of one inch from the top, right, and bottom of the page, and 1-½ inches from the left side must be met on oversized pages. Page numbers are to be placed in the same upper-right corner, one inch from the top and right side as on standard pages.

3. Horizontal folds must open toward the bottom of the book, never the top.

4. The following folding instructions should be followed closely to achieve maximum compactness, and to comply with bindery requirements. All folds should be creased by running a hard object (such as a plastic pen) along the fold.

If folding in more than one direction is necessary, fold horizontally first, then vertically, following the steps above.

ORIGINAL PAPERS, NEWS CLIPS, ETC.
Original documents of this sort should be pasted onto a page containing an appropriate figure number and title and photocopied or printed onto thesis paper. If it is necessary to reduce the size of the documents, a PMT can be made of the original as described in 7a above.

MISCELLANEOUS MATERIALS.
Ask your Graduate Department for special instructions on how to handle media such as slides, microfiche, rolled illustrations, computer readouts, sound and video tapes, films, large plates, musical scores, and overlays.

HORIZONTAL FOLDS

Step 1: Make the first fold at the bottom, 10-½ inches from the top of the page. If more folds are necessary, make the second fold ½-inch from the top of the page, and subsequent folds in line with the first two folds. Each horizontally folded section of an oversized page should, therefore, be 10 inches high, leaving a margin of ½-inch at the top and bottom of the regular size thesis page.

Step 2: Cut a one inch strip from the left edge of the entire *folded* portion of the page (shaded in the illustration), leaving a 1x10-½-inch binding strip along the top-left edge of the page. This prevents the folded portion from being caught in the binding.

VERTICAL FOLDS

Step 1: Make the first fold at the right side of the page, 8 inches from the left edge.

Step 2: If two folds are used, align the right edge of the sheet 8-½ inches from the left edge (½-inch past the first fold), and crease the fold where it falls. The entire page should be 8-½ inches wide when folded flat.

Step 3: If multiple folds are required, make the first fold as in Step 1 above, then the second fold 1-½-inch from the left edge of the page. Align each subsequent fold with the first and second folds, except for the last fold. To make the last fold, align the right edge of the sheet 8-½ inches from the left edge (½-inch past the lower folds), and crease the fold where it falls. The entire page should be 8-½ inches wide when folded flat.

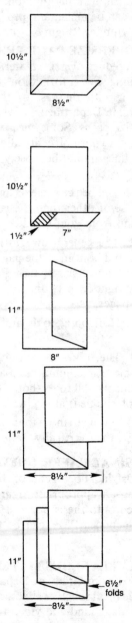

Figure 29. Folding sequence.

Chapter Seventeen

WHAT YOU NEED TO KNOW
ABOUT FOOTNOTES, ENDNOTES,
AND OTHER DOCUMENTATION STYLES

By its very nature, a thesis (or a dissertation) requires that its writer incorporate ideas or information borrowed from others. This "borrowed" material is what you will use to support your arguments and conclusions. Since one of the measures of a good thesis is the breadth and depth of the research effort, your thesis committee will closely scrutinize this area of your work. In particular, they will be looking at how well and how accurately you document the material you use. "Documentation" in a thesis means supplying exact references to the sources of authoritative information you use to support your statements or hypotheses. The reader should be able to identify, locate, and retrieve each of your sources if he wishes to do so.

In practice, documenting a thesis involves compiling a detailed list of your sources, including page numbers where the pertinent information may be found, and keying them to references in the text. Source documentation information should *always* be taken from the title and copyright pages of a work — never from the cover, which may display incomplete information.

Specific rules for documentation differ from discipline to discipline and between universities. Our study of current university guidelines shows a trend toward favoring one of four documentation forms for theses. In the order of preference expressed in the university style guides we studied they are:

1. **Endnotes,** with number citations in the text keyed to documentation notes placed at the end of chapters, and bibliographic listings at the end of the text.

2. **Footnotes,** with number citations in the text keyed to documentation notes placed at the bottom of the page where they occur, and bibliographic listings at the back of the text;

3. **Author-date citations** (author's name, publication date, and page numbers placed in the text), with full documentation/bibliographic data in a list at the end of the text;

4. **Parenthetical citations** (author's name and page numbers placed in the text), with full documentation/bibliographic data in a list at the end of the text.

The majority of universities emphasize the use of footnotes for dissertations to help readers using microform versions of the work to easily find the note listings. Each of the documentation forms listed above will be described in detail in following sections of this chapter.

There are many style manuals published that describe the documentation practices of the various study fields, their journals, and their publications. Most universities, however, have standardized their requirements for theses by specifying that students follow the documentation style in *The Chicago Manual of Style* (University of Chicago Press), *The MLA Handbook for Writers of Research Papers* (or the *MLA Style Book*, both published by the Modern Language Association of America), or the *Publication Manual of the American Psychological Association* (American Psychological Association of America). Some universities suggest the use of one of these same documentation styles for dissertations; others require that dissertation writers follow specific styles used by professional journals in their respective fields.

The selection of a documentation form and style for your thesis should be made in conjunction with your advisor and your Graduate Department. Because the Chicago (CHI), Modern Language Association (MLA), and American Psychological Association (APA) documentation forms are so widely used, we have limited the descriptions in this manual to those three. The balance of this chapter presents an outline of the rules for documentation listings under the Chicago, MLA, and APA styles. A compendium of citation examples conforming to the three documentation styles and arranged by the type of source document appears in Chapter 19, "Footnote, Endnote, and Bibliography Examples." Chapter 19 is designed to provide a quick reference for easily determining appropriate citation and reference list formats.

ENDNOTES AND FOOTNOTES

Both the Chicago and the MLA documentation styles support the use of endnotes and footnotes; they are not used with the APA documentation style. Between Chicago and MLA there are small distinctions in punctuation, shortening of publisher's names, and abbreviations in the citation notes. Some general differences are described below. Additional variations are described in Chapter 19 with the appropriate listing examples. The numbering system is the same for both styles.

Citation notes may take one of two forms: reference or content. Reference notes are intended to direct the reader to the source of authoritative information supporting an argument or hypothesis in the text. Content notes are used to comment on, amplify or qualify points in the text, or to acknowledge indebtedness, such as permission granted to use copyrighted material, and the like. They may also be used to cross-reference parts of the text. Content notes follow the same rules as reference notes, except that they consist of textual matter in paragraph form instead of source listings.

CITATION NUMBERING. Citation notes are numbered sequentially as they occur in the thesis, using Arabic numerals and beginning with number one. Reference numbers corresponding to the notes are inserted in the text immediately following the quotation, paraphrase, or statement the notes are documenting. They may be typed superscript (one-half line above the typed line[6], with no space between the number and the last word of the documented material), or be enclosed in parentheses (6). Superscript is preferred. The numbers on footnotes should match numbers typed in the text (superscript or in parentheses). Numbers for endnotes are typed in line with the first line of the listing and are followed by a period. (See figures 18 and 19.) Reference numbers should not follow an author's name or an introductory verb (According to Hemingway[6] . . . ; Johnson was the first person to describe[4] . . .). They should not be placed at the end of, or within, chapter, section, or subsection headings. Reference numbers referring to entire divisions such as these should appear at an appropriate place in the text. Reference numbers follow all internal sentence punctuation marks except the dash (which they precede), and are placed outside of parentheses and quotation marks.

CITATION NOTE CONTENTS. A book citation note contains four basic divisions:

1. The author's full name in normal order;

2. The title, underlined;

3. Publishing data, enclosed in parentheses;

4. And page references, followed by a period.

A colon separates the city where a work is published from the publisher, and a comma the publisher from the date of publication. Chicago documentation includes commas following the author's name and the publishing data. The MLA style shortens publisher's names, and the comma following the publishing data is omitted:

CHI   1. Ernest Hemingway, A Moveable Feast(New
           York: Charles Scribner's Sons, 1964), 21.

MLA   1. Ernest Hemingway, A Moveable Feast(New
           York: Scribner's, 1964) 21.

A citation for an article appearing in a journal, a magazine or other periodical contains five divisions:

1. The author's full name in normal order;

2. The title of the article, enclosed in quotation marks;

3. The name of the periodical, underlined, followed by the volume (and number, if applicable) of the periodical;

4. The date of the volume or issue, in parentheses, followed by a colon;

5. And page references, followed by a period.

For popular magazines, the volume number is usually omitted and the issue cited by date only, without parentheses. Note the differences in the date and page references in the examples below. Newspapers are also cited by the date only.

Academic or Professional Journals

CHI   89. Samuel Penter, "Recollections of an Oregon
           Pioneer," Oregon Historical Quarterly 7 (1906):
           60

MLA   89. [the same as CHI]

Popular Magazines

CHI   107. Patricia Holt, "Books Down Under,"
           Publishers Weekly, 3 July 1981, 107.

MLA   107. Patricia Holt, "Books Down Under,"
           Publishers Weekly 3 July 1981: 107

These samples illustrate the simple basics of documentation style. The listing forms used for many of the additional elements found in publication titles, such as multiple authors, editors, translators, edition, and/or volume numbers, and the like, may be determined by studying the examples in Chapter 19. If you are unable to find an exact match for a listing, locate the example closest to it and adapt it to your needs. Use the same form each time that type of listing occurs; consistency is the key to good documentation.

FOOTNOTES AND ENDNOTES, FIRST APPEARANCE. Traditionally, a full reference listing to a source is supplied the first time it appears in a footnote or endnote. In recent times, however, when a thesis or dissertation contains an alphabetical listing of references cited, the trend has been to use a shortened reference form (described below) for all such listings. Both Chicago and MLA documentation style recommendations support this trend, but your university may specify its own requirements. Your advisor or the Graduate Department should be able to tell you what is acceptable. Examples of full listings for citation notes may be found in Chapter 19.

FOOTNOTES AND ENDNOTES, SUBSEQUENT APPEARANCES. After the first note containing the full reference to a source, subsequent references to the same source may be shortened. This may be done in one of two ways: (1) listing the last name of the author(s), followed by a comma, a short version of the title, underlined, followed by a comma, and pertinent page numbers, followed by a period; or (2) listing the last name of the author(s) followed by a comma, and the page numbers only, followed by a period. This second form, without the comma separating the name and page numbers, is used by MLA. Either of the two may be used for Chicago style. *Once you adopt a form, you must use it consistently throughout your thesis.*

A shortened citation for an article in a periodical or magazine is similar, except that the shortened article title, when used, is enclosed in quotation marks instead of underlined.

The author's first name is included only if two authors with the same last name are contained in the same citation. For works with two or three authors, list all the authors; when a citation includes more than three authors, list only the first, followed by "et al." (with a period after "al." only), or "and others." When authors' names only are used, and you cite more than one work by the same author, you must include a short title with the citation. Abbreviations for editor, translator, or compiler, if used in the first citation or included in a listing at the end of the text, may be dropped from the shortened listing.

Shortened titles should contain enough information to locate the work in a Bibliography or List of References Cited; do not change the order of words in the title. Eliminating subtitles is one way to shorten titles; omitting the initial "The" or "A" is another common practice. It is not necessary to shorten titles of five words or less.

Examples of Shortened Citation Notes

Full citation note:

CHI   3. Will Irwin and Thomas M. Johnson, <u>What You Should Know About Spies And Saboteurs</u> (New York: W.W. Norton and Co., 1943), 171.

MLA   3. Will Irwin and Thomas M. Johnson, <u>What You Should Know About Spies and Saboteurs</u> (New York: Norton, 1943) 171.

Author and shortened title:

CHI   3. Irwin and Johnson, <u>Spies and Saboteurs</u>, 171.

MLA   3. Irwin and Johnson, <u>Spies and Saboteurs</u> 171.

Author and page number only:

CHI   3. Irwin and Johnson, 171.

MLA   3. Irwin and Johnson 171.

Full citation note for an article in a periodical:

CHI   91. Arnold Berleant, "Aesthetic Paradigms for an Urban Ecology,", <u>Diogenes</u>, no. 103 (Fall 1978): 7.

MLA   91. Arnold Berleant, "Aesthetic Paradigms for an Urban Ecology," <u>Diogenes</u> 103 (1978): 7.

Author and shortened title for periodical article:

CHI   91. Berleant, "Asthetic Paradigms," 7.

MLA   91. Berleant, "Asthetic Paradigms" 7.

Author and page number only for periodical article:

CHI   91. Berleant, 7.

MLA   91. Berleant 7.

CITATION NOTE PLACEMENT. Footnotes should be typed at the bottom of the page where they are cited. Endnotes are listed at the end of each chapter, or at the end of the general text. Preferred placement is at the end of the text. For a description of the typing format, see the appropriate entries in Chapter 14, "Standardizing Your Thesis Page and Text Formats."

ABBREVIATIONS IN FOOTNOTE AND ENDNOTE ENTRIES

Table 2 lists selected abbreviations commonly used in citation notes for the Chicago and MLA documentation style. Table 3 lists selected abbreviations for geographical locations used in citation notes under the Chicago and the MLA documentation styles. Table 4 lists the abbreviations used for months of the year in MLA citation notes. These table are repeated in Chapter 19 for easy access when used with the footnote and bibliography examples illustrated in that section.

1. When an abbreviation begins a sentence, the first letter is capitalized.

2. When the abbreviations ed. and comp. appear following the title, they are intended to read "edited by" and "compiled by" and the plural form is not used.

3. Chicago and MLA documentation styles no longer recommend using the abbreviations for page(s) (p., pp.) unless such references occur at the beginning of a sentence or the reference is ambiguous without it.

4. When n. or nn. is used to indicate note(s), the number of the page on which the note appears precedes the abbreviation:

CHI   31. Watzlawick, Beavin, and Jackson, <u>Pragmatics of Human Communication</u> (New York: Norton, 1967), 186n. 11, 219 nn. 15, 16.

MLA   31. Watzlawick, Beavin, and Jackson, <u>Pragmatics of Human Communication</u> (New York: Norton, 1967) 186n11, 219nn15, 16.

Omit the period and eliminate the space between the page number and the abbreviation for Chicago style when n. or nn. is used without the note number, and stands for all the notes on the page cited. MLA does not use a period after either n or nn.

TABLE 2. SELECTED ABBREVIATIONS COMMONLY USED IN CITATION NOTES AND BIBLIOGRAPHIC ENTRIES.

CHICAGO	MLA	APA	MEANING
app.	app.	app.	appendix
bk.	bk.	bk.	book
chap.	ch.	chap.	chapter
comp.	comp.	comp.	compiler, or compiled by
ed.	ed.	Ed.	editor, or edited by
ed.	ed.	ed.	edition
f. (ff.)	f. (ff.)	f. (ff.)	and the following page(s)
fig.	fig.	fig.	figure
fol.	fol.	fol.	folio
l. (ll.)	l. (ll.)	l. (ll.)	line(s)
MS (MSS)	ms. (mss.)	ms. (mss.)	manuscript(s)
n. (nn.)	n (nn)	n. (nn.)	note(s)
n.d.	n.d.	n.d.	no date (of pub.)
no.	no.	No.	number
n.p.	n.p.	n.p.	no place (of pub.) or no publisher
n.s.	ns	n.s.	new series
o.s.	os	o.s.	old series
pl.	pl.	pl.	plate
p. (pp.)	p. (pp.)	p. (pp.)	page(s)
pt.	pt.	Pt.	part
repr.	rpt.	repr.	reprint
rev.	rev.	rev.	revision, or revised by
ser.	ser.	ser.	series
suppl.	suppl.	Suppl.	supplement
trans.	trans.	Trans.	translator, or translated by
TS (TSS)	ts. (tss.)	ts. (tss.)	typescript(s)
univ.	U	univ.	University
—	UP	—	University Press
vol.	vol.	Vol. (vols.)	volume(s)

For the plural form add "s" after all but those abbreviations already listing plural forms, and n.s, n.d., n.p., ser., trans., U and UP.

CHI   31. Watzlawick, Beavin, and Jackson, <u>Pragmatics of</u>
       <u>Human Communication</u> (New York: Norton, 1967),
       186n, 219nn.

MLA   31. Watzlawick, Beavin, and Jackson, <u>Pragmatics of</u>
       <u>Human Communication</u> (New York: Norton, 1967)
       186n, 219nn.

5. Use the abbreviation vol. only when the number of the
volume stands alone, or if it is separated from the page
number, as when the title intervenes:

CHI   53. Winston Churchill, <u>Their Finest Hour</u>, vol. 2
       of <u>The Second World War</u> (Boston: Houghton
       Mifflin Co., 1949), 37.

MLA   53. Winston Churchill, <u>Their Finest Hour</u>, vol. 2
       of <u>The Second World War</u> (Boston: Houghton, 1949)
       37.

When the volume number immediately follows the title, the
comma is omitted:

CHI   57. Ellis, <u>Victory</u> 2:22.

       177. <u>Dublin Review</u> 142 (1908): 191.

MLA   57. Ellis, <u>Victory</u> 2: 22

       177. <u>Dublin Review</u> 142 (1908): 191

The abbreviation vol. is eliminated and a colon used to
separate volume and page numbers when they come together.
MLA style skips a space between the colon and the page
number.

CHI   49. Winston Churchill, <u>The Second World War</u>, 6
       vols. (Boston: Houghton Mifflin Co., 1948-53), 2:37

MLA   49. Winston Churchill, <u>The Second World War</u> 6
       vols. (Boston: Houghton, 1948-53) 2: 37.

6. Use Arabic numerals for volume numbers and for any
other Roman numerals in citation notes, except when Roman
numerals appear in titles, and when citations refer to pages
carrying lower case Roman numbers.

7. Because the letter "l" is used for the Arabic numeral "1" on some typewriters, use of the abbreviation for line(s) (l., ll.) is not recommended except in works with a large number of such references. When the citations are all for lines, the first entry should spell out "line" at the head of the column containing the line numbers.

8. The use of f. and ff. (and the following page(s)) is no longer recommended. Instead, give the first and last page numbers of references extending more than one page.

LATIN ABBREVIATIONS. Table 5 is a list of Latin words and abbreviations commonly employed as substitutes for English language phrases in citation entries. The majority of these are used to eliminate repetition of entire citations.

1. Ibid. is substituted for elements in a note that are the same as in the preceding note. It replaces the author's name, the title of the work, and as much of the balance of the entry as is the same as the original. MLA does not support the use of ibid; instead, it advocates the use of shortened titles for end-note entries when the same work is listed sequentially.

CHI   46. Alan Watts, <u>In My Own Way</u> (New York: Vantage Books, 1972), 149.

    47. Ibid., 359.   *[The same volume as in the preceding note.]*

    48. Ibid.   *[The same volume and page as in the preceding note.]*

2. Idem is used in place of the author's name in successive references within the same citation note to a number of works by the same person. Idem is a whole word and does not take a period. It is rarely used in graduate theses.

3. The use of loc. cit. and op. cit. as substitutes for the title of a work cited earlier in a chapter is no longer recommended for either the Chicago or the MLA documentation styles.

4. Passim is used as a substitute for page numbers when referring to material scattered within a section of text; it should be used only after listing inclusive pages where the cited material may be found. Passim is a whole word and does not take a period. It is rarely employed in graduate theses.

TABLE 3. SELECTED ABBREVIATIONS FOR GEOGRAPHICAL LOCATIONS.

CHICAGO	MLA & APA	CHICAGO	MLA & APA	CHICAGO	MLA & APA
Ala.	AL	Ky.	KY	N. Dak.	ND
Alaska	AK	La.	LA	Ohio	OH
Ariz.	AZ	Maine	ME	Okla.	OK
Ark.	AR	Md.	MD	Oreg.	OR
Calif.	CA	Mass.	MA	Pa.	PA
Colo.	CO	Mich.	MI	R.I.	RI
Conn.	CT	Minn.	MN	S.C.	SC
Del.	DE	Miss.	MS	S. Dak.	SD
D.C.	DC	Mo.	MO	Tenn.	TN
Fla.	FL	Mont.	MT	Tex.	TX
Ga.	GA	Nebr.	NE	Utah	UT
Hawaii	HI	Nev.	NV	Vt.	VT
Idaho	ID	N.H.	NH	Va.	VA
Ill.	IL	N.J.	NJ	Wash.	WA
Ind.	IN	N. Mex	NM	W. Va.	WV
Iowa	IA	N.Y.	NY	Wis.	WI
Kans.	KS	N.C.	NC	Wyo.	WY

TABLE 4. ABBREVIATIONS FOR MONTHS OF THE YEAR USED IN MLA DOCUMENTATION CITATIONS AND NOTES.

Jan.	May	Sept.
Feb.	June	Oct.
Mar.	July	Nov.
Apr.	Aug.	Dec.

Chicago and APA spell out months of the year.

TABLE 5. LATIN SUBSTITUTES FOR ENGLISH WORD PHRASES.

et al.	(et alii) and others
ibid.	(ibidem) in the same place
idem (id.)	the same
loc. cit.	in the place cited
op. cit.	in the work cited
passim	here and there
s.v.	(sub verbo) under the word

ABBREVIATION OF ENTIRE CITATION ENTRIES

When a work is cited throughout the thesis, it may be substituted with an abbreviation following its first entry. The first time it is cited, the documentation note should be complete. The full citation is then followed by a notation of the abbreviation to be used in subsequent citations, enclosed in parentheses:

CHI   65. Samuel I. Rosenman, ed., The Public Papers and Addresses of Franklin D. Roosevelt, 13 vols. (New York: Macmillan, 1938-50), 3:257 (hereafter cited as Roosevelt Papers).

66. Roosevelt Papers 5:132.

MLA   65. Samuel I. Rosenman, ed., The Public Papers and Addresses of Franklin D. Roosevelt, 13 vols. (New York: Macmillan, 1938-50) 3: 257 (hereafter cited as Roosevelt Papers).

66. Roosevelt Papers 5: 132.

ANNOTATED FOOTNOTES AND ENDNOTES

An annotated documentation note contains, in addition to its regular contents, author's comments appended to some or all of the entries. These comments may be typed as a continuation of the entry, or begin as a separate paragraph below the entry. Chicago is the only style that specifically supports the use of annotated documentation notes. Your university may allow annotated notes with MLA style; check with your advisor and with your graduate office. APA style does not use citation notes, and does not support annotated bibliography or reference list entries; instead APA advocates the use of content notes (see below). The following examples are adapted from *Computer Power and Human Reason*, by Joseph Weizenbaum (San Francisco: W. W. Freeman, 1976).

> 10. H. Wang, From Mathematics to Philosophy (New York: Humanities Press, 1974), p. 324. Kurt Godel himself referred to this on December 1951 as one of ''the two most interesting rigorously proved results about minds and machines.''

> 11. O. Firschein, M. A. Fischler, L.S. Coles, and J. M. Tenenbaum, ''Intelligent Machines Are on the Way,'' IEEE Spectrum, July 1974, p. 43. The opinion I have quoted here appears to be the consensus of ''41 artificial intelligence experts - including members of the International Joint Artificial Intelligence Council.'' The paper makes clear that the opinion is shared by the paper's authors.

AUTHOR-DATE CITATION SYSTEM

Chicago, MLA, and APA documentation styles all support the use of the author-date system for documenting information sources. The Chicago University Press strongly encourages it as its first choice for documentation. The APA indicates it as its only option. MLA rates the author-date system as its second choice, following parenthetical style, which will be described in the next section of this chapter. There are small differences of punctuation between the three styles for author-date citations.

The author-date system incorporates a List of References Cited alphabetized by author at the end of the text. This list is keyed to parenthetical citations inserted into the text, consisting of the author's name, the date of publication, and page numbers where the information cited may be found. The major difference between an author-date entry in the end of the text reference list, and other types of entries is that the date of publication follows the author's name instead of appearing after the publisher.

Examples of author-date listings may be found in Chapter 19, "Footnote, Endnote, and Bibliography Examples," where they are labled as APA-style entries. Chicago and MLA reference list entries may be converted to the author-date system by moving the publishing date from where it is listed following the publisher to after the author's name, and enclosing it in parentheses.

The in-text citations for the author-date system consist of the author's surname, the date of publication, and relevant page numbers.

CHI   (Churchill 1949, 37)

MLA   (Churchill 1949, 37)

APA   (Churchill, 1949, p. 37)

The "author" in an author-date citation is the name under which the work cited is listed in the List of References Cited. This may be an individual, an editor, compiler, translator, or organization. The abbreviations for editor, compiler, and the like, are not used in author-date citations. Multiple authors' names should always be listed in the order presented on the title page.

Author-date text citations should immediately follow the quotation, paraphrase, or statement they are documenting. They should not follow an introductory verb (Kent was the first to operate (Smith 1934, 67) . . .), or be placed at the end of, or within, chapter, section, or subsection headings. References to entire divisions such as these should appear at an appropriate place in the text. Author-date entries precede all internal sentence punctuation.

1. APA citations use a comma between the name and the date; Chicago and MLA do not.

2. APA uses the abbreviation p. and pp. for page(s). The Chicago and MLA styles have discontinued this practice unless the entry would be confusing without it. Other abbreviations associated with page references (chap., chapter; sec., section; vol., volume; and the like) are used in all three styles.

3. In Chicago and MLA styles, a reference that includes both volume and page numbers drops the abbreviation vol., and a colon separates the two numbers (3:46). MLA style requires that a space separate the colon and the page number in this type of entry (3: 46).

4. Information included in the text is not repeated in the author-date citation:

Author's name in text

> When Carruthers published his statistics on the
> population density of crickets (1942, 268), he
> proved . . .

[Cite date and page.]

Author's name and date in text

> In 1953 Henderson finished the first stage of his
> research (p. 372) on the fibre habitats of . . .

[Cite page only.]

Author's name and page in text

> In The Unusual Habits of the Northwest Ski Enthusiast
> Geordino states on page 196 (1986) that ski lifts
> provide an . . .

[Cite date only.]

Author's name, date, and page in text

> During the winter of 1932, Harding published Hardpack
> Hiker, and on page 54 he listed everything the
> snow camper needed to . . .

[No additional citation is required.]

5. When listing multiple authors, Chicago and MLA styles
prefer the use of the conjunction "and" to separate the last
two names in a citation. When listing more than two names, a
comma precedes "and." APA style prefers the use of the
ampersand (&).

CHI   (Kent and Washington)

MLA   (Wagner, Taft, and Carruthers)

APA   (Leonard, Brown, & Stewart)

Chicago and MLA styles allow the listing of up to three
authors for a single work in an author-date citation. For more
than three, list only the surname of the first author, followed
by "et al.," or "and others." APA style calls for listing up to
six authors for a single work the first time the work is cited. In

subsequent citations, and for more than six authors, list only the surname of the first author, followed by "et al." (do not use "and others" for APA style).

6. When your reference list includes two or more authors with the same surname, include those authors' initials in all citations:

(E. L. Hobbes, 1868, 93)

(M. C. Hobbes, 1913)

7. When two works by the same author carry the same publishing date, assign a lower case letter following the publication date to each work in the List of References Cited, and use that letter in the citation:

(DuBoff, 1985a, 45-51)

(DuBoff, 1985b, 78-103)

8. When two works by the same multiple authors carry the same publishing date, insert a short title of the work in the citation:

(Toffer, et al., First Things, 1967, 23-56)

(Toffer, et al., Believer, 1967, 89)

9. Two or more works in the same citation are separated by semicolons:

(Dent, 1864; Rob and James, 1860; Hand, 1859)

Two or more works by the same author in the same citation are listed by date only and separated by semicolons:

(Jerard, 1943, 66; 1945a, 31; 1945b, 17-20)

PARENTHETICAL CITATION STYLE

MLA lists the parenthetical style as its first choice for citing information sources in text. Chicago and APA do not use this form of citation. The parenthetical citation form is the same as the author-date form, except that the publishing date is omitted from the citation, and the end of text reference listing remains the same as for footnotes and endnotes. To use this citation form under MLA style, follow the rules for author-date citations described above, omitting the publishing date.

CONTENT NOTES WITH AUTHOR-DATE
AND PARENTHETICAL CITATIONS

Content notes are used to comment on, amplify, or qualify points in your text. They may also be used to acknowledge indebtedness, such as permission to use copyrighted material or to cross-reference parts of the text. To use content notes with author-date or parenthetical references, follow the rules for citation numbering described in the first part of this chapter, and place the corresponding content notes at the bottom of the page where they occur, at the end of each chapter, or at the end of the text, the same as you would place documentation notes under the numbering system. When using the author-date system of documentation, the content note citations are listed the same as endnotes. The list should be titled "Notes."

Chapter Eighteen

WHAT YOU NEED TO KNOW ABOUT BIBLIOGRAPHIES AND REFERENCE LISTS

All research papers require that a list of books and other references used by the author in writing the work be placed at the end of the text. This list serves several purposes: (1) it allows the reader to determine the scope of research behind the work; (2) full information is provided to identify, locate, and retrieve sources without having to search for first reference citations; (3) the use of specific references can be quickly determined; and (4) research sources may be discovered by the reader that will aid in his or her own work.

The title of your reference list will be determined by its content. Undergraduate papers traditionally use the title "Bibliography" for such lists. In scholarly works however, "Bibliography" infers a comprehensive list of all works available on the subject. Some universities make this distinction, and require the use of alternate titles for lists of reference sources. Since most thesis and dissertation reference lists will contain only works cited in the text, more appropriate titles may be "Selected Bibliography," "List of References Cited," "Works Cited," or just plain "References." If you list all the resources you consulted, some of which you do not cite in the text, you might want to use "Works Consulted," "Literature Consulted," or some other appropriate title.

Most reference lists are arranged alphabetically, by author. "Author" in this case is the name under which the work is listed on the title page, and may be an individual, an editor, compiler, translator, or organization. When a work has multiple authors, the first author's name is reversed, and the following names are listed in normal order. Multiple authors should always be listed in the order presented on the title page.

Some reference lists are divided into sections grouping sources according to types of material, subject matter, or other criteria. Entries within each section are arranged alphabetically. Examples of these groupings are:

primary sources	(original writings such as letters, diaries, manuscripts, official records, and personal interviews)
secondary sources	(publications and writings derived from primary sources)
published material	books magazines newspapers
unpublished material	

Whether or not you divide your reference list into sections will depend on the nature of your work, convenience to the reader, preferences of your advisor, and the requirements of your university. See figure 20 for an example of a divided bibliography list.

REFERENCE LIST ENTRY CONTENTS

Reference list entries for books contain the first three divisions used in full citation notes, with some minor changes in punctuation: (1) the author's full name, reversed for alphabetizing; (2) the title, underlined; (3) and the publishing data. Each division ends with a period. The MLA style requires that two spaces separate the divisions; Chicago and APA use only one space. A colon separates the place of publication from the publisher, and a comma separates the publisher's name from the date of publication APA lists books "library" style, with only the first word and proper nouns capitalized.

For APA style, and when using the author-date system with Chicago or MLA, the publication date follows the author's name and is enclosed in parentheses. MLA and APA styles both shorten the publisher's name. For APA style, the author's surname is listed first, followed by his initials. The differences between styles are illustrated in the examples below.

CHI   Hemingway, Ernest. <u>A Moveable Feast</u>. New York:
         Charles Scribner's Sons, 1964.

MLA   Hemingway, Ernest. <u>A Moveable Feast</u>. New York:
         Scribner's, 1964.

APA   Hemingway, E. (1964). <u>A Moveable Feast</u>. New York:
         Scribner's.

An entry for an article appearing in a journal, a magazine, or other periodical contains three similar divisions: (1) the author's name, reversed for alphabetizing; (2) the title, enclosed in quotation marks; (3) the name of the periodical, underlined, followed by the volume (and number, if applicable) of the periodical, the date of the volume or issue enclosed in parentheses, and the page numbers containing the article. For popular magazines, the volume number is usually omitted and the issue cited by date only, without parentheses. Each division ends with a period. For MLA style two spaces separate the divisions; Chicago and APA use only one space.

When citing popular magazines, Chicago style requires that a comma separate the periodical title from the date; the comma is omitted in MLA style. When following the APA style, and when using the author-date system with Chicago or MLA, the publication date follows the author's name and is enclosed in parentheses; APA lists the year before the date, and the author's initials are used instead of the full name. As with books, APA lists article titles in periodicals "library" style, with only the first word and proper nouns capitalized, and quotation marks are not used to enclose the title. APA style also requires that the volume number be underlined. The differences between entries for the three styles are illustrated in the examples below.

Academic or professional journals

CHI   Penter, Samuel. "Recollections of an Oregon Pioneer."
         <u>Oregon Historical Quarterly</u> 7 (1906): 56-61.

MLA   Penter, Samuel. "Recollections of an Oregon Pioneer."
         <u>Oregon Historical Quarterly</u> 7 (1906): 56-61.

APA   Penter, S. (1906). Recollections of an Oregon pioneer.
         <u>Oregon Historical Quarterly</u>, <u>7</u>, 56-61.

Popular Magazines

CHI   Holt, Patricia. "Books Down Under." <u>Publishers</u>
          <u>Weekly</u>, 3 July 1981, 55-109.

MLA   Holt, Patricia. "Books Down Under." <u>Publishers</u>
          <u>Weekly</u> 3 July 1981: 55-109.

APA   Holt, P. (1981, July 3). Books down under.
          <u>Publishers Weekly</u>, pp. 55-109.

These samples illustrate the simple basics of reference list entries. The form for additional elements, such as multiple authors, editors, translators, edition and/or volume number, and the like, may be determined by studying the examples in Chapter 19. If you are unable to find an exact match for a listing, locate the example closest to it and adapt it to your needs. Use the same form each time that type of entry occurs; consistency is the key to a well-constructed reference list. See the appropriate section of Chapter 14, "Standardizing Your Thesis Page and Text Formats" for a description of the reference list typing format.

If you have been careful to record complete information on your sources when taking notes, you should be able to compile your reference list by alphabetizing the bibliographic information on your note cards. Use the examples in Chapter 19 to determine the correct listing form of your sources. Cross-check your entries to be sure they contain the same exact information used in your citation notes if you use that form of documentation.

ANNOTATED REFERENCE LISTS

An annotated reference list contains, in addition to its regular contents described above, author's comments appended to some or all of the entries. These comments may be typed as a continuation of the entry, or begin as a separate paragraph below the entry. Chicago and MLA styles support the use of annotated reference lists; APA does not. The examples below are adapted from *Computer Power and Human Reason*, by Joseph Weizenbaum (San Francisco: W. W. Freeman, 1976).

Kaplan, A. The Conduct of Inquiry. San Francisco:
    Chandler, 1964. This important book contains an
    excellent discussion of models and theories in
    the social sciences. See especially chapters
    three and four.

Orstein, Robert E. The Psychology of Consciousness.
    San Francisco: W. W. Freeman, 1972. Chapter
    three is particularly relevant to the discussion
    in the text. It is written in plain English. The
    references it cites open the door to the entire
    area of research.

Chapter Nineteen

FOOTNOTE, ENDNOTE, AND BIBLIOGRAPHY EXAMPLES

The principal purpose of documentation notes and bibliographies is to provide the reader with sufficient information to identify, locate, and retrieve the source documents used to support the arguments in a text. Secondary purposes are to illustrate the depth and breadth of research, and to provide others with information sources for their work in the same or related fields. To achieve these ends, publishers and scholars have formulated documentation styles that they feel are appropriate for their respective fields. While the styles differ from discipline to discipline, distinctions between documentation listings are generally limited to variations in punctuation, abbreviations, and spacing. Each documentation style aspires to present an orderly listing of information for each source, and each presents it in the same general sequence.

There appears to be an effort by universities to standardize the documentation of research and term papers and graduate theses. This may be a recognition that few of these works will be published in professional journals, thereby requiring specialized documentation, or it may be an acknowledgement that it is more important for students to learn good documentation practices than to simply adhere to the special documentation requirements of those journals. A growing number of universities appear to be applying this same reasoning to doctoral dissertations.

Most of the university style guides we studied during the writing of this manual recommend the use of one of three documentation styles:

1. **Chicago (CHI)**, from the *Chicago Manual of Style*, 13th ed. (Chicago: Chicago University Press, 1982);

2. **MLA**, from *The MLA Handbook for Writers of Research Papers*, 2nd ed. (1984), or *The MLA Style Manual* (1985), (New York: Modern Language Association); or

3. **APA**, from *The Publication Manual of The American Psychological Association*, 3rd ed. (New York: The American Psychological Association, 1985).

Each of these books describes a number of style variations. The four variations most frequently suggested, in the order of preference expressed in the university style guides are:

1. **Endnotes**, with number citations in the text keyed to documentation notes placed at the end of chapters, and bibliographic listings at the end of the text;

2. **Footnotes**, with number citations in the text keyed to documentation notes placed at the bottom of the page where they occur, and bibliographic listings at the back of the text;

3. **Author-date citations** (author's name, publication date, and page numbers placed in the text), with full documentation/bibliographic data in a list at the back of the text;

4. **Parenthetical citations** (author's name and page numbers placed in the text), with full documentation/bibliographic data in a list at the back of the text.

You will be required to select one of the documentation styles, combined with one of the variations listed above, and use it throughout your thesis. All of the style manuals emphasize that their rules for documentation are flexible, and that accuracy, clarity, and consistency are the most important factors when citing information sources. The university style guides also reflect this concept. You should keep this in mind as you prepare your work, and resist becoming overwhelmed by the seeming technicality of documentation listings.

This chapter has been designed to relieve you of some of the more difficult aspects of determining how to formulate footnote, endnote, bibliographic, and author-date entries. It is in two parts: (1) a short reference section containing abbreviations and rules specific to individual documentation styles; and (2) a compendium of citation note and bibliographic entries arranged by documentation style and information source. The examples in the compendium were formulated according to Chicago, MLA, and APA styles using the style guides listed above, and are labeled accordingly. The basics of documentation entry formulation are discussed in Chapters 17 and 18. Typing format instructions for documentation styles and bibliographic entries may be found in Chapter 14.

To use the compendium, simply look up the type of entry you need (book, magazine, government publication, etc.) and use it as an example for the sequence of data and punctuation in your entry. When you cannot locate an exact match, find one close to it and modify it to fit your needs. Underlining of titles is presented in the listing examples as it would appear in a typewritten manuscript. In a typeset book, the underlined titles would be set in an italic typeface.

REFERENCE DATA

DATA LISTING SEQUENCE. Table 6 (following page) lists the order in which data is entered in individual citation note and bibliography entries.

ABBREVIATIONS. Tables 2, 3, 4, and 5 from Chapter 17 are repeated on the pages following Table 6 to provide a ready reference section adjacent to the documentation examples.

TABLE 6. BASIC SEQUENCE AND CONTENTS OF DATA FOR INDIVIDUAL DOCUMENTATION ENTRIES.

FOR CITATION NOTES

Books

1. Name of author (may be an editor, translator, compiler or organization).
2. Title of part of the work, if appropriate.
3. Full title of the work, including subtitle, if any.
4. Editor, translator, or compiler, if any, and if not listed as author.
5. Series title, if any, and volume or number in the series.
6. Edition, when other than the original.
7. Number of volumes, if more than one.
8. City where published.
9. Publisher's name.
10. Year of publication.
11. Volume number, if required.
12. Page number(s) of information cited.

Periodicals

1. Name of author.
2. Title of article.
3. Name of periodical.
4. Volume or issue number.
5. Date of issue.
6. Page numbers of the information cited.

TABLE 6. CONTINUED

FOR BIBLIOGRAPHIC ENTRIES

Books

1. Name of author (may be an editor, translator, compiler, or organization).
2. Title of part of the work, if appropriate.
3. Full title of the work, including subtitle, if any.
4. Editor, translator, or compiler, if any, and if not listed as author.
5. Series title, if any, and volume or number in the series.
6. Volume number or total volumes in a multivolume work.
7. Edition, when other than the original.
8. City where published.
9. Publisher's name.
10. Year of publication.

Periodicals

1. Name of author.
2. Title of article.
3. Name of periodical.
4. Volume or issue number.
5. Date of issue.
6. Inclusive page numbers.

TABLE 2. SELECTED ABBREVIATIONS COMMONLY USED IN CITATION NOTES AND BIBLIOGRAPHIC ENTRIES.

CHICAGO	MLA	APA	MEANING
app.	app.	app.	appendix
bk.	bk.	bk.	book
chap.	ch.	chap.	chapter
comp.	comp.	comp.	compiler, or compiled by
ed.	ed.	Ed.	editor, or edited by
ed.	ed.	ed.	edition
f. (ff.)	f. (ff.)	f. (ff.)	and the following page(s)
fig.	fig.	fig.	figure
fol.	fol.	fol.	folio
l. (ll.)	l. (ll.)	l. (ll.)	line(s)
MS (MSS)	ms. (mss.)	ms. (mss.)	manuscript(s)
n. (nn.)	n (nn)	n. (nn.)	note(s)
n.d.	n.d.	n.d.	no date (of pub.)
no.	no.	No.	number
n.p.	n.p.	n.p.	no place (of pub.) or no publisher
n.s.	ns	n.s.	new series
o.s.	os	o.s.	old series
pl.	pl.	pl.	plate
p. (pp.)	p. (pp.)	p. (pp.)	page(s)
pt.	pt.	Pt.	part
repr.	rpt.	repr.	reprint
rev.	rev.	rev.	revision, or revised by
ser.	ser.	ser.	series
suppl.	suppl.	Suppl.	supplement
trans.	trans.	Trans.	translator, or translated by
TS (TSS)	ts. (tss.)	ts. (tss.)	typescript(s)
univ.	U	univ.	University
—	UP	—	University Press
vol.	vol.	Vol. (vols.)	volume(s)

For the plural form add "s" after all but those abbreviations already listing plural forms, and n.s, n.d., n.p., ser., trans., U and UP.

TABLE 3. SELECTED ABBREVIATIONS FOR GEOGRAPHICAL LOCATIONS.

CHICAGO	MLA & APA	CHICAGO	MLA & APA	CHICAGO	MLA & APA
Ala.	AL	Ky.	KY	N. Dak.	ND
Alaska	AK	La.	LA	Ohio	OH
Ariz.	AZ	Maine	ME	Okla.	OK
Ark.	AR	Md.	MD	Oreg.	OR
Calif.	CA	Mass.	MA	Pa.	PA
Colo.	CO	Mich.	MI	R.I.	RI
Conn.	CT	Minn.	MN	S.C.	SC
Del.	DE	Miss.	MS	S. Dak.	SD
D.C.	DC	Mo.	MO	Tenn.	TN
Fla.	FL	Mont.	MT	Tex.	TX
Ga.	GA	Nebr.	NE	Utah	UT
Hawaii	HI	Nev.	NV	Vt.	VT
Idaho	ID	N.H.	NH	Va.	VA
Ill.	IL	N.J.	NJ	Wash.	WA
Ind.	IN	N. Mex	NM	W. Va.	WV
Iowa	IA	N.Y.	NY	Wis.	WI
Kans.	KS	N.C.	NC	Wyo.	WY

TABLE 4. ABBREVIATIONS FOR MONTHS OF THE YEAR USED IN MLA DOCUMENTATION CITATIONS AND NOTES.

Jan.	May	Sept.
Feb.	June	Oct.
Mar.	July	Nov.
Apr.	Aug.	Dec.

Chicago and APA spell out months of the year.

TABLE 5. LATIN SUBSTITUTES FOR ENGLISH WORD PHRASES.

et al.	(et alii) and others
ibid.	(ibidem) in the same place
idem (id.)	the same
loc. cit.	in the place cited
op. cit.	in the work cited
passim	here and there
s.v.	(sub verbo) under the word

A COMPENDIUM OF CITATION NOTE AND BIBLIOGRAPHIC ENTRY EXAMPLES, AND AUTHOR-DATE CITATIONS

To convert Chicago and MLA styles to the author-date documentation style or MLA to the parenthetical documentation style, see the appropriate entries in Chapter 17, "What You Need To Know About Footnotes, Endnotes, and Other Documentation Styles."

LIST OF DOCUMENTATION EXAMPLES

BOOKS: GENERAL

BASIC FORM

CHI   1. Ernest Hemingway, <u>A Moveable Feast</u> (New York: Charles Scribner's Sons, 1964), 21.

MLA   2. Ernest Hemingway, <u>A Moveable Feast</u> (New York: Scribner's, 1964) 21.

APA   (Hemingway, 1964, p. 21)

TWO AUTHORS

CHI   3. Will Irwin and Thomas M. Johnson, <u>What You Should Know About Spies And Saboteurs</u> (New York: W. W. Norton and Co., 1943), 171.

MLA   4. Will Irwin and Thomas M. Johnson, <u>What You Should Know About Spies And Saboteurs</u> (New York: Norton, 1943) 171.

APA   (Irwin & Johnson, 1943, p. 171)

THREE AUTHORS

CHI   5. R. Charles Moyer, James R. McGuigan, and William J. Kretlow, <u>Contemporary Financial Management</u> (St. Paul: West Publishing Co., 1981), 133.

MLA   6. R. Charles Moyer, James R. McGuigan, and William J. Kretlow, <u>Contemporary Financial Management</u> (St. Paul: West, 1981) 133.

BOOKS: GENERAL

BASIC FORM

CHI   Hemingway, Ernest. A Moveable Feast. New York: Charles
      Scribner's Sons, 1964.

MLA   Hemingway, Ernest.   A Moveable Feast.   New York:
      Scribner's, 1964.

*[MLA requires two spaces after periods or other punctuation
separating main sections of a listing.]*

APA   Hemingway, E. (1964). A moveable feast. New York:
      Scribner's.

*[For APA style, include the surname and initials for all authors. The
year the work was copyrighted follows the author(s) name, enclosed
in parentheses. Capitalize the first word and the first letters of proper nouns and adjectives in titles and subtitles.]*

TWO AUTHORS

CHI   Irwin, Will, and Thomas M. Johnson. What You Should
      Know About Spies And Saboteurs. New York: W. W.
      Norton and Co., 1943.

*[Reverse only the name of the first author in multiple author listings
(Chicago and MLA).]*

MLA   Irwin, Will, and Thomas M. Johnson.   What You Should
      Know About Spies And Saboteurs.   New York: Norton,
      1943.

APA   Irwin, W. & Johnson, T. M. (1943). What you should know
      about spies and saboteurs. New York: Norton.

*[For APA, list the last name first for all authors in multiple author
listings. Use an ampersand (&) before the last author in place of
"and."]*

THREE AUTHORS

CHI   Moyer, R. Charles, James R. McGuigan, and William J.
      Kretlow. Contemporary Financial Management. St.
      Paul: West Publishing Co., 1981.

MLA   Moyer, R. Charles, James R. McGuigan, and William J.
      Kretlow.   Contemporary Financial Management.   St.
      Paul: West, 1981.

APA   (Moyer, McGuigan, & Kretlow, 1981, p. 133)

APA   (Moyer, et al., 1981, p. 133)

MORE THAN THREE AUTHORS

CHI   7. Zeb Taylor et al., How To Bathe Your Cat (New York:
        Paws Press, 1987), 10.

MLA   8. Zeb Taylor et al., How To Bathe Your Cat (New York:
        Paws, 1987) 10.

APA   (Taylor, Miller, Mitlor, & Thibault, 1987, p. 10)

APA   (Taylor, et al., 1987, p. 10)

PSEUDONYM, REAL NAME SUPPLIED

CHI   9. Charles Sealsfield, Life in the New World; or
        Sketches of American Society, trans. Gustavus C. Hebbe and
        James Mackay (New York, 1844), 13.

   *[Treat the pseudonym as if it were the author's real name unless the
   context of the text requires the real name (Chicago).]*

MLA   10. Charles Sealsfield [Karl Anton Postl], Life in
        the New World; or Sketches of American Society, trans.
        Gustavus C. Hebbe and James Mackay (New York, 1844) 13.

   *[The pseudonym should be placed in brackets when used with the
   author's real name.]*

APA   (Sealsfield, 1844, p. 13)

PSEUDONYM, REAL NAME UNKNOWN

CHI   11. Luke Shortfield, Wild Western Scenes: A Narrative
        of Adventures in the Western Wilderness, the Nearest and Best
        California. Wherein the Exploits of Daniel Boone, the Great
        American Pioneer, Are Particularly Described (Philadelphia,
        1849), 3.

APA   Moyer, R. C., McGuigan, J. R., & Kretlow, W. J. (1981).
      Contemporary financial management. St. Paul: West.

MORE THAN THREE AUTHORS

CHI   Taylor, Zeb, Alfred Miller, Oscar Mitlor, and Cynthia
      Thibault. How To Bathe Your Cat. New York: Paws
      Press, 1987.

MLA   Taylor, Zeb, et al.   How To Bathe Your Cat.   New York:
      Paws, 1987.

APA   Taylor, Z., Miller, A., Mitlor, O., & Thibault, C.
      (1987). How to bathe your cat. New York: Paws.

PSEUDONYM, REAL NAME SUPPLIED

CHI   Sealsfield, Charles [Karl Anton Postl]. Life in the
      New World; or Sketches of American Society. New
      York, 1844.

*[The author's real name, if known, may be added after the
pseudonym, and enclosed in brackets in the bibliography. Place and
date, or date alone, are sufficient for older works (as in the listing
above); use a comma instead of a colon between the place and date
(for Chicago and MLA styles).]*

MLA   Sealsfield, Charles [Karl Anton Postl].   Life in the
      New World; or Sketches of American Society.   New
      York, 1844.

APA   Sealsfield, C. (1844). Life in the new world; Or
      sketches of American society. New York: n.p.

*[For APA style, treat pseudonyms the same as ordinary author's
names. Indicate no publisher with "n.p."]*

PSEUDONYM, REAL NAME UNKNOWN

CHI   Shortfield, Luke [pseud.]. Wild Western Scenes: A
      Narrative of Adventures in the Western Wilderness,
      the Nearest and Best California. Wherein the
      Exploits of Daniel Boone, the Great American
      Pioneer, Are Particularly Described. Philadelphia,
      1849.

MLA   12. Luke Shortfield, <u>Wild Western Scenes: A Narrative of Adventures in the Western Wilderness, the Nearest and Best California. Wherein the Exploits of Daniel Boone, the Great American Pioneer, Are Particularly Described</u> (Philadelphia, 1849) 3.

APA   (Shortfield, 1849, p. 3)

AUTHOR'S NAME MISSING, ANONYMOUS

CHI   13. <u>5500 Questions and Answers on the Holy Bible</u> (Grand Rapids: Zondervan Publishing House, 1967), 40.

MLA   14. <u>5500 Questions and Answers on the Holy Bible</u> (Grand Rapids: Zondervan, 1967) 40.

APA   (<u>5500 Questions and Answers</u>, 1967, p. 40)

AUTHOR OF INTRODUCTION, PREFACE, OR FORWARD EMPHASIZED

CHI   15. Lyman Bryson, forward to <u>The Art of Plain Talk</u>, by Rudolf Flesch (New York: Harper and Brothers Publishers, 1946), ix.

MLA   16. Lyman Bryson, forward, <u>The Art of Plain Talk</u>, by Rudolf Flesch (New York: Harper, 1946) ix.

APA   (Bryson, 1946, p. ix)

GROUP, CORPORATION, ORGANIZATION, OR ASSOCIATION AS AUTHOR

CHI   17. Diagram Group, <u>Comparisons</u> (New York: St. Martin's Press, 1980), 81.

MLA   18. Diagram Group, <u>Comparisons</u> (New York: St. Martin's, 1980) 81.

APA   (Diagram Group, 1980, p. 81)

MLA   Shortfield, Luke. Wild Western Scenes: A Narrative of
      Adventures in the Western Wilderness, the Nearest
      and Best California.   Wherein the Exploits of Daniel
      Boone, the Great American Pioneer, Are Particularly
      Described. Philadelphia, 1849.

APA   Shortfield, L. (1849). Wild western scenes: A narrative
      of adventures in the western wilderness, the nearest
      and best California. Wherein the exploits of Daniel
      Boone, the great American pioneer, are particularly
      described. Philadelphia: n.p.

AUTHOR'S NAME MISSING, ANONYMOUS

CHI   5500 Questions and Answers on the Holy Bible. Grand
      Rapids: Zondervan Publishing House, 1967.

MLA   5500 Questions and Answers on the Holy Bible. Grand
      Rapids: Zondervan, 1967.

APA   5500 questions and answers on the Holy Bible. (1967).
      Grand Rapids: Zondervan.

*[Alphabetize bibliography entries by the first significant word in the
title.]*

AUTHOR OF INTRODUCTION, PREFACE,
OR FOREWORD EMPHASIZED

CHI   Bryson, Lyman. Foreword to The Art of Plain Talk, by
      Rudolf Flesch. New York: Harper and Brothers
      Publishers, 1946.

MLA   Bryson, Lyman. Foreword. The Art of Plain Talk. By
      Rudolf Flesch. New York: Harper, 1946. ix-xi.

APA   Bryson, L. (1946). [Foreword]. In R. Flesch, The art of
      plain talk. New York: Harper.

GROUP, CORPORATION, ORGANIZATION,
OR ASSOCIATION AS AUTHOR

CHI   Diagram Group. Comparisons. New York: St. Martin's
      Press, 1980.

MLA   Diagram Group. Comparisons. New York: St. Martin's,
      1980.

APA   Diagram Group. (1980). Comparisons. New York: St.
      Martin's.

*[For APA, when the author and publisher are the same, use the word
"Author" as the publisher's name.]*

EDITOR OR TRANSLATOR AND AUTHOR, EMPHASIS ON AUTHOR

CHI   19. Adolf Hitler, <u>Mein Kampf</u>, trans. Ralph Manheim (Boston: Houghton, Mifflin Co., 1943), 13.

MLA   20. Adolf Hitler, <u>Mein Kampf</u>, trans. Ralph Manheim (Boston: Houghton, 1943) 13.

APA   (Hitler, 1943, p. 13)

EDITOR OR TRANSLATOR AND AUTHOR, EMPHASIS ON TRANSLATOR OR EDITOR

CHI   21. Louis P. Lochner, ed. and trans., <u>The Goebbles Diaries 1942-1943</u>, by Joseph P. Goebbles (Garden City, N.Y.: Doubleday and Co., 1948), 150-51.

MLA   22. Louis P. Lochner, ed. and trans., <u>The Goebbles Diaries 1942-1943</u>, by Joseph P. Goebbles (Garden City, NY: Doubleday) 150-51.

APA   (Lochner, 1948, pp. 150-151)

EDITOR OR TRANSLATOR, NO AUTHOR

CHI   23. Joachim Remak, ed., <u>The Nazi Years: A Documentary History</u> (Englewood Cliffs, N.J.: Prentice-Hall, 1969), 73.

MLA   24. Joachim Remak, ed., <u>The Nazi Years: A Documentary History</u> (Englewood Cliffs, NJ: Prentice, 1969) 73.

APA   (Remak, 1969, p. 73)

TWO EDITORS, TRANSLATORS, OR COMPILERS

CHI   25. Kathryn Paulsen and Ryan A. Kuhn, comps. and eds., <u>Woman's Almanac</u> (Philadelphia: Armitage Press and Information House, 1976), 69.

MLA   26. Kathryn Paulsen and Ryan A. Kuhn, comps. and eds., <u>Woman's Almanac</u> (Philadelphia: Armitage Press and Information House, 1976) 69.

APA   (Paulsen & Kuhn, 1976, p. 69)

EDITOR OR TRANSLATOR AND AUTHOR, EMPHASIS ON AUTHOR

CHI   Hitler, Adolf. Mein Kampf. Translated by Ralph
           Manheim. Boston: Houghton, Mifflin Co., 1943.

MLA   Hitler, Adolf. Mein Kampf. Trans. Ralph Manheim.
           Boston: Houghton, 1943.

APA   Hitler, A. (1943). Mein kampf. (R. Manheim, Trans.).
           Boston: Houghton.

EDITOR OR TRANSLATOR AND AUTHOR, EMPHASIS ON TRANSLATOR OR EDITOR

CHI   Lochner, Louis P., ed. and trans. The Goebbles Diaries
           1942-1943, by Joseph P. Goebbles. Garden City,
           N.Y.: Doubleday and Co., 1948.

MLA   Lochner, Louis P., ed. and trans. The Goebbles Diaries
           1942-1943. By Joseph P. Goebbles. Garden City:
           NY: Doubleday, 1948.

APA   Lochner, L. P. (Ed. and Trans.). (1948). The Goebbles
           diaries 1942-1943, by J. P. Goebbles. Garden City,
           NY: Doubleday.

EDITOR OR TRANSLATOR, NO AUTHOR

CHI   Remak, Joachim, ed. The Nazi Years: A Documentary
           History. Englewood Cliffs, N.J.: Prentice-Hall,
           1969.

MLA   Remak, Joachim, ed. The Nazi Years: A Documentary
           History. Englewood Cliffs, NJ: Prentice, 1969.

APA   Remak, J. (Ed.). (1969). The Nazi years: A documentary
           history. Englewood Cliffs, NJ: Prentice.

TWO EDITORS, TRANSLATORS, OR COMPILERS

CHI   Paulsen, Kathryn, and Ryan A. Kuhn, comps. and eds.
           Woman's Almanac. Philadelphia: Armitage Press and
           Information House, 1975.

MLA   Paulsen, Kathryn, and Ryan A. Kuhn, comps. and eds.
           Woman's Almanac. Philadelphia: Armitage Press and
           Information House, 1975.

APA   Paulsen, K. & Kuhn, R. A. (Comps. and Eds.). (1975).
           Woman's Almanac. Philadelphia: Armitage Press and
           Information House.

COMPILATION, EMPHASIS ON EDITOR

CHI   27. Gordon A. Craig and Felix Gilbert, eds., The Diplomats 1919-1939 (Princeton: Princeton University Press, 1953), 400.

MLA   28. Gordon A. Craig and Felix Gilbert, eds., The Diplomats 1919-1939 (Princeton: Princeton UP, 1953) 400.

APA   (Craig & Gilbert, 1953, p. 400)

COMPILATION, EMPHASIS ON AUTHOR OF ONE ARTICLE, CHAPTER, OR SECTION

CHI   29. Carl E. Schorske, "Two German Ambassadors: Dirksen and Schulenburg," in The Diplomats 1919-1939, ed. Gordon A. Craig and Felix Gilbert (Princeton: Princeton University Press, 1953), 478.

MLA   30. Carl E. Schorske, "Two German Ambassadors: Dirksen and Schulenburg," The Diplomats 1919-1939, ed. Gordon A. Craig and Felix Gilbert (Princeton: Princeton UP, 1953) 478.

APA   (Schorske, 1953, p. 478)

COMPILATION, EDITOR AND AUTHOR THE SAME

CHI   31. Bryn Williams, "Karate-do," in his Martial Arts of the Orient (London: Hamlyn Publishing Group, 1975), 128.

MLA   32. Bryn Williams, "Karate-do," Martial Arts of the Orient (London: Hamlyn, 1975) 128.

APA   (Williams, 1975, p. 128)

COMPILATION, EMPHASIS ON EDITOR

CHI   Craig, Gordon A., and Felix Gilbert, eds. The Diplomats 1919-1939. Princeton: Princeton University Press, 1953.

MLA   Craig, Gordon A., and Felix Gilbert, eds. The Diplomats 1919-1939. Princeton: Princeton UP, 1953.

APA   Craig, G. A. & Gilbert, F. (Eds.). (1953). The diplomats 1919-1939. Princeton: Princeton University Press.

COMPILATION, EMPHASIS ON AUTHOR OF ONE ARTICLE, CHAPTER OR SECTION

CHI   Schorske, Carl E. "Two German Ambassadors: Dirksen and Schulenburg." In The Diplomats 1919-1939, edited by Gordon A. Craig and Felix Gilbert. Princeton: Princeton University Press, 1953. 475-511.

[The names of editors, translators, and compilers, when not in the author position, are not reversed (all styles).]

MLA   Schorske, Carl E. "Two German Ambassadors: Dirksen and Schulenburg." The Diplomats 1919-1939. Ed. Gordon A. Craig and Felix Gilbert. Princeton: Princeton UP, 1953. 475-511.

APA   Schorske, C. E. (1953). Two German ambassadors: Dirksen and Schulenburg. In G. A. Craig & F. Gilbert (Eds.), The diplomats 1919-1939 (pp. 475-511). Princeton: Princeton University Press.

COMPILATION, EDITOR AND AUTHOR THE SAME

CHI   Williams, Bryn. "Karate-do." In Martial Arts of the Orient, edited by Bryn Williams. London: Hamlyn Publishing Group, 1975.

MLA   Williams, Bryn. "Karate-do." Martial Arts of the Orient. Ed. Bryn Williams. London: Hamlyn, 1975. 128-47

APA   Williams, B. (1975). Karate-do. In B. Williams (Ed.), Martial arts of the orient (pp. 128-147). London: Hamlyn.

COMPILATION, REPRINT OF MATERIAL (ARTICLE, CHAPTER, BOOK) PREVIOUSLY PUBLISHED ELSEWHERE

CHI   33. J. Edgar Hoover, "The Spy Who Double-Crossed Hitler," American Magazine, May 1946, 23-25; reprinted in Secrets and Spies: Behind-the-Scenes Stories of World War II (Pleasantville, N.Y.: Reader's Digest Association, 1964), 283.

MLA   34. J. Edgar Hoover, "The Spy Who Double-Crossed Hitler," American Magazine, May 1946: 23-25; rpt. in Secrets and Spies: Behind-the-Scenes Stories of World War II (Pleasantville, NY: Reader's Digest Assn., 1964) 283.

APA   (Hoover, 1946/1964, p. 283)

SUBTITLE, OPTIONAL IN NOTE CITATION; MUST APPEAR IN BIBLIOGRAPHY

CHI   35. Barbara W. Tuchman, A Distant Mirror: The Calamitous Fourteenth Century (New York: Alfred A. Knopf, 1978), 11.

MLA   36. Barbara W. Tuchman, A Distant Mirror: The Calamitous Fourteenth Century (New York: Knopf, 1978) 11.

[Spell out the names of centuries in titles.]

APA   (Tuchman, 1978, p. 11)

Without subtitle

CHI   35. Barbara W. Tuchman, A Distant Mirror (New York: Alfred A. Knopf, 1978), 11.

MLA   36. Barbara W. Tuchman, A Distant Mirror (New York: Knopf, 1978) 11.

EDITION OTHER THAN THE FIRST

CHI   37. Thomas A. Bailey, A Diplomatic History of the American People, 10th ed. (Englewood Cliffs, N.J.: Prentice-Hall, 1980), 816-17.

COMPILATION, REPRINT OF MATERIAL (ARTICLE, CHAPTER, BOOK) PREVIOUSLY PUBLISHED ELSEWHERE

CHI   Hoover, J. Edgar. "The Spy Who Double-Crossed Hitler."
       American Magazine, May 1946, 23-25. Reprinted in
       Secrets and Spies: Behind-the-Scenes Stories of
       World War II, 283-87. Pleasantville, N.Y.: Reader's
       Digest Association, 1964.

MLA   Hoover, J. Edgar. "The Spy Who Double-Crossed Hitler."
       American Magazine, May 1946: 23-25. Rpt. in
       Secrets and Spies: Behind-the-Scenes Stories of
       World War II. Pleasantville, NY: Reader's Digest
       Assn., 1964.   283-87.

APA   Hoover, J. E. (1964). The spy who double-crossed Hitler.
       In Secrets and spies: Behind-the-scenes stories of
       World War II (pp. 283-287). Pleasantville, NY:
       Reader's Digest Assn. (Reprinted from American
       Magazine, 1946, May, 23-25).

SUBTITLE, OPTIONAL IN NOTE CITATION; MUST APPEAR IN BIBLIOGRAPHY

CHI   Tuchman, Barbara W. A Distant Mirror: The Calamitous
       Fourteenth Century. New York: Alfred A. Knopf,
       1978.

MLA   Tuchman, Barbara W. A Distant Mirror: The Calamitous
       Fourteenth Century. New York: Knopf, 1978.

APA   Tuchman, B. W. (1978). A distant mirror: The calamitous
       fourteenth century. New York: Knopf.

EDITION OTHER THAN THE FIRST

CHI   Bailey, Thomas A. A Diplomatic History of the American
       People. 10th ed. Englewood Cliffs, N.J.:
       Prentice-Hall, 1980.

MLA   38. Thomas A. Bailey, A Diplomatic History of the
American People, 10th ed. (Englewood Cliffs, NJ: Prentice,
1980) 816-17.

APA   (Bailey, 1980, pp. 816-817)

REPRINT

CHI   39. Lucy S. Dawidowicz, The War Against the Jews
1933-1945 (1975; reprint, New York: Bantam Books, 1976),
270.

CHI   39. Lucy S. Dawidowicz, The War Against the Jews
1933-1945 (New York: Holt, Rinehart and Winston, 1975; New
York: Bantam Books, 1976), 270.

*[When the original publication data is known, it should be included,
as in the second example above (Chicago).]*

MLA   40. Lucy S. Dawidowicz, The War Against the Jews
1933-1945 (1975; New York: Bantam, 1976) 270.

APA   (Dawidowicz, 1976, p. 270)

FACTS OF PUBLICATION MISSING

No date

CHI   41. Harold Lamb, The March of the Barbarians (New
York: Literary Guild of America, n.d.), 105.

MLA   42. Harold Lamb, The March of the Barbarians (New
York: Literary Guild, n.d.) 105.

APA   (Lamb, n.d., p. 105)

No Place

CHI   41. Harold Lamb, The March of the Barbarians (N.p.:
Literary Guild of America, 1940), 105.

MLA   42. Harold Lamb, The March of the Barbarians (N.p.:
Literary Guild, 1940) 105.

APA   (Lamb, 1940, p. 105)

MLA   Bailey, Thomas A. A Diplomatic History of the American
         People. 10th ed. Englewood Cliffs, NJ: Prentice,
         1980.

APA   Bailey, T. A. (1980). A diplomatic history of the
         American people (10th ed.). Englewood Cliffs, NJ:
         Prentice.

REPRINT

CHI   Dawidowicz, Lucy S. The War Against the Jews
         1933-1945. 1975. Reprint. New York: Bantam Books,
         1976.

CHI   Dawidowicz, Lucy S. The War Against the Jews
         1933-1945. New York: Holt, Rinehart and Winston,
         1975; New York: Bantam Books, 1976.

   *[When the original publication data is known, it should be included,
   as in the second example above (Chicago).]*

MLA   Dawidowicz, Lucy S. The War Against the Jews
         1933-1945. 1975. New York: Bantam, 1976.

APA   Dawidowicz, L. (1976). The war against the Jews
         (Reprint). New York: Bantam.

FACTS OF PUBLICATION MISSING

No date

CHI   Lamb, Harold. The March of the Barbarians. New York:
         Literary Guild of America, n.d.

MLA   Lamb, Harold. The March of the Barbarians. New York:
         Literary Guild of America, n.d.

APA   Lamb, H. (n.d.). The march of the barbarians. New
         York: Literary Guild of America.

No place

CHI   Lamb, Harold. The March of the Barbarians. N.p.:
         Literary Guild of America, 1940.

MLA   Lamb, Harold. The March of the Barbarians. N.p.:
         Literary Guild of America, 1940.

APA   Lamb, H. (1940). The march of the barbarians. N.p.:
         Literary Guild of America.

   *[Note that the first letter in abbreviations is capitalized when the ab-
   breviation follows a period.]*

No Publisher

CHI   41. Harold Lamb, The March of the Barbarians (New York: n.p., 1940), 105.

MLA   42. Harold Lamb, The March of the Barbarians (New York: n.p., 1940) 105.

APA   (Lamb, 1940, p. 105)

No Page Number

CHI   41. Harold Lamb, The March of the Barbarians (New York: Literary Guild of America, 1940), unpaginated.

MLA   42. Harold Lamb, The March of the Barbarians (New York: Literary Guild, 1940) n. pag.

APA   (Lamb, 1940)

None of the Above

CHI   41. Harold Lamb, The March of the Barbarians (N.p., n.d.), unpaginated.

MLA   42. Harold Lamb, The March of the Barbarians (N.p.: n.p., n.d.) N. pag.

APA   (Lamb, The March)

TITLE NORMALLY UNDERLINED
WITHIN THE MAIN TITLE

CHI   43. William S. Gleim, The Meaning of "Moby Dick" (New York: Russell and Russell, 1938), 121.

[Chicago style adds quotation marks before and after the title within a title.]

MLA   44. William S. Gleim, The Meaning of Moby Dick (New York: Russell, 1938) 121.

[MLA drops the underline from beneath the title within a title.]

APA   (Gleim, 1938, p. 121)

No publisher

CHI   Lamb, Harold. <u>The March of the Barbarians</u>. New York:
            n.p., 1940.

MLA   Lamb, Harold. <u>The March of the Barbarians</u>. New York:
            n.p., 1940.

APA   Lamb, H. (1940). <u>The march of the barbarians</u>. New
            York: n.p.

No page number

*[MLA uses the abbreviation "n. pag." to indicate that no page
references were supplied with the documentation, and why they were
missing from the note citations. Chicago and APA do not address
this for bibliographic listings.]*

None of the above

CHI   Lamb, Harold. <u>The March of the Barbarians</u>. N.p.,
            n.d.

MLA   Lamb, Harold. <u>The March of the Barbarians</u>. N.p.:
            n.p., n.d.

APA   Lamb, H. (n.d.). <u>The march of the barbarians</u>. N.p.:
            n.p.

TITLE NORMALLY UNDERLINED
WITHIN THE MAIN TITLE

CHI   Gleim, William S. <u>The Meaning of "Moby Dick."</u> New
            York: Russell and Russell, 1938.

[Chicago style adds quotation marks to the title within a title.]

MLA   Gleim, William S. <u>The Meaning of</u> Moby Dick. New
            York: Russell, 1938.

[MLA drops the underline from beneath the title within a title.]

APA   Gleim, W. S. (1938). <u>The meaning of "Moby Dick."</u> New
            York: Russell.

TITLE NORMALLY ENCLOSED IN QUOTATION MARKS WITHIN THE MAIN TITLE

CHI   45. Portius Hadden, Comments on Poe's "Eldorado"
        (Newport News, Va.: Cross Gap Publishing, 2011), 101.

MLA   46. Portius Hadden, Comments on Poe's "Eldorado"
        (Newport News, VA: Cross Gap, 2011) 101.

APA   (Hadden, 2011, p. 101)

OLDER TITLES

CHI   47. Thomas Hutchins, An Historical Narrative and
        Topographical Description of Louisiana and West Florida
        (Philadelphia, 1784), 97.

        *[For older works, place and date, or date alone, are sufficient
        (Chicago and MLA).]*

MLA   48. Thomas Hutchins, An Historical Narrative and
        Topographical Description of Louisiana and West Florida
        (Philadelphia, 1784) 97.

APA   (Hutchins, 1784, p. 97)

FOREIGN TITLES

Follow the capitalization conventions of the language being used.
If a translation is included, it follows the original title, and is enclosed
in parentheses for Chicago and in brackets for MLA and APA styles.
Capitalize the first word, proper nouns, and adjectives in the
translated title and subtitle.

CHI   49. Werner Baumbach, Zu Spät? Aufstieg und Untergang
        der deutschen Luftwaffe (Too late? The rise and fall of the
        German airforce) (Munich: Pflaum, 1949), 290.

MLA   50. Werner Baumbach, Zu Spät? Aufstieg und Untergang
        der deutschen Luftwaffe [Too late? The rise and fall of the
        German airforce] (Munich: Pflaum, 1949) 290.

APA   (Baumbach, 1949, p. 290)

TITLE NORMALLY ENCLOSED IN QUOTATION MARKS WITHIN THE MAIN TITLE

CHI   Hadden, Portius. Comments on Poe's "Eldorado." Newport News, Va.: Cross Gap Publishing, 2011.

MLA   Hadden, Portius. Comments on Poe's "Eldorado." Newport News, VA: Cross Gap, 2011.

APA   Hadden, P. (2011). Comments on Poe's "Eldorado." Newport News, VA: Cross Gap.

OLDER TITLES

CHI   Hutchins, Thomas. An Historical Narrative and Topographical Description of Louisiana, and West-Florida. Philadelphia, 1784.

[For older works, place and date, or date alone, are sufficient (Chicago and MLA).]

MLA   Hutchins, Thomas. An Historical Narrative and Topographical Description of Louisiana, and West-Florida. Philadelphia, 1784.

APA   Hutchins, T. (1784). An historical narrative and topographical description of Louisiana, and west-Florida. Philadelphia: n.p.

FOREIGN TITLES

Follow the capitalization conventions of the language being used. If a translation is included, it follows the original title, and is enclosed in parentheses for Chicago and in brackets for MLA and APA styles. Capitalize the first word, proper nouns, and adjectives in the translated title and subtitle.

CHI   Baumbach, Werner. Zu Spät? Aufstieg und Untergang der deutschen Luftwaffe (Too late? The rise and fall of the German airforce). Munich: Pflaum, 1949.

MLA   Baumbach, Werner. Zu Spät? Aufstieg und Untergang der deutschen Luftwaffe [Too late? The rise and fall of the German airforce). Munich: Pflaum, 1949

APA   Baumbach, W. (1949). Zu spät? Aufstieg und untergang der deutschen luftwaffe [Too late? The rise and fall of the German airforce]. Munich: Pflaum.

[APA requires that an English translation of a foreign title be included in the bibliography listing. It is optional with Chicago and MLA.]

BOOKS: MULTIVOLUME WORKS

GENERAL TITLE, AUTHOR

CHI   51. Winston Churchill, The Second World War, 6 vols. (Boston: Houghton Mifflin Co., 1948-53), 2:37.

MLA   52. Winston Churchill, The Second World War, 6 vols. (Boston: Houghton, 1948-53) 2: 37.

APA   (Churchill, 1948-1953, vol. 2, p. 37)

GENERAL TITLE, EDITOR

CHI   53. Samuel I. Rosenman, ed., The Public Papers and Addresses of Franklin D. Roosevelt, 13 vols. (New York: Macmillan Co., 1938-50), 7:115.

MLA   54. Samuel I. Rosenman, ed., The Public Papers and Addresses of Franklin D. Roosevelt 13 vols. (New York: Macmillan, 1938-50) 7: 115.

APA   (Rosenman, 1938-1950, vol. 7, p. 115)

INDIVIDUAL TITLES (AUTHOR OR EDITOR)

CHI   55. Winston Churchill, Their Finest Hour, vol. 2 of The Second World War (Boston: Houghton Mifflin Co., 1949), 37.

CHI   55. Winston Churchill, The Second World War, vol. 2, Their Finest Hour (Boston: Houghton Mifflin Co., 1949), 37.

MLA   56. Winston Churchill, Their Finest Hour, vol. 2 of The Second World War, 6 vols. (Boston: Houghton, 1949) 37.

APA   (Churchill, 1949, p. 37)

MULTIVOLUME WORK IN A SERIES

CHI   57. L.F. Ellis, Victory in the West, 2 vols., History of the Second World War: United Kingdom Military Series (London: HMSO, 1968), 2:22.

BOOKS: MULTIVOLUME WORKS

GENERAL TITLE, AUTHOR

CHI   Churchill, Winston. The Second World War.
        6 vols. Boston: Houghton Mifflin Co., 1948-53.

MLA   Churchill, Winston. The Second World War.
        6 vols. Boston: Houghton, 1948-53.

APA   Churchill, W. (1948-1953). The Second World War
        (6 Vols.). Boston: Houghton.

GENERAL TITLE, EDITOR

CHI   Rosenman, Samuel I., ed. The Public Papers and
        Addresses of Franklin D. Roosevelt. 13 vols. New York:
        Macmillan Co., 1938-50.

MLA   Rosenman, Samuel I., ed. The Public Papers and
        Addresses of Franklin D. Roosevelt. 13 vols. New York:
        Macmillan, 1938-50.

APA   Rosenman, S. I. (Ed.). (1938-1950). The public papers
        and addresses of Franklin D. Roosevelt (13 Vols).
        New York: Macmillan.

INDIVIDUAL TITLES (AUTHOR OR EDITOR)

CHI   Churchill, Winston. Their Finest Hour. Vol 2 of The
        Second World War. Boston: Houghton Mifflin Co., 1949.

CHI   Churchill, Winston. The Second World War. Vol. 2,
        Their Finest Hour. Boston: Houghton Mifflin Co., 1949.

MLA   Churchill, Winston. Their Finest Hour. Vol. 2 of
        The Second World War. 6 vols. Boston: Houghton, 1949.

APA   Churchill, W. (1949). The Second World War: Vol. 2.
        Their finest hour. Boston: Houghton.

MULTIVOLUME WORK IN A SERIES

CHI   Ellis, L. F. Victory in the West. 2 vols. History of
        the Second World War: United Kingdom Military Series.
        London: HMSO, 1968.

MLA   58. L. F. Ellis, <u>Victory in the West</u>, 2 vols., History
of the Second World War: United Kingdom Military Series
(London: HMSO, 1968) 2: 22.

APA   (Ellis, 1968, vol. 2, p. 22)

BOOKS: SERIES WORKS

BASIC FORM

CHI   59. Oscar Osburn Winther, <u>The Old Oregon Country: A
History of Frontier Trade, Transportation, and Travel</u>,
Indiana University Social Science Series no. 7 (Bloomington:
Indiana University Press, 1950), 11.

MLA   60. Oscar Osburn Winther, <u>The Old Oregon Country: A
History of Frontier Trade, Transportation, and Travel</u>,
Indiana U Social Science Series No. 7 (Bloomington:
Indiana UP, 1950) 11.

APA   (Winther, 1950, p. 11)

AUTHOR, WITH SERIES EDITOR INCLUDED

CHI   61. David W. Noble, <u>The Progressive Mind, 1890-1917</u>,
ed. David D. Van Tassel, Rand McNally Series on the History
of American Thought and Culture (Chicago: Rand McNally and
Co., 1970), 83.

MLA   62. David W. Noble, <u>The Progressive Mind, 1890-1917</u>,
ed. David D. Van Tassel, Rand McNally Series on the History
of American Thought and Culture (Chicago: Rand, 1970) 83.

APA   (Noble, 1970, p. 83)

MLA   Ellis, L. F.   Victory in the West.   2 vols.   History
          of the Second World War: United Kingdom Military Series.
          London: HMSO, 1968.

APA   Ellis, L. F. (1968). Victory in the west (2 Vols.).
          History of the Second World War: United Kingdom Military
          Series. London: HMSO.

BOOKS: SERIES WORKS

BASIC FORM

CHI   Winther, Oscar Osburn.   The Old Oregon Country:
          A History of Frontier Trade, Transportation, and Travel.
          Indiana University Social Science Series no. 7. Bloomington:
          Indiana University Press, 1950.

MLA   Winther, Oscar Osburn.   The Old Oregon Country:
          A History of Frontier Trade, Transportation, and Travel.
          Indiana U Social Science Series No. 7.   Bloomington:
          Indiana UP, 1950.

APA   Winther, O. O. (1950). The old Oregon country:
          A history of frontier trade, transportation, and travel
          (Indiana University Social Science Series No. 7).
          Bloomington: Indiana University Press.

AUTHOR, WITH SERIES EDITOR INCLUDED

CHI   Noble, David W. The Progressive Mind, 1890-1917.
          Edited by David D. Van Tassel. Rand McNally Series on the
          History of American Thought and Culture. Chicago: Rand
          McNally Co., 1970.

MLA   Noble, David W.   The Progressive Mind, 1890-1917.
          Ed. David D. Van Tassel.   Rand McNally Series on the
          History of American Thought and Culture.   Chicago: Rand,
          1970.

APA   Noble, D. W. (1970). The progressive mind, 1890-1917
          (D. D. Van Tassel, Ed.). Rand McNally Series on the
          History of American Thought and Culture, Chicago: Rand.

TRANSLATOR, EDITOR, OR BOTH

CHI   63. Theodore S. Hamerow, ed., Otto von Bismark: A Historical Assessment, 2d ed., Problems in European Civilization Series (Lexington, Mass.: D. C. Heath and Co., 1972), 130-31.

MLA   64. Theodore S. Hamerow, ed., Otto von Bismark: A Historical Assessment, 2nd ed., Problems in European Civilization Series (Lexington, MA: D. C. Heath, 1972) 130-31.

APA   (Hamerow, 1972, pp. 130-131)

MULTIVOLUME WORKS IN A SERIES (SEE BOOKS: MULTIVOLUME WORKS)

YEARBOOK

CHI   65. U.S. Department of Agriculture, Yearbook of Agriculture, 1914 (Washington, D.C.: GPO, 1915), 27.

MLA   66. United States, Dept. of Agriculture, Yearbook of Agriculture, 1914 (Washington: GPO, 1915) 27.

APA   (U.S. Department of Agriculture, 1915, p. 27)

CHAPTER IN A YEARBOOK

CHI   67. Edward B. Mitchell, "The American Farm Woman As She Sees Herself," in Yearbook of Agriculture, 1914, U.S. Department of Agriculture (Washington, D.C.: GPO, 1915), 5.

MLA   68. Edward B. Mitchell, "The American Farm Woman As She Sees Herself," Yearbook of Agriculture, 1914, U.S., Dept. of Agriculture (Washington: GPO, 1915) 5.

APA   (Mitchell, 1915, p. 5)

TRANSLATOR, EDITOR, OR BOTH

CHI   Hamerow, Theodore S., ed. Otto von Bismark:
          A Historical Assessment. 2d ed. Problems in European
          Civilization Series. Lexington, Mass.: D. C. Heath and Co.,
          1972.

MLA   Hamerow, Theodore S., ed. Otto von Bismark:
          A Historical Assessment. 2nd ed. Problems in European
          Civilization Series. Lexington, MA: Heath, 1972.

APA   Hamerow, T. S. (Ed.). (1972). Otto von Bismark:
          A historical assessment (2nd ed.). Problems in European
          Civilization Series. Lexington, MA: Heath.

MULTIVOLUME WORK IN A SERIES
(SEE BOOKS: MULTIVOLUME WORKS)

YEARBOOK

CHI   U.S. Department of Agriculture. Yearbook of
          Agriculture, 1914. Washington, D.C.: GPO, 1915.

MLA   United States. Dept. of Agriculture. Yearbook of
          Agriculture, 1914. Washington: GPO, 1915.

APA   U.S. Department of Agriculture. (1915). Yearbook of
          agriculture, 1914. Washington, D.C.: GPO.

CHAPTER IN A YEARBOOK

CHI   Mitchell, Edward B. "The American Farm Woman As She Sees
          Herself." In Yearbook of Agriculture, 1914, U.S.
          Department of Agriculture. Washington, D.C.: GPO, 1915.

MLA   Mitchell, Edward B. "The American Farm Woman As She
          Sees Herself." Yearbook of Agriculture, 1914. U.S.
          Dept. of Agriculture. Washington: GPO, 1915.

APA   Mitchell, E. B. (1915). The American farm woman as she
          sees herself. In U.S. Department of Agriculture, Yearbook of
          agriculture, 1914 . Washington, D.C.: GPO.

CATALOGS

CHI   69. Recreational Equipment, Inc., catalog, <u>REI:
        Spring 1986</u> (Seattle: Recreational Equipment, Inc., 1985), 23.

MLA   70. Recreational Equipment, Inc., catalog, <u>REI:
        Spring 1986</u> (Seattle: Recreational Equipment, Inc., 1985) 23.

APA   (Recreational Equipment, Inc. [REI], 1985, p. 23)

APA   (REI, 1985, p. 23)   *[subsequent reference]*

   [Corporate authors may be abbreviated in subsequent references (all styles).]

CONVENTION OR CONFERENCE PROCEEDINGS

CHI   71. Conference on Manifestations of Jewish Resistance,
        <u>Jewish Resistance During The Holocaust: Proceedings</u>
        (Jerusalem: n.p., 1971), 13.

CHI   71. Henry Bradley, "On the Relations between Spoken and
        Written Language," <u>Proceedings of the British Academy</u>
        6 (1913-14): 212.

MLA   72. Conference on Manifestations of Jewish Resistance,
        <u>Jewish Resistance During the Holocaust: Proceedings</u>
        (Jerusalem: n.p., 1971) 13.

MLA   72. Henry Bradley, "On the Relations between Spoken and
        Written Language," <u>Proceedings of the British Academy</u>
        6 (1913-14): 212.

APA   (Bradley, 1913-1914, p. 212)

CATALOGS

CHI   Recreational Equipment, Inc. Catalog. <u>REI:</u>
        <u>Spring 1986</u>. Seattle: Recreational Equipment, Inc., 1985.

MLA   Recreational Equipment, Inc. Catalog. <u>REI:</u>
        <u>Spring 1986</u>. Seattle: Recreational Equipment, Inc., 1985.

APA   Recreational Equipment, Inc. [Catalog]. (1985). <u>REI:</u>
        <u>Spring 1986</u>. Seattle: Author.

CONVENTION OR CONFERENCE PROCEEDINGS

CHI   Conference on Manifestations of Jewish Resistance.
        <u>Jewish Resistance During the Holocaust: Proceedings</u>.
        Jerusalem: n.p., 1971.

CHI   Bradley, Henry. "On the Relations between Spoken and
        Written Language." <u>Proceedings of the British Academy</u>
        6 (1913-14): 212-32.

MLA   Conference on Manifestations of Jewish Resistance.
        <u>Jewish Resistance During the Holocaust: Proceedings</u>.
        Jerusalem: n.p., 1971.

MLA   Bradley, Henry. "On the Relations between Spoken and
        Written Language." <u>Proceedings of the British Academy</u>
        6 (1913-14): 212-32.

APA   Bradley, H. (1913-14). On the relations between spoken
        and written language. <u>Proceedings of the British Academy</u>,
        <u>6</u>, 212-232.

*[List published proceedings the same as a book, but add information
about the conference if it is not included in the title. Cite a particular
presentation as you would a work in a collection of articles by individual authors (all styles).]*

DISSERTATIONS AND THESES

For the purpose of bibliographic and footnote listings, theses and dissertations are treated as unpublished works unless copies have been reproduced for sale or distribution. Dissertations and theses commercially sold or distributed on microfilm are treated as published books. (See Copyright Act of 1976, Sec 101.) The form of the publication is given at the end of the entry (if it is not included as part of the publisher's name). A sponsoring organization may be listed in addition to the publisher.

OBTAINED FROM THE DEGREE-GRANTING UNIVERSITY, OR FROM UNIVERSITY MICROFILMS INTERNATIONAL (PUBLISHED)

CHI   73. Barbara Greenblatt Landau, Language Learning in Blind Children: Relationships Between Perception and Language, Ph.D diss., University of Pennsylvania, 1982 (Ann Arbor: University Microfilms International, 1982), 96. PR182-17143.

MLA   74. Barbara Greenblatt Landau, Language Learning in Blind Children: Relationships Between Perception and Language, diss., U of Pennsylvania, 1982 (Ann Arbor: UMI, 1982) 96.   PR182-17143.

APA   (Landau, 1982, p. 96)

UNPUBLISHED

CHI   75. Ralph Dewar Bald, Jr., "The Development of Expansionist Sentiment in the United States, 1885-1895" (Ph.D. diss., University of Pittsburgh, 1953), 200.

CHI   75. Arthur Barcan, "American Imperialism and the Spanish American War" (Master's thesis, Columbia University, 1940), 65.

[Treat the title of unpublished papers the same as journal articles; the label "unpublished" is not required.]

DISSERTATIONS AND THESES

For the purpose of bibliographic and footnote listings, theses and dissertations are treated as unpublished works unless copies have been reproduced for sale or distribution. Dissertations and theses commercially sold or distributed on microfilm are treated as published books. (See Copyright Act of 1976, Sec 101.) The form of the publication is given at the end of the entry (if it is not included as part of the publisher's name). A sponsoring organization may be listed in addition to the publisher.

OBTAINED FROM THE DEGREE-GRANTING UNIVERSITY, OR FROM UNIVERSITY MICROFILMS INTERNATIONAL (PUBLISHED)

CHI Landau, Barbara Greenblatt. Language Learning in Blind Children: Relationships Between Perception and Language. Ph.D. diss., University of Pennsylvania, 1982. Ann Arbor: University Microfilms International, 1982. PR182-17143.

MLA Landau, Barbara Greenblatt. Language Learning in Blind Children: Relationships Between Perception and Language. Diss. U of Pennsylvania, 1982. Ann Arbor: UMI, 1982. PR182-17143.

APA Landau, B. G. (1982). Language learning in blind children: Relationships between perception and language (Doctoral dissertation, University of Pennsylvania, 1982). (University Microfilms No. PR182-17143).

[Add pertinent dissertation information where appropriate and, where the work is published by University Microfilms International, include the order number (all styles).]

UNPUBLISHED

CHI Bald, Ralph Dewar, Jr. "The Development of Expansionist Sentiment in the United States, 1885-1895." Ph.D. diss., University of Pittsburgh, 1953.

CHI Barcan, Arthur. "American Imperialism and the Spanish American War." Master's thesis, Columbia University, 1940.

MLA   76. Ralph Dewar Bald, Jr., "The Development of
Expansionist Sentiment in the United States, 1885-1895,"
diss., U of Pittsburgh, 1953, 200.

MLA   76. Arthur Barcan, "American Imperialism and the Spanish
American War," thesis, Columbia U, 1940, 65.

APA   (Bald, 1953, p. 200)

APA   (Barcan, 1940, p. 65)

ABSTRACT, PUBLISHED IN
DISSERTATION ABSTRACTS INTERNATIONAL

CHI   77. Grace Carroll Massey, "Self-Concept, Personal
Control and Social Context Among Students in Inner-City High
Schools," DAI 36 (1975): sec. 5, 2738A (Stanford
University).

MLA   78. Grace Carroll Massey, "Self-Concept, Personal
Control and Social Context Among Students in Inner-City High
Schools," DAI 36 (1975): sec. 5, 2738A (Stanford U).

APA   (Massey, 1975, p. 2738A)

GOVERNMENT AND OTHER
OFFICIAL PUBLICATIONS

Both houses of Congress, the Executive Departments, and independent government agencies all issue publications. The Government

MLA   Bald, Ralph Dewar, Jr.   "The Development of Expansionist
      Sentiment in the United States, 1885-1895."   Diss.
      U of Pittsburgh, 1953.

MLA   Barcan, Arthur.   "American Imperialism and the Spanish
      American War."   Thesis.   Columbia U, 1940.

APA   Bald, R. D., Jr. (1953). The development of
      expansionist sentiment in the United States,
      1885-1895. Unpublished doctoral dissertation,
      University of Pittsburgh, Pittsburgh.

APA   Barcan, A. (1940). American imperialism and the Spanish
      American war. Unpublished master's thesis, Columbia
      University, New York.

*[APA style underlines the titles of unpublished dissertations and
theses. Titles of published dissertations and theses are neither
underlined nor enclosed in quotation marks.]*

ABSTRACT, PUBLISHED IN
DISSERTATION ABSTRACTS INTERNATIONAL

CHI   Massey, Grace Carroll.   "Self-Concept, Personal Control
      and Social Context Among Students in Inner-City High
      Schools."   DAI 36 (1975): sec. 5, 2738A. Stanford
      University.

MLA   Massey, Grace Carroll.   "Self-Concept, Personal Control
      and Social Context Among Students in Inner-City High
      Schools."   DAI 36 (1975): sec. 5, 2738A.
      Stanford U.

APA   Massey, G. C. (1975). Self-concept, personal control and
      social context among students in inner city high
      schools. Dissertation Abstracts International,
      36, sec. 5, 2738A.

GOVERNMENT AND OTHER
OFFICIAL PUBLICATIONS

Both houses of Congress, the Executive Departments, and independent government agencies all issue publications. The Government

Printing Office (GPO) prints and distributes most of these, and is usually listed as the publisher.

CONGRESSIONAL COMMITTEE REPORT

CHI   79. Senate Committee on Interstate Commerce, Promotion of Export Trade: Hearings On H.R. 17350, 64th Cong., 2d sess., January, 1917, 10.

CHI   79. U.S. Congress, Senate Committee on Interstate Commerce, Promotion of Export Trade: Hearings on H.R. 17350, 64th Cong., 2d sess. (Washington, D.C.: GPO, 1917), 10

[When it is difficult to determine the country and issuing body from the text, a more complete reference may be used (second example).]

MLA   80. United States, Cong., Senate, Committee on Interstate Commerce, Promotion of Export Trade: Hearings on H.R. 17350. 64th Cong., 2nd sess. (Washington: GPO, 1917) 10.

[Spell out "United States" if it is in the author position (MLA).]

APA   (Promotion of Export Trade, 1917, p. 10)

CONGRESSIONAL HOUSE OR SENATE REPORT

CHI   81. House Interstate and Foreign Commerce Committee, Securities Exchange Bill of 1934, 73d Cong., 2d sess., 1934, H. Rept. 1383, 3.

MLA   82. United States, Cong., House, Interstate and Foreign Commerce Committee, Securities Exchange Bill of 1934, 73rd Cong., 2nd sess., H. Rept. 1383 (Washington: GPO, 1934) 3.

APA   (Securities Exchange Bill, 1934, p. 3)

CONGRESSIONAL RECORD

CHI   83. Congressional Record, 99th Cong., 2nd sess., 1 August, 1986, H5321.

Printing Office (GPO) prints and distributes most of these, and is usually listed as the publisher.

CONGRESSIONAL COMMITTEE REPORT

CHI   U.S. Congress. Senate. Committee on Interstate Commerce. Promotion of Export Trade: Hearings on H.R. 17350. 64th Cong., 2d sess. Washington, D.C.: GPO, 1917.

MLA   United States. Cong. Senate. Committee on Interstate Commerce. Promotion of Export Trade: Hearings on H.R. 17350. 64th Cong., 2nd sess. Washington: GPO, 1917.

[Spell out "United States" if it is in the author position (MLA).]

APA   U.S. Congress. Senate. Committee on Interstate Commerce. (1917, January). Promotion of export trade: Hearings on H.R. 17350. 64th Cong., 2nd sess. Washington, D.C.: GPO.

CONGRESSIONAL HOUSE OR SENATE REPORT

CHI   U.S. Congress. House. Interstate and Foreign Commerce Committee. Securities Exchange Bill of 1934. 73d Cong., 2d sess., 1934. H. Rept. 1383. Washington, D.C.: GPO, 1934.

MLA   United States. Cong. House. Interstate and Foreign Commerce Committee. Securities Exchange Bill of 1934. 73rd Cong., 2nd sess. H. Rept. 1383. Washington: GPO, 1934.

APA   U.S. Congress. House. Interstate and Foreign Commerce Committee (1934). Securities exchange bill of 1934. (H. Rept. 1383). 73rd Cong., 2nd sess. Washington, D.C.: GPO.

CONGRESSIONAL RECORD

CHI   Congressional Record. 99th Cong., 2nd sess., 1986. vol. 132, No. 103.

MLA   84. <u>Cong. Rec.</u>, 1 August 1986: H5321.

APA   (<u>Congressional Record</u>, 1986, p. H5321)

*[The authors of this handbook disagree with the Congressional
Record listing forms described in the Chicago and MLA style
manuals on the basis that they do not present adequate information.
The Congressional Record, from 1874 to the present, has been
organized in a semi-magazine format, with titles heading each of the
activities recorded. To locate a specific item, the documentation, we
feel, should include the title of the article, the date of presentation,
and the page number. None of the current styles include the title in
the documentation. The APA manual does not describe or present
an example for this catagory; we have composed one from their
general rules. Following are examples of Congressional Record
listings as we would present them using the three styles.]*

CHI   83. <u>Congressional Record</u>, "Legislation Amending The
Debt Ceiling Legislation," August 1, 1986, H5321.

MLA   84. <u>Cong. Rec</u>, "Legislation Amending The Debt Ceiling
Legislation," 1 Aug. 1986: H5321.

APA   (<u>Congressional Record</u>, Legislation amending the debt
ceiling, 1986, August 1, p. H5321)

EXECUTIVE DEPARTMENTS OR INDEPENDENT AGENCIES, BASIC FORM

CHI   85. U.S. Department of Education, National Center for
Education Statistics, <u>Digest of Education Statistics</u>
<u>1983-84</u> (Washington, D.C.: GPO, 1985), 93.

MLA   86. United States, Dept. of Education, National Center
for Education Statistics, <u>Digest of Education Statistics</u>
<u>1983-84</u> (Washington: GPO, 1985) 93.

APA   (U.S. Department of Education, 1985, p. 93)

EXECUTIVE DEPARTMENTS OR INDEPENDENT AGENCIES, WORK IN A SERIES

CHI   87. U.S. Department of Health and Human Services, Public
Health Service, <u>Exercise and Your Heart</u>, National
Institutes of Health Publication no. 83-1677 (May 1981;
reprint, Washington, D.C.: GPO, January 1983), 22-23.

MLA   Cong. Rec. 1 Aug. 1986: H5321.

APA   Congressional Record. (1986, August 1). p. H5321

[The authors of this handbook disagree with the Congressional Record listing forms described in the Chicago and MLA style manuals on the basis that they do not present adequate information. The Congressional Record, from 1874 to the present, has been organized in a semi-magazine format, with titles heading each of the activities recorded. To locate a specific item, the documentation, we feel, should include the title of the article, the date of presentation, and the page number. None of the current styles include the title in the documentation. The APA manual does not describe or present an example for this catagory; we have composed one from their general rules. Following are examples of Congressional Record listings as we would present them using the three styles.]

CHI   Congressional Record. "Legislation Amending The Debt Ceiling Legislation." August 1, 1986. H5321.

MLA   Cong. Rec. "Legislation Amending The Debt Ceiling Legislation." 1 Aug. 1986: H5321.

APA   Congressional Record. Legislation amending the debt ceiling legislation. (1986, August 1). p.H5321

EXECUTIVE DEPARTMENTS OR INDEPENDENT AGENCIES, BASIC FORM

CHI   U.S. Department of Education. National Center for Education Statistics. Digest of Education Statistics 1983-84. Washington, D.C.: GPO, 1985.

MLA   United States. Dept. of Education. National Center for Education Statistics. Digest of Education Statistics 1983-84. Washington: GPO, 1985.

APA   U.S. Department of Education. National Center for Education Statistics. (1985). Digest of education statistics 1983-84. Washington, D.C.: GPO.

EXECUTIVE DEPARTMENTS OR INDEPENDENT AGENCIES, WORK IN A SERIES

CHI   U.S. Department of Health and Human Services. Public Health Service. Exercise and Your Heart. National Institutes of Health Publication no. 83-1677. May 1981. Reprint. Washington, D.C.: GPO, January 1983.

MLA   88. United States, Dept. of Health and Human Services, Public Health Service, Exercise and Your Heart, National Institutes of Health Publication No. 83-1677 (May 1981; Washington: GPO, January 1983) 22-23.

APA   (U.S. Department of Health and Human Services, 1983, pp. 22-23)

EXECUTIVE DEPARTMENTS OR INDEPENDENT AGENCIES, LEAFLET

CHI   89. General Services Administration, National Archives and Records Service, Select List of Publications of the National Archives and Records Service, rev. ed., General Services Administration General Information Leaflet no. 3 (Washington, D.C., 1982), 32.

[If the publisher is other than the issuing body, you should include this information (see the statement about the GPO as publisher at the beginning of this section).]

MLA   90. General Services Administration, National Archives and Records Service, Select List of Publications of the National Archives and Records Service, rev. ed., General Services Administration [GSA] General Information Leaflet No. 3 (Washington: GSA, 1982) 32.

APA   (General Services Administration, 1982, p. 32)

EXECUTIVE DEPARTMENTS OR INDEPENDENT AGENCIES, AUTHOR(S) INCLUDED

CHI   91. U.S. State Department, European Affairs Division, National Socialism: Basic Principles, Their Application by the Nazi Party's Foreign Organization, and the Use of Germans Abroad for Nazi Aims, by Raymond E. Murphey et al. (Washington, D.C.: GPO, 1943), 345.

MLA   United States. Dept. of Health and Human Services.
Public Health Service. <u>Exercise and Your Heart</u>.
National Institutes of Health Publication No.
83-1677. May 1981. Washington: GPO, January 1983.

APA   U.S. Department of Health and Human Services. Public
Health Service. (1983, January). <u>Exercise and your
heart</u> (Reprint). (National Institutes of Health
Publication No. 83-1677). Washington, D.C.: GPO.

EXECUTIVE DEPARTMENTS OR
INDEPENDENT AGENCIES, LEAFLET

CHI   General Services Administration. National Archives and
Records Service. <u>Select List of Publications of the
National Archives and Records Service</u>. Rev. ed.
General Services Administration General Information
Leaflet no. 3. Washington, D.C., 1982.

*[If the publisher is other than the issuing body, you should include
this information (see the statement about the GPO as publisher at
the beginning of this section).]*

MLA   General Services Administration. National Archives and
Records Service. <u>Select List of Publications of
the National Archives and Records Service</u>. Rev.
ed. GSA General Information Leaflet No. 3.
Washington: GSA, 1982.

APA   General Services Administration. National Archives and
Records Service. (1982). <u>Select list of
publications of the National Archives and Records
Service</u> (rev. ed.). (GSA General Information
Leaflet No. 3). Washington, D.C.: Author.

EXECUTIVE DEPARTMENTS OR
INDEPENDENT AGENCIES, AUTHOR(S) INCLUDED

CHI   U.S. State Department. European Affairs Division.
<u>National Socialism: Basic Principles, Their
Application by the Nazi Party's Foreign
Organization, and the Use of Germans Abroad for Nazi
Aims</u>, by Raymond E. Murphy, Francis B. Stevens,
Howard Trivers, and Joseph M. Roland. Washington,
D.C.: GPO, 1943.

CHI   91. Raymond E. Murphy et al., <u>National Socialism: Basic Principles, Their Application by the Nazi Party's Foreign Organization, and the Use of Germans Abroad for Nazi Aims</u>, prepared for the State Department, European Affairs Division (Washington, D.C.: GPO, 1943), 345.

[A citation may begin with the author or the sponsoring agency when listing Executive Department or government agency publications, whichever will serve the reader best to locate the document (Chicago).]

MLA   92. United States, State Dept., European Affairs Division, <u>National Socialism: Basic Principles, Their Application by the Nazi Party's Foreign Organization, and the Use of Germans Abroad for Nazi Aims</u>, by Raymond E. Murphy et al. (Washington: GPO, 1943) 345.

MLA   92. Raymond E. Murphy et al., <u>National Socialism: Basic Principles, Their Application by the Nazi Party's Foreign Organization, and the Use of Germans Abroad for Nazi Aims</u>, U.S., State Dept., European Affairs Division (Washington: GPO, 1943) 345.

[When a government publication lists one or more authors on the title page, the citation may follow the format applicable for a book (MLA).]

APA   (Murphy, Stevens, Trivers, & Roland, 1943, p. 345)

APA   (Murphy et al., 1943, p. 345)

EXECUTIVE DEPARTMENTS OR INDEPENDENT AGENCIES, WORK IN A SERIES, AUTHOR(S) INCLUDED

CHI   93. Elizabeth M. Sorbet, <u>Do You Know the Results of Your Advertising?</u>, U.S. Small Business Administration, Management Assistance Support Services, Management Aids no. 4.020 (1979; reprint, Washington, D.C.: GPO, 1984), 5.

CHI   Murphy, Raymond E., Francis B. Stevens, Howard Trivers, and Joseph M. Roland. National Socialism: Basic Principles, Their Application by the Nazi Party's Foreign Organization, and the Use of Germans Abroad for Nazi Aims. Prepared for the State Department, European Affairs Division. Washington, D.C.: GPO, 1943.

[A citation may begin with the author or the sponsoring agency when listing Executive Department or government agency publications, whichever will serve the reader best to locate the document (Chicago).]

MLA   United States.   State Dept.   European Affairs Division. National Socialism: Basic Principles, Their Application by the Nazi Party's Foreign Organization, and the Use of Germans Abroad for Nazi Aims.   By Raymond E. Murphy, et al.   Washington: GPO, 1943.

MLA   Murphy, Raymond E., et al.   National Socialism: Basic Principles, Their Application by the Nazi Party's Foreign Organization, and the Use of Germans Abroad for Nazi Aims.   U.S.   State Dept.   European Affairs Division.   Washington: GPO, 1943.

[When a government publication lists one or more authors on the title page, the citation may follow the format applicable for a book (MLA).]

APA   Murphy, R. E., Stevens, F. B., Trivers, H., & Roland, J. M. (1943). National Socialism: Basic principles, their application by the Nazi party's foreign organization, and the use of Germans abroad for Nazi aims. Prepared for the U.S. State Department, European Affairs Division. Washington, D.C.: GPO.

EXECUTIVE DEPARTMENTS OR INDEPENDENT AGENCIES, WORK IN A SERIES, AUTHOR(S) INCLUDED

CHI   Sorbet, Elizabeth M. Do You Know the Results of Your Advertising? U.S. Small Business Administration. Management Assistance Support Services. Management Aids no. 4.020. 1979. Reprint. Washington, D.C.: GPO, 1984.

MLA   94. Elizabeth M. Sorbet, Do You Know the Results of
      Your Advertising?, U.S., Small Business Administration,
      Management Assistance Support Services, Management Aids No.
      4.020 (1979; Washington: GPO, 1984) 5.

APA   (Sorbet, 1984, p. 5)

STATE AND LOCAL GOVERNMENTS, STATE LEGISLATURE

CHI   95. Oregon, Legislative Interim Committee on Local
      Government, The Problems of the Urban Fringe: Portland Area
      (Salem, Ore., July 1956), 20.

MLA   96. Oregon, Legislative Interim Committee on Local
      Government, The Problems of the Urban Fringe: Portland Area
      (Salem, OR: Legislative Interim Committee, July 1956) 20.

APA   (Oregon, Legislative Interim Committee, 1956, p. 20)

APA   (Problems of the Urban Fringe, 1956, p. 20)

STATE AND LOCAL GOVERNMENTS,
WORK IN A SERIES, AUTHOR(S) INCLUDED

CHI   97. Roy F. Bessey, The Public Issues of Middle Snake
      River Development; the Controversy Over Hell's Canyon and Nez
      Perce Reaches, Washington, Division of Power Resources,
      Bulletin no. 9 (Olympia, 1964), 5.

MLA   98. Roy F. Bessey, The Public Issues of Middle Snake
      River Development; the Controversy Over Hell's Canyon and Nez
      Perce Reaches, Washington, Division of Power Resources,
      Bulletin No. 9 (Olympia: Division of Power Resources, 1964)
      5.

APA   (Bessey, 1964, p. 5)

MLA   Sorbet, Elizabeth M. Do You Know the Results of Your
       Advertising? U.S. Small Business Administration.
       Management Assistance Support Services. Management
       Aids No. 4.020. 1979. Washington: GPO, 1984.

APA   Sorbet, E. M. (1984). Do you know the results of your
       advertising? (Reprint). U.S. Small Business
       Administration. Management Assistance Support
       Services. (Management Aids No. 4.020). Washington,
       D.C.: GPO.

STATE AND LOCAL GOVERNMENTS, STATE LEGISLATURE

CHI   Oregon. Legislative Interim Committee on Local
       Government. The Problems of the Urban Fringe:
       Portland Area. Salem, Ore., July 1956.

MLA   Oregon. Legislative Interim Committee on Local
       Government. The Problems of the Urban Fringe:
       Portland Area. Salem, OR: Legislative Interim
       Committee, July 1956.

APA   Oregon. Legislative Interim Committee on Local
       Government. (1956, July). The problems of the urban
       fringe: Portland area. Salem, OR: Author.

STATE AND LOCAL GOVERNMENTS,
WORK IN A SERIES, AUTHOR(S) INCLUDED

CHI   Bessey, Roy F. The Public Issues of Middle Snake River
       Development; the Controversy Over Hell's Canyon and
       Nez Perce Reaches. Washington. Division of Power
       Resources, Bulletin no. 9. Olympia, 1964.

MLA   Bessey, Roy F. The Public Issues of Middle Snake River
       Development; the Controversy Over Hell's Canyon and
       Nez Perce Reaches. Washington. Division of Power
       Resources. Bulletin No. 9. Olympia: Division of
       Power Resources, 1964.

APA   Bessey, R. F. (1964). The public issues of middle Snake
       River development; The controversy over Hell's
       Canyon and Nez Perce Reaches. Washington. Division
       of Power Resources (Bulletin No. 9). Olympia:
       Division of Power Resources.

JOURNALS

Journals are periodicals intended for an academic or professional audience. Periodicals for the general public are usually called magazines.

BASIC FORM

CHI   99. Samuel Penter, "Recollections of an Oregon Pioneer," <u>Oregon Historical Quarterly</u> 7 (1906): 60.

CHI   99. Gerhard Weinberg, "Hitler's Image of the United States," <u>American Historical Review</u> 69 (July 1964): 1007.

MLA   100. Samuel Penter, "Recollections of an Oregon Pioneer," <u>Oregon Historical Quarterly</u> 7 (1906): 60.

MLA   100. Gerhard Weinberg, "Hitler's Image of the United States," <u>American Historical Review</u> 69 (1964): 1007.

APA   (Penter, 1906, p. 60)

APA   (Weinberg, 1964, p. 1007)

ISSUE NUMBER DESIGNATION

CHI   101. Arnold Berleant, "Aesthetic Paradigms for an Urban Ecology," <u>Diogenes</u>, no. 103 (Fall 1978): 7.

MLA   102. Arnold Berleant, "Aesthetic Paradigms for an Urban Ecology," <u>Diogenes</u> 103 (1978): 7.

APA   (Berleant, 1978, p. 7)

SERIES DESIGNATION

CHI   103. Chester E. Eisinger, "The Freehold Concept in Eighteenth-Century American Letters," <u>William and Mary Quarterly</u>, 3d ser., 4 (January 1947): 50.

[Long running series sometimes number their volumes over again and must be designated new series (n.s.), old series (o.s.), or if by number, second, third, or fourth series (2d ser., 3d ser., 4th ser. for CHI; MLA uses 2nd ser., 3rd ser., 4th ser.) between the title and the volume number (all styles).]

JOURNALS

Journals are periodicals intended for an academic or professional audience. Periodicals for the general public are usually called magazines.

BASIC FORM

CHI   Penter, Samuel. "Recollections of an Oregon Pioneer." Oregon Historical Quarterly 7 (1906): 56-61

CHI   Weinberg, Gerhard. "Hitler's Image of the United States." American Historical Review 69 (July 1964): 1006-21.

MLA   Penter, Samuel. "Recollections of an Oregon Pioneer." Oregon Historical Quarterly 7 (1906): 56-61.

MLA   Weinberg, Gerhard. "Hitler's Image of the United States." American Historical Review 69 (1964): 1006-21.

APA   Penter, S. (1906). Recollections of an Oregon pioneer. Oregon Historical Quarterly, 7, 56-61.

APA   Weinberg, G. (1964). Hitler's image of the United States. American Historical Review, 69, 1006-1021.

ISSUE NUMBER DESIGNATION

CHI   Berleant, Arnold. "Aesthetic Paradigms for an Urban Ecology." Diogenes, no. 103 (Fall 1978): 1-28.

MLA   Berleant, Arnold. "Aesthetic Paradigms for an Urban Ecology." Diogenes 103 (1978): 1-28.

APA   Berleant, A. (1978). Aesthetic paradigms for an urban ecology. Diogenes, (103), 1-28.

SERIES DESIGNATION

CHI   Eisinger, Chester E. "The Freehold Concept in Eighteenth-Century American Letters." William and Mary Quarterly, 3d ser. 4 (January 1947): 42-59.

[Long running series sometimes number their volumes over again and must be designated new series (n.s.), old series (o.s.), or if by number, second, third, or fourth series (CHI uses 2d ser., 3d ser., 4th ser.; MLA uses 2nd ser., 3rd ser., 4th ser.) between the title and the volume number (all styles).]

MLA   104. Chester E. Eisinger, "The Freehold Concept in Eighteenth-Century American Letters," William and Mary Quarterly 3rd ser. 4 (1947): 50.

APA   (Eisinger, 1947, p. 50)

ARTICLE WITH A QUOTATION OR A TITLE WITHIN QUOTATION MARKS IN THE MAIN TITLE

CHI   105. Lisa Keylor, "Images of Time in Frost's 'Birches,' " American Quarterly 4 (May 1990): 260.

[A title within a title is enclosed with single quotation marks; the complete title uses normal quotation marks. When the title within a title is underlined, retain the underlining and enclose the complete title in quotation marks (Chicago and MLA).]

MLA   106. Lisa Keylor, "Images of Time in Frost's 'Birches,' " American Quarterly 4 (1990): 260.

APA   (Keylor, 1990, p. 260)

ARTICLE IN PRESS

CHI   107. Lisa Keylor, "Images of Time in Frost's 'Birches,' " American Quarterly (In press).

[When an article has been accepted for publication but the issuing date has not been determined, "In Press" takes the place of publication facts (all styles).]

MLA   108. Lisa Keylor, "Images of Time in Frost's 'Birches,' " American Quarterly (In press).

APA   (Keylor, in press)

INTERVIEWS, EDITORIALS, OR LETTERS TO THE EDITOR

CHI   109. Gerhard Weinberg, editorial, American Historical Review 69 (July 1964): 1022.

MLA   110. Gerhard Weinberg, editorial, American Historical Review 69 (1964): 1022.

APA   (Weinberg, 1964, p. 1022)

MLA   Eisinger, Chester E.   "The Freehold Concept in Eighteenth-Century American Letters."   <u>William and Mary Quarterly</u> 3rd ser.   4 (1947): 42-59.

APA   Eisinger, C. E. (1947). The freehold concept in eighteenth-century American letters. <u>William and Mary Quarterly, 4</u> (3rd ser.), 42-59.

ARTICLE WITH A QUOTATION OR A TITLE WITHIN QUOTATION MARKS IN THE MAIN TITLE

CHI   Keylor, Lisa. "Images of Time in Frost's 'Birches.' " <u>American Quarterly</u> 4 (1990): 255-80.

[A title within a title is enclosed with single quotation marks; the complete title uses normal quotation marks. When the title within a title is underlined, retain the underlining and enclose the complete title in quotation marks (Chicago and MLA).]

MLA   Keylor, Lisa.   "Images of Time in Frost's 'Birches' " <u>American Quarterly</u> 4 (1990): 255-80.

APA   Keylor, L. (1990). Images of time in Frost's "Birches." <u>American Quarterly, 4</u>, 255-280.

ARTICLE IN PRESS

CHI   Keylor, Lisa. "Images of Time in Frost's 'Birches' " <u>American Quarterly</u> (In press).

[When an article has been accepted for publication but the issuing date has not been determined, "In Press" takes the place of publication facts (all styles).]

MLA   Keylor, Lisa.   "Images of Time in Frost's 'Birches.' " <u>American Quarterly</u> (In press).

APA   Keylor, L. (in press). Images of time in Frost's "Birches." <u>American Quarterly</u>.

INTERVIEWS, EDITORIALS, OR LETTERS TO THE EDITOR

CHI   Weinberg, Gerhard. Editorial. <u>American Historical Review</u> 69 (July 1964): 1022.

MLA   Weinberg, Gerhard.   Editorial.   <u>American Historical Review</u> 69 (1964): 1022.

APA   Weinberg, G. (1964). [Editorial]. <u>American Historical Review, 69</u>, 1022.

FOREIGN LANGUAGE JOURNALS

CHI   111. Jürgen Rohwer, "La Radiotélégraphie: Auxiliaire du commandement dans la guerre sousmarin," Revue d'Histoire de la deuxiéme guerre mondiale 18 (January 1968): 60.

MLA   112. Jürgen Rohwer, "La Radiotélégraphie: Auxiliaire du commandement dans la guerre sousmarin," Revue d'Histoire de la deuxiéme guerre mondiale 18 (1968): 60.

APA   (Rohwer, 1968, p. 60)

LEGAL REFERENCES

U.S. CODE

CHI   113. 17 U.S.C. [United States Code], sec. 302(a), 1976.

MLA   114. 17 US Code, sec. 302(a), 1976.

[For MLA style, laws, acts, and similar documents (Declaration of Independence, the Constitution, Sherman Antitrust Act) are not underlined or enclosed in quotation marks in either the text or in documentation listings.]

APA   (Copyright Act of 1976)

APA   (Copyright Act of 1976, sec. 302(a))

[For APA style, use the name of the act and the year introduced (as opposed to the year codified).]

COURT CASES

List the name of the case, volume number of the law report, the page number, and the year, in that order (example 1 below). When a decision is cited in both an official and an unofficial report, include them both if you have that information, with the official report listed first (example 2). Older reports are frequently named for court

FOREIGN LANGUAGE JOURNALS

CHI   Rohwer, Jürgen. "La Radiotélégraphie: Auxiliaire du commandement dans la guerre sousmarin." Revue d'Histoire de la deuxiéme guerre mondiale 18 (January 1968): 41-66.

MLA   Rohwer, Jürgen. "La Radiotélégraphie: Auxiliaire du commandement dans la guerre sousmarin." Revue d'Histoire de la deuxiéme guerre mondiale 18 (1968): 41-66.

APA   Rohwer, J. (1968). La radiotélégraphie: Auxiliaire du commandement dans la guerre sousmarin. Revue d'Histoire de la deuxiéme guerre mondiale, 18, 41-66.

LEGAL REFERENCES

U.S. CODE

CHI   *[For Chicago style, statutory notes and court decisions are cited in the text only, and not listed separately in the bibliography.]*

MLA   17 USC. Sec. 302(a). 1976.

[For MLA style, laws, acts, and similar documents (Declaration of Independence, the Constitution, Sherman Antitrust Act) are not underlined or enclosed in quotation marks in either the text or in documentation listings.]

APA   Copyright Act of 1976, 17 U.S.C. Sec. 302(a) (1978).

COURT CASES

List the name of the case, volume number of the law report, the page number, and the year, in that order (example 1 below). When a decision is cited in both an official and an unofficial report, include them both if you have that information, with the official report listed first (example 2). Older reports are frequently named for court reporters ("Wheat." for Wheaton in example 3); U.S. should appear after the name of a U.S. Supreme Court reporter; a state abbreviation after that of a state reporter. Add the jurisdiction to reports cited to court reporters that do not contain that information (example 3).

This section provides only a brief overview for documenting court cases. If your thesis contains a large number of court citations, obtain a copy of *A Uniform System of Citations*, Cambridge: Harvard Law Review Association, from your library, and follow its recommendations.

CHI   115. Mandeville Island Farms v. American Crystal Sugar Co., 334 U.S. 219 (1948).

CHI   115. American Can Co. v. Oregon Liquor Control Commission, 15 Ore. App. 618, 517 P2d 691 (1973).

CHI   115. Parrott v. Wells-Fargo Co., 15 Wheat. (U.S.) 524 (1872).

MLA   116. Mandeville Island Farms v. American Crystal Sugar Co., 334 US 219 (1948).

MLA   116. American Can Co. v. Oregon Liquor Control Commission, 15 Ore. App 618, 517 P2d 691 (1973).

MLA   116. Parrott v. Wells-Fargo Co., 15 Wheat. (US) 524 (1872).

[MLA underlines the names of cases when used in text, but not in documentation listings.]

APA   (Mandeville Island Farms v. American Crystal Sugar Co., 1948)

APA   (American Can Co. v. Oregon Liquor Control Commission, 1973)

APA   (Parrott v. Wells-Fargo Co., 1872)

LETTERS, PUBLISHED

CHI   117. John Steinbeck to Adlai Stevenson, 20 November 1962, Steinbeck: A Life in Letters, ed. Elaine Steinbeck and Robert Wallsten (New York: Viking Press, 1975), 755-56.

reporters ("Wheat." for Wheaton in example 3). U.S. should appear after the name of a U.S. Supreme Court reporter; a state abbreviation after that of a state reporter. Add the jurisdiction to reports cited to court reporters that do not contain that information (example 3).

This section provides only a brief overview for documenting court cases. If your thesis contains a large number of court citations, obtain a copy of *A Uniform System of Citations*, Cambridge: Harvard Law Review Association, from your library, and follow its recommendations.

CHI   *[For Chicago style, statutory notes and court decisions are cited in the text, or in notes to the text only, and not listed separately in the bibliography.]*

MLA   Mandeville Island Farms v. American Crystal Sugar Co. 334 US 219. 1948.

MLA   American Can Co. v. Oregon Liquor Control Commission. 15 Ore. App 618. 517 P2d 691. 1973.

MLA   Parrott v. Wells-Fargo Co. 15 Wheat. (US) 524. 1872.

APA   Mandeville Island Farms v. American Crystal Sugar Co., 334 U.S. 219 (1948).

APA   American Can Co. v. Oregon Liquor Control Commission, 15 Ore. App 618, 517 P2d 691 (1973).

APA   Parrott v. Wells-Fargo Co., 15 Wheat. (U.S.) 524 (1872).

LETTERS, PUBLISHED

CHI   Steinbeck, John. Letter to Adlai Stevenson. 20 November 1962. Steinbeck: A Life in Letters. Edited by Elaine Steinbeck and Robert Wallsten. New York: Viking Press, 1975

MLA   118. John Steinbeck, "To Adlai Stevenson," 20 Nov. 1962, Steinbeck: A Life in Letters, ed. Elaine Steinbeck and Robert Wallsten (New York: Viking, 1975) 755-56.

APA   (Steinbeck, 1962/1975, pp. 755-756)

[When a collection of letters is reprinted or republished, cite the date of the original and the secondary source dates, separated by a slash.]

LITERATURE, WORKS OF

PLAY; ACT, SCENE, LINE

CHI   119. The Comedy of Errors, act 2, sc. 1, lines 19-22.

[For Chicago style, text citations of classical plays and poems using section and line or stanza numbers do not require publication data unless it is important to identify a specific text.]

MLA   120. William Shakespeare, The Comedy of Errors, The Complete Works of William Shakespeare (New York: Avenel, 1975) 2.1.19-22.

APA   (Shakespeare, 1975, act 2, sc. 1, lines 19-22)

POEM; BOOK, CANTO, LINE

CHI   121. The Divine Comedy: Purgatory, canto 10, lines 73-75.

MLA   122. Dante Alighieri, The Divine Comedy: Purgatory, trans. Dorothy L. Sayers (Harmondsworth, Eng.: Penguin, 1976) 10.73-75.

APA   (Alighieri, 1976, canto 10, lines 73-75)

POEM; STANZA, LINE

CHI   123. Sir Gawain and The Green Knight, stanza *[or st.]* 56, lines 1405-7.

MLA   Steinbeck, John. "To Adlai Stevenson." 20 Nov. 1962. <u>Steinbeck: A Life in Letters</u>. Ed. Elaine Steinbeck and Robert Wallsten. New York: Viking, 1975.

APA   Steinbeck, J. (1962, November 20/1975). [Letter to A. Stevenson]. In E. Steinbeck & R. Wallsten (Eds.), <u>Steinbeck: A life in letters</u> (pp. 755-756). New York: Viking.

LITERATURE, WORKS OF

PLAY; ACT, SCENE, LINE

CHI   Shakespeare, William. <u>The Comedy of Errors</u>. In <u>The Complete Works of William Shakespeare</u>. New York: Avenel Books, 1975.

MLA   Shakespeare, William. <u>The Comedy of Errors</u>. <u>The Complete Works of William Shakespeare</u>. New York: Avenel, 1975.

APA   Shakespeare, W. (1975). <u>The complete works of William Shakespeare: The comedy of errors</u>. New York: Avenel.

POEM; BOOK, CANTO, LINE

CHI   Alighieri, Dante. <u>The Divine Comedy: Purgatory</u>. Translated by Dorothy L. Sayers. Harmondsworth, England: Penguin Books, 1976.

MLA   Alighieri, Dante. <u>The Divine Comedy: Purgatory</u>. Trans. Dorothy L. Sayers. Harmondsworth, Eng.: Penguin, 1976.

APA   Alighieri, D. (1976). <u>The divine comedy: Purgatory</u> (D. S. Sayers, Trans.). Harmondsworth, England: Penguin.

POEM; STANZA, LINE

CHI   Stone, Brian, trans. <u>Sir Gawain and the Green Knight</u>. 2d ed. Harmondsworth, England: Penguin Books, 1974.

MLA   124. Brian Stone, trans., <u>Sir Gawain and the Green Knight</u>, 2nd ed. (Harmondsworth, Eng.: Penguin, 1974) 56.1405-07.

APA   (Stone, 1974, st. 56, lines 1405-1407)

CLASSICAL TRANSLATION

CHI   125. Homer, <u>Odyssey</u>, trans. Robert Fitzgerald (1961; reprint, New York: Anchor Books, 1963), bk. 8, lines 26-42.

MLA   126. Homer, <u>Odyssey</u>, trans. Robert Fitzgerald (1961; New York: Anchor, 1963) 8.26-42.

APA   (Homer, 1963, book 8, lines 26-42)

BIBLICAL CITATIONS; CHAPTER, VERSE

CHI   127. Isa. 6:8.

CHI   127. 1 Pet. 4:8.

MLA   128. Isa. 6.8 (RSV).   *[Revised Standard Version]*

MLA   128. 1 Pet. 4.8 (RSV).

APA   (Isa. 6:8)

APA   (1 Pet. 6:8)

MAGAZINES

WEEKLY, BASIC FORM

CHI   129. Patricia Holt, "Books Down Under," <u>Publishers Weekly</u>, 3 July 1981, 107.

MLA   130. Patricia Holt, "Books Down Under," <u>Publishers Weekly</u> 3 July 1981: 107.

APA   (Holt, 1981, p. 107)

MONTHLY, BASIC FORM

CHI   131. Christopher M. DeBracy, "RCPMs: Settling the Frontier," <u>Profiles</u>, December 1985, 57.

MLA   132. Christopher M. DeBracy, "RCPMs: Settling the Frontier," <u>Profiles</u> Dec. 1985: 57.

MLA Stone, Brian, trans. <u>Sir Gawain and the Green Knight</u>. 2nd ed. Harmondsworth, Eng.: Penguin, 1974.

APA Stone, B. (Trans.). (1974). <u>Sir Gawain and the green knight</u> (2nd ed.). Harmondsworth, England: Penguin.

CLASSICAL TRANSLATION

CHI Homer. <u>Odyssey</u>. Translated by Robert Fitzgerald. 1961. Reprint. New York: Anchor Books, 1963.

MLA Homer. <u>Odyssey</u>. Trans. Robert Fitzgerald. 1961. New York: Anchor, 1963.

APA Homer. (1963). <u>Odyssey</u> (R. Fitzgerald, Trans.). (Reprint). New York: Anchor Books.

BIBLICAL CITATIONS; CHAPTER, VERSE

CHI The Bible. Revised Standard Version. New York: Thomas Nelson and Sons, 1952.

MLA The Bible. Revised Standard Version. New York: Nelson, 1952.

APA The Bible. (1952). (Revised Standard Version). New York: Nelson.

MAGAZINES

WEEKLY, BASIC FORM

CHI Holt, Patricia. "Books Down Under." <u>Publishers Weekly</u>, 3 July 1981, 55-109.

MLA Holt, Patricia. "Books Down Under." <u>Publishers Weekly</u> 3 July 1981: 55-109.

APA Holt, P. (1981, July 3). Books down under. <u>Publishers Weekly</u>, pp. 55-109.

MONTHLY, BASIC FORM

CHI DeBracy, Christopher M. "RCPMs: Settling the Frontier." <u>Profiles</u>, December 1985, 55-59.

MLA DeBracy, Christopher M. "RCPMs: Settling the Frontier." <u>Profiles</u> Dec. 1985: 55-59.

APA   (DeBracy, 1985, p. 57)

UNSIGNED ARTICLE

CHI   133. "Reagan's Tax Revolution: What It Means For Investors," <u>Changing Times</u>, August 1985, 44.

MLA   134. "Reagan's Tax Revolution: What It Means For Investors," <u>Changing Times</u> Aug. 1985: 44.

APA   ("Reagan's Tax Revolution," 1985, p. 44)

WEEKLY OR MONTHLY COLUMN ITEM, NO AUTHOR

CHI   135. News Scan, "QMS Offers Low-cost Laser," <u>Computer Decisions</u>, 17 December 1985, 17.

MLA   136. News Scan, "QMS Offers Low-cost Laser," <u>Computer Decisions</u> 17 Dec. 1985: 17.

APA   ("QMS offers," 1985, p. 17)

EDITORIALS, INTERVIEWS, OR LETTERS TO THE EDITOR

CHI   137. David Gregory, letter, <u>American History Illustrated</u>, February 1986, 5.

MLA   138. David Gregory, letter, <u>American History Illustrated</u> Feb. 1986: 5.

APA   (Gregory, 1986, p. 5)

ARTICLE PUBLISHED IN TWO OR MORE PARTS, IN TWO OR MORE ISSUES

CHI   139. Stuart Cohen, "Photography for Writers," <u>Writer's Digest</u>, November 1985, 36.

MLA   140. Stuart Cohen, "Photography for Writers," <u>Writer's Digest</u> Nov. 1985: 36.

APA   (Cohen, 1985a, p. 36)

APA   DeBracy, C. M. (1985, December). RCPMs: Settling the
       frontier. Profiles, pp. 55-59.

UNSIGNED ARTICLE

CHI   "Reagan's Tax Revolution: What It Means For Investors."
       Changing Times, August 1985, 40-44.

MLA   "Reagan's Tax Revolution: What It Means For Investors."
       Changing Times Aug. 1985: 40-44.

APA   Reagan's tax revolution: What it means for investors.
       (1985, August). Changing Times, pp. 40-44.

WEEKLY OR MONTHLY COLUMN ITEM,
NO AUTHOR

CHI   News Scan. "QMS offers low-cost laser." Computer
       Decisions, 17 December 1985, 17.

MLA   News Scan.   "QMS offers low-cost laser." Computer
       Decisions 17 Dec. 1985: 17.

APA   QMS offers low-cost laser. (1985, December 17).
       [Column]. Computer Decisions, p. 17.

EDITORIALS, INTERVIEWS,
OR LETTERS TO THE EDITOR

CHI   Gregory, David. Letter. American History Illustrated,
       February 1986, 5.

MLA   Gregory, David. Letter. American History Illustrated
       Feb. 1986: 5.

APA   Gregory, D. (1986, February). [Letter]. American
       History Illustrated, p. 5.

ARTICLE PUBLISHED IN TWO OR MORE PARTS,
IN TWO OR MORE ISSUES

CHI   Cohen, Stuart. "Photography for Writers." Parts 1, 2.
       Writer's Digest, November, December 1985, 36-38,
       26-29.

MLA   Cohen, Stuart. "Photography for Writers." Writer's
       Digest Nov. 1985: 36-38; Dec. 1985: 26-29.

APA   Cohen, S. (1985a, November). Photography for writers.
       [Part 1]. Writer's Digest, pp. 36-38.

APA   Cohen, S. (1985b, December). Photography for writers.
       [Part 2] Writer's Digest, pp. 26-29.

MICROFORM, COMPUTER
AND DATABASE MATERIAL

COMPUTER SOFTWARE

CHI   141. Perfect Writer, computer software, Perfect
        Software, 1983.

MLA   142. Perfect Writer, computer software, Perfect
        Software, 1983.

APA   (Perfect Writer, 1983)

> *[Ideally, a commercially produced computer program entry will list
> the writer, if known, the title, the description "Computer software"
> (not enclosed in quotation marks or underlined), and the year of
> publication. Additional information, such as the computer the soft-
> ware is designed for, the amount of memory required and the
> operating system may be added to the end of the entry if pertinent.]*

MATERIAL FROM DIALOG DATABASE

CHI   143. William R. Hambrecht, "Venture Capital and the
        Growth of Silicon Valley," California Management Review,
        Winter 1984, 75 (DIALOG file 15, item 84011837).

MLA   144. William R. Hambrecht, "Venture Capital and the
        Growth of Silicon Valley," California Management Review
        Winter 1984: 75 (DIALOG file 15, item 84011837).

APA   (Hambrecht, 1984, p. 75)

MATERIAL FROM ERIC
INFORMATION SERVICE DATABASE

CHI   145. Elaine El-Khawas, Campus Trends, 1984, Higher
        Education Panel Report no. 65 (Washington, D.C.: American
        Council on Education, Higher Education Panel, 1985), 2 (ERIC
        ED 252171).

MLA   146. Elaine El-Khawas, Campus Trends, 1984, Higher
        Education Panel Rept. 65 (Washington: American Council on
        Education, Higher Education Panel, 1985) 2 (ERIC ED 252171)

MICROFORM, COMPUTER,
AND DATABASE MATERIAL

COMPUTER SOFTWARE

CHI   Perfect Writer. Computer software. Perfect Software,
        1983.

MLA   Perfect Writer. Computer software. Perfect Software,
        1983.

APA   Perfect writer. (1983). [Computer software].
        Berkeley: Perfect Software.

*[Ideally, a commercially produced computer program entry will list
the writer, if known, the title, the description "Computer software"
(not enclosed in quotation marks or underlined), and the year of
publication. Additional information, such as the computer the software is designed for, the amount of memory required, and the
operating system may be added to the end of the entry if pertinent.]*

MATERIAL FROM DIALOG DATABASE

CHI   Hambrecht, William R. "Venture Capital and the Growth of
        Silicon Valley." California Management Review,
        Winter 1984, 74-82. DIALOG file 15, item 84011837.

MLA   Hambrecht, William R. "Venture Capital and the Growth of
        Silicon Valley." California Management Review
        Winter 1984: 74-82. DIALOG file 15, item 84011837.

APA   Hambrecht, W. R. (1984, Winter). Venture capital and the
        growth of Silicon Valley. California Management
        Review, pp. 74-82. (DIALOG file 15, item 84011837).

MATERIAL FROM ERIC
INFORMATION SERVICE DATABASE

CHI   El-Khawas, Elaine. Campus Trends, 1984. Higher
        Education Panel Report no. 65. Washington, D.C.:
        American Council on Education, Higher Education
        Panel, 1985. ERIC ED 252171.

MLA   El-Khawas, Elaine. Campus Trends, 1984. Higher
        Education Panel Rept. 65. Washington: American
        Council on Education, Higher Education Panel, 1985.
        ERIC ED 252171.

APA   (El-Khawas, 1985, p. 2)

MULTIVOLUME WORKS
(SEE BOOKS: MULTIVOLUME WORKS)

NEWSPAPERS

ARTICLE FROM A DAILY NEWSPAPER, CITY OR STATE INTERPOLATED

CHI   147. Elizabeth Coonrod, "Protestors Delay Flight To
        Portland," Oregonian (Oregon), 17 Dec. 1985,
        sec. B, p. 10.

MLA   148. Elizabeth Coonrod, "Protestors Delay Flight To
        Portland," Oregonian [Oregon] 17 Dec. 1985,
        sec. B: 10.

*[If the city of publication is not included in the name of the
newspaper, add it in square brackets for MLA style, or in parentheses for Chicago style.]*

APA   ("Coonrod," 1985, p. 10)

APA   El-Khawas, E. (1985). <u>Campus trends, 1984</u> (Higher
          Education Panel Report No. 65). Washington, D.C.:
          American Council on Education, Higher Education
          Panel. (ERIC Document Reproduction Service No. ED
          252171).

MULTIVOLUME WORKS
(SEE BOOKS: MULTIVOLUME WORKS)

NEWSPAPERS

ARTICLE FROM A DAILY NEWSPAPER,
CITY OR STATE INTERPOLATED

*[For Chicago style, articles from daily newspapers are generally cited
in-text or in notes to the text, and are seldom listed individually in
the bibliography. Instead, the name of the paper and the inclusive
dates used are included in the bibliography, as in the first example
below. However, if the number of newspaper articles used as
references is small, the articles may be listed separately in the
bibliography. Page numbers are usually omitted when citing
newspapers, but when included, the abbreviation "p." or "pp." is
used with Chicago style.]*

CHI   <u>New York Times</u>. March 1936-January 1945.

CHI   Coonrod, Elizabeth. "Protestors Delay Flight To
          Portland." <u>Oregonian</u> (Oregon), 17 Dec. 1985,
          sec. B, p. 10

MLA   Coonrod, Elizabeth. "Protestors Delay Flight To
          Portland." <u>Oregonian</u> [Oregon] 17 Dec. 1985,
          sec. B: 10

APA   Coonrod, E. (1985, December 17). Protestors delay flight
          to Portland. <u>Oregonian</u> (Oregon), sec. B, p. 10.

AUTHOR, TITLE, EDITION, NO CITY

CHI   149. Steve Weiner, "Book Chains Look for Big Author, Great Cover and, Sometimes, Merit," <u>Wall Street Journal</u>, 27 June 1985, Western ed., sec. 2, p. 33.

MLA   150. Steve Weiner, "Book Chains Look for Big Author, Great Cover and, Sometimes, Merit," <u>Wall Street Journal</u> 27 June 1985, western ed., sec. 2: 33.

[For large newspapers that print several editions a day, include the edition in the citation (Chicago and MLA).]

APA   (Weiner, 1985, p. 33)

EDITORIAL

CHI   151. "Counterproductive Policing," editorial, <u>Oregonian</u>, 15 Dec. 1985, sec. C, p. 2.

MLA   152. "Counterproductive Policing," editorial, <u>Oregonian</u> 15 Dec. 1985, sec. C: 2.

APA   ("Counterproductive Policing," 1985, p. 2)

LETTER

CHI   153. Stephen Lawrence, letter, <u>Oregonian</u>, 15 Dec. 1985, sec C, p. 2.

MLA   154. Stephen Lawrence, letter, <u>Oregonian</u> 15 Dec. 1985, sec. C: 2.

APA   (Lawrence, 1985, p. 2)

NONPRINT SOURCES

FILM

CHI   155. William Wyler (director), <u>The Best Years of Our Lives</u>, with Frederic March, Goldwyn, RKO, 1946.

MLA   156. William Wyler, dir., <u>The Best Years of Our Lives</u>, with Frederic March, Goldwyn, RKO, 1946.

APA   (Wyler, 1946)

AUTHOR, TITLE, EDITION, NO CITY

CHI   Weiner, Steve. "Book Chains Look for Big Author, Great
       Cover and, Sometimes, Merit." <u>Wall Street Journal</u>,
       27 June 1985, Western edition, sec. 2, p. 33.

MLA   Weiner, Steve. "Book Chains Look for Big Author, Great
       Cover and, Sometimes, Merit." <u>Wall Street Journal</u>
       27 June 1985, western ed., sec. 2: 33.

APA   Weiner, S. (1985, June 27). Book chains look for big
       author, great cover and, sometimes, merit. <u>Wall
       Street Journal</u>, western ed., sec. 2, p. 33.

EDITORIAL

CHI   "Counterproductive Policing." Editorial. <u>Oregonian</u>, 15
       Dec. 1985, sec. C, p. 2.

MLA   "Counterproductive Policing." Editorial. <u>Oregonian</u>
       15 Dec. 1985, sec. C: 2.

APA   Counterproductive policing. (1985, December 15).
       [Editorial]. <u>Oregonian</u>, sec. C, p. 2.

LETTER

CHI   Lawrence, Stephen. Letter. <u>Oregonian</u>, 15 Dec. 1985,
       sec. C, p. 2.

MLA   Lawrence, Stephen. Letter. <u>Oregonian</u> 15 Dec. 1985,
       sec. C: 2.

APA   Lawrence, S. (1985, December 15). [Letter].
       Oregonian, sec. C, p. 2.

NONPRINT SOURCES

FILM

CHI   Wyler, William (director). <u>The Best Years of Our
       Lives</u>. With Frederic March. Goldwyn, RKO, 1946.

MLA   Wyler, William, dir. <u>The Best Years of Our Lives</u>.
       With Frederic March. Goldwyn, RKO, 1946.

APA   Wyler, W. (Director). (1946). <u>The best years of our
       lives</u> [Film]. Los Angeles: Goldwyn, RKO.

PERFORMANCE, MUSICAL THEATER

CHI   157. Martin Charnin (director), <u>Annie</u>, Alvin Theatre, New York, 21 April 1977.

MLA   158. Martin Charnin, dir., <u>Annie</u>, Alvin Theatre, New York, 21 Apr. 1977.

APA   (Charnin, 1977) *[or]* (<u>Annie</u>, 1977)

PERFORMANCE, ORCHESTRA

CHI   159. James DePriest (conductor), Oregon Symphony, concert, Arlene Schnitzer Concert Hall, Portland, 5 January 1986.

MLA   160. James DePriest, cond., Oregon Symphony, concert, Arlene Schnitzer Concert Hall, Portland, 5 Jan. 1986.

APA   (DePriest, 1986)

PERFORMANCE, DRAMA, EMPHASIS ON AUTHOR

CHI   161. Noel Coward, <u>Blithe Spirit</u>, dir. Pat Patton, with Richard Elmore, Angus Bowmer Theatre, Ashland, Ore., 25 March 1982.

MLA   162. Noel Coward, <u>Blithe Spirit</u>, dir. Pat Patton, with Richard Elmore, Angus Bowmer Theatre, Ashland, OR, 25 Mar. 1982.

APA   (Coward, 1982) *[or]* (<u>Blithe Spirit</u>, 1982)

MUSICAL COMPOSITIONS AND SONGS

CHI   163. Johann Sebastian Bach, Concerto in G Minor for Flute and Strings, BWV. 1056.

[The titles of long compositions are underlined. Titles of short compositions and songs are enclosed in quotation marks. Compositions identified by the name of a musical form have the first letter of main words in the title capitalized (as in the above example), but are neither underlined nor enclosed in quotation marks (Chicago and MLA).]

PERFORMANCE, MUSICAL THEATER

CHI   Charnin, Martin (director). Annie. Alvin Theatre, New
         York. 21 April 1977.

MLA   Charnin, Martin, dir. Annie. Alvin Theatre, New
         York.   21 Apr. 1977.

APA   Charnin, M. (Director). (1977, April 21). Annie
         [Musical performance]. Alvin Theatre, New York.

PERFORMANCE, ORCHESTRA

CHI   DePriest, James (conductor). Oregon Symphony. Concert.
         Arlene Schnitzer Concert Hall, Portland. 5 January
         1986.

MLA   DePriest, James, cond. Oregon Symphony. Concert.
         Arlene Schnitzer Concert Hall, Portland.   5 Jan.
         1986.

APA   DePriest, J. (Conductor). (1986, January 5). Oregon
         Symphony [Concert]. Arlene Schnitzer Concert Hall,
         Portland.

PERFORMANCE, DRAMA, EMPHASIS ON AUTHOR

CHI   Coward, Noel. Blithe Spirit. Directed by Pat Patton.
         With Richard Elmore. Angus Bowmer Theatre, Ashland,
         Ore. 25 March 1982.

MLA   Coward, Noel. Blithe Spirit. Dir. Pat Patton. With
         Richard Elmore. Angus Bowmer Theatre, Ashland, OR.
         25 Mar. 1982.

APA   Coward, N. (Author). (1982, March 25). Blithe spirit
         [Dramatic performance]. (P. Patton, Dir.). Angus
         Bowmer Theatre, Ashland, OR.

MUSICAL COMPOSITIONS AND SONGS

CHI   Bach, Johann Sebastian. Concerto in G Minor for Flute
         and Strings, BWV. 1056.

[The titles of long compositions are underlined. Titles of short compositions and songs are enclosed in quotation marks. Compositions identified by the name of a musical form have the first letter of main words in the title capitalized (as in the above example), but are neither underlined nor enclosed in quotation marks (Chicago and MLA).]

MLA   164. Johann Sebastian Bach, Concerto in G minor for
        Flute and Strings, BWV. 1056.

APA   (Bach, BWV. 1056) *[or]* (Bach, Concerto in G Minor for
        Flute and Strings) *[or]* (Bach, n.d.)

*[The initials at the end of the citation indicate the abbreviation of the
individual composer's catalog of works (All styles).]*

MUSICAL COMPOSITION WITH DESCRIPTIVE TITLE

CHI   165. Wolfgang Amadeus Mozart, Symphony no. 41 in C
        Major, K. 551 (Jupiter).

MLA   166. Wolfgang Amadeus Mozart, Symphony No. 41 in C
        major, K. 551 (Jupiter).

APA   (Mozart, K. 551) *[or]* (Mozart, Symphony No. 41 in C Major)
        [or] (Mozart, Jupiter) *[or]* (Mozart, n.d.)

RECORDING, EMPHASIS ON COMPOSER

CHI   167. Ferde Grofé, Grand Canyon Suite, cond. Eugene
        Ormandy, Philadelphia Orchestra, Columbia ML 5286.

MLA   168. Ferde Grofé, Grand Canyon Suite, cond. Eugene
        Ormandy, Philadelphia Orchestra, Columbia, ML 5286, n.d.

APA   (Grofé, Grand Canyon Suite) or (Grofé, ML 5286) *[or]*
        (Grofé, n.d.)

RECORDING, EMPHASIS ON CONDUCTOR

CHI   169. Zubin Mehta (conductor), The Rite of Spring, New
        York Philharmonic, Columbia M 34557.

MLA   170. Zubin Mehta, cond., The Rite of Spring, New York
        Philharmonic, Columbia, M 34557, 1978.

APA   (Mehta, The Rite of Spring) *[or]* (Mehta, M 34557) *[or]*
        (Mehta, 1978)

RECORDING, EMPHASIS ON PERFORMER

CHI   171. Cyndi Lauper, "Money Changes Everything," She's So
        Unusual, Portrait FR 38930.

MLA   172. Cyndi Lauper, "Money Changes Everything," She's So
        Unusual, Portrait, FR 38930, 1983.

MLA   Bach, Johann Sebastian.   Concerto in G minor for Flute and Strings, BWV. 1056.

APA   Bach, J. S. (Composer). (N.d.). Concerto in G minor for flute and strings [Musical composition]. BWV. 1056.

[The initials at the end of the citation indicate the abbreviation of the individual composer's catalog of works (all styles).]

MUSICAL COMPOSITION WITH DESCRIPTIVE TITLE

CHI   Mozart, Wolfgang Amadeus. Symphony no. 41 in C Major, K. 551 (Jupiter).

MLA   Mozart, Wolfgang Amadeus.   Symphony no. 41 in C major, K. 551 (Jupiter).

APA   Mozart, W. A. (Composer). (N.d.). Symphony no. 41 in C major [Musical composition]. K. 551 (Jupiter).

RECORDING, EMPHASIS ON COMPOSER

CHI   Grofé, Ferde. Grand Canyon Suite. Conducted by Eugene Ormandy. Philadelphia Orchestra. Columbia ML 5286.

MLA   Grofé, Ferde.   Grand Canyon Suite.   Cond. Eugene Ormandy.   Philadelphia Orchestra.   Columbia, ML 5286, n.d.

APA   Grofé, F. (Composer). (N.d.). Grand canyon suite (Stereo record ML 5286). (E. Ormandy, Cond.). Philadelphia Orchestra. New York: Columbia.

RECORDING, EMPHASIS ON CONDUCTOR

CHI   Mehta, Zubin (conductor). The Rite of Spring. New York Philharmonic. Columbia M 34557.

MLA   Mehta, Zubin, cond.   The Rite of Spring.   New York Philharmonic.   Columbia, M 34557, 1978.

APA   Mehta, Z. (Conductor). (1978). The rite of spring (Stereo record M 34557). New York Philharmonic. New York: Columbia.

RECORDING, EMPHASIS ON PERFORMER

CHI   Lauper, Cyndi. "Money Changes Everything." She's So Unusual. Portrait FR 38930.

MLA   Lauper, Cyndi.   "Money Changes Everything."   She's So Unusual.   Portrait, FR 38930, 1983.

APA   (Lauper, 1983)

RECORDING, SPOKEN

CHI   173. W. C. Fields, "The Philosophy of W. C. Fields,"
        W. C. Fields: The Original Voice Tracks From His
        Greatest Movies, Decca Records DL 79164.

MLA   174. W. C. Fields, "The Philosophy of W. C. Fields,"
        W. C. Fields: The Original Voice Tracks From His
        Greatest Movies, Decca Records, DL 79164, n.d.

APA   (Fields, "The Philosophy") *[or]* (Fields, n.d.)

CASSETTE RECORDING

CHI   175. Cat Stevens, Teaser and the Firecat, A and M
        CS-4313, cassette.

MLA   176. Cat Stevens, Teaser and the Firecat, cassette,
        A and M, CS-4313, n.d.

APA   (Stevens, n.d.)

JACKET NOTES ON RECORDS

CHI   177. Russ Wilson, jacket notes to The Kingston Trio
        From the "Hungry i," Capital M-11968.

MLA   178. Russ Wilson, jacket notes, the Kingston Trio From
        the "Hungry i," Capital, M-11968, n.d.

APA   (Wilson, n.d.)

WORK OF ART

CHI   179. Vincent van Gogh, A Cornfield, with Cypresses,
        National Gallery, London.

MLA   180. Vincent van Gogh, A Cornfield, with Cypresses,
        National Gallery, London.

APA   Lauper, C. (Singer *[or Performer]*). (1983) Money changes
        everything. She's so unusual (Stereo record FR
        38930). New York: Portrait.

RECORDING, SPOKEN

CHI   Fields, W. C. "The Philosophy of W. C. Fields." W. C.
        Fields: The Original Voice Tracks From His Greatest
        Movies. Decca Records DL 79164.

MLA   Fields, W. C.   "The Philosophy of W. C. Fields."   W. C.
        Fields: The Original Voice Tracks From His Greatest
        Movies.   Decca Records, DL 79164, n.d.

APA   Fields, W. C. (Speaker). (N.d.). The philosophy of W. C.
        Fields. W. C. Fields: The original voice tracks
        from his greatest movies (Stereo record DL 79164).
        New York: Decca Records.

CASSETTE RECORDING

CHI   Stevens, Cat. Teaser and the Firecat. A and M CS-4313.
        Cassette.

MLA   Stevens, Cat.   Teaser and the Firecat.   Cassette.   A
        and M, CS-4313, n.d.

APA   Stevens, C. (Singer *[or Performer]*). (N.d.) Teaser and
        the firecat (Cassette recording CS-4313). Beverly
        Hills: A and M.

JACKET NOTES ON RECORDS

CHI   Wilson, Russ. Jacket notes to The Kingston Trio From
        the "Hungry i." Capital M-11968.

MLA   Wilson, Russ.   Jacket notes.   The Kingston Trio From
        the "Hungry i."   Capital, M-11968, n.d.

APA   Wilson, R. (N.d.). [Jacket notes]. The Kingston Trio
        from the "Hungry i." (Stereo record M-11968).
        Hollywood: Capital.

WORK OF ART

CHI   Gogh, van Vincent. A Cornfield, with Cypresses.
        National Gallery, London.

MLA   Gogh, van Vincent.   A Cornfield, with Cypresses.
        National Gallery, London.

APA   (Gogh, <u>A Cornfield</u>) *[or]* (Gogh, n.d.)

WORK OF ART, REPRODUCED IN A BOOK

CHI   181. Pierre-Auguste Renoir, <u>Les Parapluies</u>, National
         Gallery, London, in <u>The National Gallery</u>, by Michael
         Levey (London: Pitkin Pictorials, 1972), 27.

MLA   182. Pierre-Auguste Renoir, <u>Les Parapluies</u>, National
         Gallery, London, page 27 of <u>The National Gallery</u>, by
         Michael Levey (London: Pitkin Pictorials, 1972).

APA   (Renoir, 1972, p. 27)

TELEVISION PROGRAM

CHI   183. "Wild America," dir. and prod. Marty Stouffer, PBS,
         KOAP, Portland, 7 January 1986.

MLA   184. <u>Wild America</u>, dir. and prod. Marty Stouffer, PBS,
         KOAP, Portland, 7 Jan. 1986.

APA   (Stouffer, 1986)

TELEVISION PROGRAM, EPISODE IN A SERIES

CHI   185. "Keep Smiling," writ. and dir. Michael Landon,
         "Highway to Heaven," NBC, KGW, Portland, 5 February
         1986.

MLA   186. "Keep Smiling," writ. and dir. Michael Landon,
         <u>Highway to Heaven</u>, NBC, KGW, Portland, 5 Feb. 1986.

APA   Gogh, van V. (Artist). (N.d.). <u>A cornfield, with cypresses</u> [Work of art, painting]. National Gallery, London.

WORK OF ART, REPRODUCED IN A BOOK

CHI   Renoir, Pierre-Auguste. <u>Les Parapluies</u>. National Gallery, London. In <u>The National Gallery</u>, by Michael Levey. London: Pitkin Pictorials, 1972.

MLA   Renoir, Pierre-Auguste. <u>Les Parapluies</u>. National Gallery, London. Page 27 of <u>The National Gallery</u>. By Michael Levey. London: Pitkin, 1972.

APA   Renoir, P. A. (Artist). (1972) <u>Les parapluies</u> [Work of art, painting]. National Gallery, London. In M. Levey, <u>The National Gallery</u> (p. 71). London: Pitkin Pictorials.

TELEVISION PROGRAM

CHI   "Wild America." Directed and produced by Marty Stouffer. PBS. KOAP, Portland. 7 January 1986.

[Chicago style requires that titles of television and radio programs be enclosed in quotation marks.]

MLA   <u>Wild America</u>. Dir. and prod. Marty Stouffer. PBS. KOAP, Portland. 7 Jan. 1986.

[MLA style requires that titles of television and radio programs be underlined, but the title of a television episode is enclosed in quotation marks and the title of the program is underlined when included in the same entry.]

APA   Stouffer, M. (Director and producer). (1986, January 7). <u>Wild America</u> [Television program]. PBS. KOAP, Portland.

TELEVISION PROGRAM, EPISODE IN A SERIES

CHI   "Keep Smiling." Written and directed by Michael Landon. "Highway to Heaven." NBC. KGW, Portland, Ore. 5 February 1986.

MLA   "Keep Smiling." Writ. and dir. Michael Landon. <u>Highway To Heaven</u>. NBC. KGW, Portland, OR. 5 Feb. 1986.

APA   (Landon, 1986)

RADIO PROGRAM

CHI   187. "Bread and Roses," KBOO, Portland, 25 February 1986.

MLA   188. Bread and Roses, KBOO, Portland, 25 Feb. 1986.

APA   (Bread and Roses, 1986)

PAPER READ AT A MEETING

CHI   189. Bruce J. Taylor, "Some Remarks on the Uses and Abuses of Press Releases" (Paper presented at the Northwest Association of Book Publishers meeting, Portland, Ore., 26 February 1985).

MLA   190. Bruce J. Taylor, "Some Remarks on the Uses and Abuses of Press Releases," Northwest Association of Book Publishers, Portland, OR, 26 Feb. 1985.

APA   (Taylor, 1985)

INTERVIEW, TELEPHONE

CHI   191. Mikhail Sergeyvich Gorbachev, telephone interview with author, 1 January 1996.

MLA   192. Mikhail Sergeyvich Gorbachev, telephone interview, 1 Jan. 1996.

APA   (M. S. Gorbachev, telephone interview, January 1, 1996)

INTERVIEW, PERSONAL

CHI   193. Galileo Galilei, interview with author, Pisa, Italy, 20 July 1630.

MLA   194. Galileo Galilei, personal interview, 20 July 1630.

APA   Landon, M. (Writer and director). (1986, February 5).
      Keep smiling. <u>Highway to Heaven</u> [Television
      program]. NBC. KGW, Portland, OR.

RADIO PROGRAM

CHI   "Bread and Roses." KBOO, Portland. 25 February 1986.

MLA   Bread and Roses. KBOO, Portland. 25 Feb. 1986.

APA   Bread and Roses [Radio program]. (1986, February
      25). KBOO, Portland.

PAPER READ AT A MEETING

CHI   Taylor, Bruce J. "Some Remarks on the Uses and Abuses of
      Press Releases." Paper presented at the Northwest
      Association of Book Publishers meeting, Portland,
      Ore., 26 February 1985.

MLA   Taylor, Bruce J. "Some Remarks on the Uses and Abuses
      of Press Releases." Northwest Association of Book
      Publishers. Portland, OR, 26 Feb. 1985.

APA   Taylor, B. J. (1985, February 26). <u>Some remarks on the
      uses and abuses of press releases.</u> Paper presented
      at the Northwest Association of Book Publishers
      meeting, Portland, OR.

INTERVIEW, TELEPHONE

CHI   Gorbachev, Mikhail Sergeyvich. Telephone interview with
      author. 1 January 1996.

MLA   Gorbachev, Mikhail Sergeyvich. Telephone Interview.
      1 Jan. 1996.

APA   *[Because of the nature of the information, APA cites
      personal communications in the text only, and does
      not provide a separate bibiliography listing.]*

INTERVIEW, PERSONAL

CHI   Galilei, Galileo. Interview with author. Pisa, Italy,
      20 July 1630.

MLA   Galilei, Galileo. Personal interview. 20 July 1630.

APA   (G. Galilei, personal interview *[or personal communication]* , July 20, 1630)

PAMPHLETS

CHI   195. <u>Fort Vancouver</u> (Washington, D.C.: 1982), 1.

MLA   196. <u>Fort Vancouver</u> (Washington: GPO, 1982) 1.

APA   (Fort Vancouver, 1982, p. 1)

REFERENCE WORKS

ENCYCLOPEDIA ENTRY, UNSIGNED

CHI   197. <u>Academic American Encyclopedia</u>, s.v. "Seven Weeks' War."

[For Chicago style, publication facts for well-known books are not required, but the edition must be specified if not the first. For alphabetically arranged information, such as in a dictionary or an encyclopedia, enter "s.v." (sub verbo, "under the word") in front of the item; the volume and page number are not required.]

MLA   198. "Seven Weeks' War," <u>Academic American Encyclopedia</u>, 1981 ed.   *[or 1st ed.]*

[For MLA style, full publication information is not required for well-known books; give the edition, if other than the first, and the year published.]

APA   ("Seven Weeks' War," 1981)

ENCYCLOPEDIA ENTRY, SIGNED

CHI   199. <u>Collier's Encyclopedia</u>, 1966 ed., s.v. "Dogger Bank Arbitration," by Michael Kraus.

MLA   200. Michael Kraus, "Dogger Bank Arbitration," <u>Collier's Encyclopedia</u>, 1966 ed.

APA   (Kraus, 1966)

APA   *[Because of the nature of the information, APA cites
personal communications in the text only, and does
not provide a separate bibiliography listing.]*

PAMPHLETS

CHI   <u>Fort Vancouver</u>. Washington, D.C.: GPO, 1982.

MLA   <u>Fort Vancouver</u>. Washington: GPO, 1982

APA   <u>Fort Vancouver</u>. (1982). Washington, D.C.,: GPO.

REFERENCE WORKS

ENCYCLOPEDIA ENTRY, UNSIGNED

CHI   <u>Academic American Encyclopedia</u>. S.v. "Seven Weeks'
War."

*[For Chicago style, publication facts for well-known books are not
required, but the edition must be specified, if not the first. For
alphabetically arranged information in a dictionary or an encyclopedia, enter "s.v." (sub verbo, "under the word") in front of
the item; the volume and page number are not required.]*

MLA   "Seven Weeks' War."   <u>Academic American Encyclopedia</u>.

*[For MLA style, full publication information is not required for
well-known books; give the edition, if other than the first, and the
year published.]*

APA   Seven weeks' war. (1981). <u>Academic American
encyclopedia</u>.

ENCYCLOPEDIA ENTRY, SIGNED

CHI   <u>Collier's Encyclopedia</u>, 1966 ed. S.v. "Dogger Bank
Arbitration," by Michael Kraus.

MLA   Kraus, Michael. "Dogger Bank Arbitration."   <u>Collier's
Encyclopedia</u>. 1966 ed.

APA   Kraus, M. (1966). Dogger bank arbitration. <u>Collier's
encyclopedia</u>.

ENCYCLOPEDIA ENTRY, INITIALED, NAME SUPPLIED

CHI   201. Encyclopaedia Britannica, 1971 ed., s.v. "English
       History," by H[erbert] G[eorge] N[icholas].

MLA   202. Herbert George Nicholas, "English History,"
       Encyclopaedia Britannica, 1971 ed.

APA   (Nicholas, 1971)

DICTIONARY ENTRY

CHI   203. Webster's New Collegiate Dictionary, 1974 ed.,
       s.v. "gyroplane."

MLA   204. "Gyroplane," Webster's New Collegiate Dictionary,
       1973 ed.

APA   ("Gyroplane," 1974)

DICTIONARY, NOT WIDELY KNOWN

CHI   205. Mitford M. Mathews, ed., s.v. "Moonshine Bank,"
       A Dictionary of Americanisms on Historical Principles
       (Chicago: University of Chicago Press, 1951), 1078.

MLA   206. Mitford M. Mathews, ed., "Moonshine Bank,"
       A Dictionary of Americanisms on Historical Principles
       (Chicago: U of Chicago P, 1951) 1078.

APA   (Mathews, 1951, p. 1078)

REFERENCE WORK, NOT WIDELY KNOWN, SIGNED ARTICLE

CHI   207. Hans E. Gruen, s.v. "Hypha," Encyclopedia of the
       Biological Sciences, ed. Peter Gray (New York: Reinhold
       Publishing, 1961), 500-501.

MLA   208. Hans E. Gruen, "Hypha," Encyclopedia of the
       Biological Sciences, ed. Peter Gray (New York:
       Reinhold, 1961) 500-01.

APA   (Gruen, 1961, pp. 500-501)

ENCYCLOPEDIA ENTRY, INITIALED, NAME SUPPLIED

CHI   Encyclopaedia Britannica, 1971 ed. S.v. "English
      History," by H[erbert] G[eorge] N[icholas].

MLA   Nicholas, Herbert George. "English History."
      Encyclopaedia Britannica. 1971 ed.

APA   Nicholas, H. G. (1971). English history. Encyclopedia
      Britannica.

DICTIONARY ENTRY

CHI   Webster's New Collegiate Dictionary, 1974 ed. S.v.
      "gyroplane."

MLA   "Gyroplane." Webster's New Collegiate Dictionary.
      1974 ed.

APA   Gyroplane. (1974). Webster's new collegiate
      dictionary.

DICTIONARY, NOT WIDELY KNOWN

CHI   Mathews, Mitford M., ed. S.v. "Moonshine Bank." A Dictionary
      of Americanisms on Historical Principles. Chicago:
      University of Chicago Press, 1951.

MLA   Mathews, Mitford M., ed. "Moonshine Bank." A
      Dictionary of Americanisms on Historical
      Principles. Chicago: U of Chicago P, 1951.

APA   Mathews, M. M. (Ed.). (1951). Moonshine bank. In A
      dictionary of americanisms on historical principles
      (p. 1078). Chicago: University of Chicago Press.

REFERENCE WORK NOT WIDELY KNOWN, SIGNED ARTICLE

CHI   Gruen, Hans. S.v. "Hypha." Encyclopedia of the Biological
      Sciences, edited by Peter Gray. New York: Reinhold
      Publishing, 1961.

MLA   Gruen, Hans. "Hypha." Encyclopedia of the Biological
      Sciences. Ed. Peter Gray. New York: Reinhold,
      1961.

APA   Gruen, H. (1961). Hypha. In P. Gray (Ed.), Encyclopedia
      of the biological sciences (pp. 500-501). New York:
      Reinhold.

ATLAS ENTRY

CHI   209. National Geographic Atlas of the World, 1963 ed., "Historic and Scenic America."

MLA   210. "Historic and Scenic America," National Geographic Atlas of the World, 1963 ed.

APA   ("Historic and Scenic," 1963)

MAPS OR CHARTS

CHI   211. Washington, map (Falls Church, Va.: American Automobile Association, 1982).

MLA   212. Washington, map (Falls Church, VA: American Automobile Association, 1982).

APA   (Washington, 1982)

REVIEWS

UNSIGNED, UNTITLED

CHI   213. Review of Dante and His Italy, by Lonsdale Ragg, Dublin Review 142 (January 1908): 191.

MLA   214. Rev. of Dante and His Italy, by Lonsdale Ragg, Dublin Review 142 (1908): 191.

APA   ([Review of Dante and His Italy], 1908, p. 191)

[If the review is untitled, use a description enclosed in brackets as the title (APA).]

SIGNED, WITH TITLE

CHI   215. Noel Annan, "Carlyle, Our Hero?" review of The Seventh Hero: Thomas Carlyle and the Theory of Radical Activism, by Philip Rosenberg, New York Review of Books, 27 June 1974, 6.

MLA   216. Noel Annan, "Carlyle, Our Hero?" rev. of The Seventh Hero: Thomas Carlyle and the Theory of Radical Activism, by Philip Rosenberg, New York Review of Books 27 June 1974: 6.

ATLAS ENTRY

CHI   National Geographic Atlas of the World, 1963 ed.
        "Historic and Scenic America."

MLA   "Historic and Scenic America." National Geographic
        Atlas of the World. 1963 ed.

APA   Historic and scenic America. (1963). National
        geographic atlas of the world.

MAPS OR CHARTS

CHI   Washington. Map. Falls Church, Va.: American
        Automobile Association, 1982.

MLA   Washington. Map. Falls Church, VA: American
        Automobile Association, 1982.

APA   Washington. (1982). [Map]. Falls Church, VA:
        American Automobile Association.

REVIEWS

UNSIGNED, UNTITLED

CHI   Review of Dante and His Italy, by Lonsdale Ragg.
        Dublin Review 142 (January 1908): 191-92.

MLA   Rev. of Dante and His Italy, by Lonsdale Ragg.
        Dublin Review 142 (1908): 191-92.

APA   [Review of Dante and his Italy, by L. Ragg]. (1908).
        Dublin Review, 142, 191-192.

[If the review is untitled, use the description enclosed in brackets as the title (APA).]

SIGNED, WITH TITLE

CHI   Annan, Noel. "Carlyle, Our Hero?" Review of The Seventh
        Hero: Thomas Carlyle and the Theory of Radical
        Activism, by Philip Rosenberg. New York Review of
        Books, 27 June 1974, 6-9.

MLA   Annan, Noel. "Carlyle, Our Hero?" Rev. of The Seventh
        Hero: Thomas Carlyle and the Theory of Radical
        Activism, by Philip Rosenberg. New York Review of
        Books 27 June 1974: 6-9.

APA   (Annan, 1974, p. 6)

SIGNED, UNTITLED

CHI   217. Paul A. Varg, review of The United States and the Far Eastern Crisis of 1933-1938: From the Manchurian Incident through the Initial Stage of the Undeclared Sino-Japanese War, by Dorothy Borg, Journal of American History 51 (March 1965): 751.

MLA   218. Paul A. Varg, rev. of The United States and the Far Eastern Crisis of 1933-1938: From the Manchurian Incident through the Initial Stage of the Undeclared Sino-Japanese War, by Dorothy Borg, Journal of American History 51 (1965): 751.

APA   (Varg, 1965, p. 751)

SERIES WORKS
(SEE BOOKS: SERIES WORKS)

UNPUBLISHED SOURCES

LETTER IN A MANUSCRIPT COLLECTION

CHI   219. Anna Hall to Elliott Roosevelt, 12 March 1882, Halsted Collection, Franklin D. Roosevelt Library, Hyde Park, New York.

MLA   220. Anna Hall, Letter to Elliott Roosevelt, 12 Mar. 1882, Halsted Collection, Franklin D. Roosevelt Library, Hyde Park, NY.

APA   Annan, N. (1974, June 27). Carlyle, our hero? [Review
      of The seventh hero: Thomas Carlyle and the theory
      of radical activism, by P. Rosenberg]. New York
      Review of Books, pp. 6-9.

   [Note that APA uses "pp." for magazines, but not for journals.]

SIGNED, UNTITLED

CHI   Varg, Paul A. Review of The United States and the Far
      Eastern Crisis of 1933-1938: From the Manchurian
      Incident through the Initial Stage of the Undeclared
      Sino-Japanese War, by Dorothy Borg. Journal of
      American History 51 (March 1965): 750-52.

MLA   Varg, Paul A.   Rev. of The United States and the Far
      Eastern Crisis of 1933-1938: From the Manchurian
      Incident through the Initial Stage of the Undeclared
      Sino-Japanese War, by Dorothy Borg.   Journal of
      American History 51 (1965): 750-52.

APA   Varg, P. A. (1965). [Review of The United States and
      the far eastern crisis of 1933-1938: From the
      Manchurian incident through the initial stage of the
      undeclared Sino-Japanese war, by D. Borg].
      Journal of American History, 51, 750-752.

SERIES WORKS
(SEE BOOKS: SERIES WORKS)

UNPUBLISHED SOURCES

LETTER IN A MANUSCRIPT COLLECTION

CHI   Hall, Anna. Letter to Elliott Roosevelt. 12 March 1882.
      Halsted Collection. Franklin D. Roosevelt Library,
      Hyde Park, New York.

MLA   Hall, Anna.   Letter to Elliott Roosevelt.   12 Mar.
      1882.   Halsted Collection.   Franklin D. Roosevelt
      Library, Hyde Park, NY.

APA   (Hall, 1882)

PERSONAL COMMUNICATION, LETTER

CHI   221. Evan Thomas, letter to author, 4 June 1978.

MLA   222. Evan Thomas, letter to the author, 4 June 1978.

APA   (E. Thomas, letter to author, June 4, 1978)

DIARY, NOTEBOOK, OR MANUSCRIPT IN A COLLECTION

CHI   223. William Kahler, diary, 1 January 1852, MS, Beinecke
        Library, Yale University.

MLA   224. William Kahler, Diary, ms., 1 Jan. 1852, Beinecke
        Library, Yale U.

APA   (Kahler, 1852)

DIARY, NOTEBOOK, OR MANUSCRIPT
NOT IN A COLLECTION

CHI   225. Johanna Quade, notebook 1911, handwritten MS, in
        the author's possession, 20.

*[If the entry is handwritten or a typescript (TS), this may be in-
dicated by a descriptive title. Labeling a manuscript as handwritten
or typewritten is optional. Add "handwritten" to MS; or substitute
TS for MS in the entry.]*

MLA   226. Johanna Quade, Notebook 1911, handwritten ms, in
        the author's possession, 20.

APA   (Quade, 1911, p. 20)

APA   Hall, A. (1882, March 12). [Letter to E. Roosevelt].
       Halsted Collection, Franklin D. Roosevelt Library,
       Hyde Park, NY.

*[Note that the brackets contain a description of contents, not a title.
Additional information required to locate and retrieve the work may
also be included in the bracketed description (APA).]*

PERSONAL COMMUNICATION, LETTER

CHI   Thomas, Evan. Letter to author, 4 June 1978.

MLA   Thomas, Evan. Letter to author. 4 June 1978.

APA   *[Because of the nature of the information, APA cites
       personal communications in the text only, and does
       not provide a separate bibliography listing.]*

DIARY, NOTEBOOK, OR MANUSCRIPT IN A COLLECTION

CHI   Kahler, William. Diary. MS. Beinecke Library, Yale
       University.

CHI   Kahler, William. Diary. MS. 1 January 1852. Beinecke
       Library, Yale University.

MLA   Kahler, William. Diary, ms. Jan.-Dec. 1852. Beinecke
       Library, Yale U.

APA   Kahler, W. (1852). [Diary, manuscript]. Beinecke
       Library, Yale University, New Haven.

DIARY, NOTEBOOK, OR MANUSCRIPT
NOT IN A COLLECTION

CHI   Quade, Johanna. Notebook 1911. Handwritten MS. In the
       author's possession.

*[If the entry is handwritten or a typescript (TS), this may be in-
dicated by a descriptive title. Labeling a manuscript as handwritten
or typewritten is optional. Add "handwritten" to MS; or substitute
TS for MS in the entry.]*

MLA   Quade, Johanna. Notebook 1911. Handwritten ms. In the
       author's possession.

APA   Quade, J. (1911). [Notebook 1911. Handwritten MS]. In the
       author's possession.

232   FOOTNOTE EXAMPLES

DATA FROM A STUDY

CHI   227. Emily Barnett, "Diet and Stress," (unpublished data, 1965).

MLA   228. Emily Barnett, "Diet and Stress," unpublished data, 1965.

APA   (Barnett, 1965)

UNPUBLISHED WORK COPIED BY A DUPLICATING PROCESS (PHOTOCOPY, MIMEOGRAPH, DITTO)

CHI   229. Katherine Dunlap, Journal, n.d., MS, Bancroft Library, University of California, Berkeley (photocopy of typescript), 4.

MLA   230. Katherine Dunlap, Journal, ms., photocopy of typescript, Bancroft Library, U of California, Berkeley, 4.

APA   (Dunlap, n.d., p. 4)

NATIONAL ARCHIVES SOURCES

CHI   231. Hans Thomsen to German Foreign Ministry, 22 May 1940, German Foreign Ministry Records, Record Group 242, Serial 765, frames 270416-417; National Archives Microfilm Publication T-120, roll 371.

MLA   232. Hans Thomsen to German Foreign Ministry, 22 May 1940, German Foreign Ministry Records, Record Group 242, Serial 765, frames 270416-417; National Archives Microfilm Publication T-120, roll 371.

APA   (Thomsen, 1940)

DATA FROM A STUDY

CHI   Barnett, Emily. "Diet and Stress." Unpublished data.
         1965.

MLA   Barnett, Emily. "Diet and Stress." Unpublished data.
         1965.

APA   Barnett, E. (1965). Diet and stress. Unpublished data.

APA   Barnett, E. (1965). [Diet and stress]. Unpublished
         data.

[Underline topic only if it is a true title. When it is a description of contents, enclose in brackets (APA only).]

UNPUBLISHED WORK COPIED BY A DUPLICATING PROCESS (PHOTOCOPY, MIMEOGRAPH, DITTO)

CHI   Dunlap, Katherine. Journal. MS. Bancroft Library,
         University of California, Berkeley. Photocopy of
         typescript.

MLA   Dunlap, Katherine. Journal, ms. Photocopy of
         typescript. Bancroft Library, U of California,
         Berkeley.

APA   Dunlap, K. (N.d.). [Journal, manuscript, photocopy of
         typescript]. Bancroft Library, University of
         California, Berkeley.

NATIONAL ARCHIVES SOURCES

CHI   Thomsen, Hans. Letter to the German Foreign Ministry.
         22 May 1940. National Archives. Collection of World
         War II Seized Enemy Records. Record Group 242.
         German Foreign Ministry Records. Microfilm
         Publication T-120, 5,055 rolls.

MLA   Thomsen, Hans. Letter to the German Foreign Ministry.
         22 May 1940. National Archives. Collection of World
         War II Seized Enemy Records. Record Group 242.
         German Foreign Ministry Records. Microfilm
         Publication T-120, 5,055 rolls.

APA   Thomsen, H. (1940, May 22). [Letter to the German
         foreign ministry]. National Archives. [Collection
         of World War II seized enemy records: German foreign
         ministry records]. Record group 242, microfilm
         publication T-120, 5,055 rolls.

APPENDIX

The Punctuation Handbook

by
Joan I. Miller and Bruce J. Taylor

Alcove Publishing Company
West Linn, Oregon

237

238

CONTENTS

INTRODUCTION

Punctuation brings to written language what facial expression, body movement, tone of voice, sound level, and emotion provide for the spoken language. All of these help the writer or speaker to convey ideas to his audience.

Humans communicate with one another by the use of symbols. When we speak, we express what we want to say with a set of symbolic sounds, which, by common agreement, are strung together to form words. The words, in turn, are symbolic of—that is, they represent—ideas or images formed in the speaker's mind. When we listen, we hear the spoken sounds, and our mind translates them into thoughts or pictorial images. Assuming both speaker and listener are using a common language, a communication from one to the other has begun. But how effectively is the message being transmitted?

When you watch TV, notice how professional actors and announcers communicate. They gesticulate with their arms and hands. They move their bodies expressively. Their faces show emotion to reflect what they are saying. Their voices rise and fall to convey meaning, and they use frequent pauses to convey expression.

In contrast, notice people who do not have the training in enunciation and delivery of the professionals; usually people being interviewed. More often than not, they will speak in a monotone, with little or no expression in their voice. Their bodies will be stiff, expressing nervousness or fear. There is no life in their message; you probably wouldn't want to listen to them for very long.

Enunciation, facial expression, animation, gesturing, rising and falling tone of voice, and timing in the form of pauses are the punctuation marks of the spoken word. Their use improves the transfer of ideas and information when we talk to one another.

When we write, we employ a set of symbolic letters drawn or printed on paper in agreed-upon shapes. The letters are strung together to make words representing ideas, actions, or things, and we assemble the words in series to construct sentences. Completed sentences are then used to communicate ideas and information from writer to reader. Also among the symbols we use for our written language are punctuation marks; devices used to convey expression and to improve clarity.

Every punctuation mark is a shorthand device that conveys meaning to the reader. A question mark, for example, conveys the rising voice inflection used when speaking to indicate that a question is being asked. An exclamation mark, along with the choice of words used, may indicate surprise, anger, determination, or command. A comma can be used as a short pause, for dramatic effect, or to separate or highlight ideas within a sentence. Commas can also be employed as housekeeping devices, as when they separate items in a list, or divide parts of compound sentences expressing more than one idea or thought.

A dash indicates a longer pause than a comma, thereby emphasizing part of a sentence. A semicolon calls for an even longer pause, and signals a possible shift in an idea, an upcoming definition or explanation, or the attachment of a closely related, but separate statement. A colon signals the end of an introduction and the beginning of related information; a period indicates the end of an idea or statement; apostrophes are used to show possession. All of these examples, and other punctuation marks, have their counterparts in speech.

In both written and spoken English, the meaning of a sentence is usually determined by the position of the words within it. But the sequence of words expressing the same thought can vary considerably. Punctuation is indispensable here, to indicate the word-groupings and relationships that will convey clear meaning. Punctuation marks show the reader what words to read together, where to pause for emphasis or importance, when to separate closely-related throughts, and where one statement ends and another begins. Punctuation regulates the "flow" of reading, and ensures that each thought is carried to the reader in the manner intended by the writer.

Punctuation marks are the means by which we clarify what we want to say by adding expression to our words on paper. A person who can punctuate effectively, can write effectively.

A NO-FRILLS APPROACH TO PUNCTUATION

For most of us, what we know about punctuation is derived from early education, and from subconsciously absorbing how punctuation is used in the material we read. This has provided us with the knowledge to get by in most situations. To progress from that point to a reasonable mastery of punctuation is a fairly simple task using the following framework.

The basic element of the English language is the sentence. Sentences may be of any length, from one word, to hundreds. No matter how long or short, sentences always contain three basic elements: (1) subject (who or what), (2) verb (what the subject did), and (3) object (who or what the subject did it to).

John drove the car.

In the sentence above, John (who) is the subject, drove (what John did) is the verb, and the car (what John drove) is the object. The sentence is terminated with a period, which indicates to the reader that it is a simple statement of fact. If the sentence were to end in a question mark:

John drove the car?

the reader would read the sentence as a question, and mentally add a rise in tone to match the way it would sound if spoken. If the sentence were to end in an exclamation point:

John drove the car!

the reader could read the sentence as if it was said in anger, as if the speaker were surprised, or if the speaker were elated. The true intention of the sentence would depend on how it was used in context.

The period, the question mark, and the exclamation point are terminating punctuation marks. Commas, colons, dashes, and ellipses may also be used as terminating marks.

Commas, colons, and dashes are frequently used to terminate introductory elements added to a sentence:

There was no denying it, John drove the car.

The sheriff was sure of it: John drove the car.

They all agreed on one point—John drove the car.

Dashes and ellipses are used to terminate incomplete statements in dialogue:

> "John drove the car; I'm convinced of—" George stopped as John entered the room.
>
> "They all say John drove the car, but what if . . ." The inspector's voice trailed off as he contemplated a new line of thought.

Punctuation marks are also used to separate parts of sentences. Termination of introductory elements, illustrated above, is one example of how punctuation separates one part of a sentence from another. Commas, semicolons, and dashes are all employed as separating devices. Commas are also used to separate main clauses in a sentence:

> Dave supplied the gas, but John drove the car.
>
> *[Main clauses are complete sentences, able to stand alone if separated.]*

Semicolons separate independent statements when they are joined in a compound sentence because of their close relationship:

> John drove the car; Joyce and Debbie only went along for the ride.

Dashes are used to separate parts of a sentence the writer wishes to emphasize:

> One fact stands out above all else—John drove the car!

A third function of punctuation is to enclose parts of sentences or independent statements to improve clarity. Used in pairs, commas, dashes, parentheses, quotation marks, both double and single, and brackets are employed for this purpose.

A large portion of the enclosing function is to set apart parenthetical elements in sentences. These are words, phrases, or clauses that amplify or explain something in the main sentence, or offer a digressive statement related to it.

Incidental parenthetical elements in a sentence are enclosed by commas.

> John, in fact, drove the car.
>
> *[A transitional parenthetical expression.]*

John, the boy who dated Julia last summer, drove the car.

[A parenthetical appositive. An appositive restates, amplifies, explains, or further identifies the noun or pronoun that precedes or follows it.]

Dashes are employed when the writer wishes to emphasize a parenthetical element:

John—boy would I like to get my hands on that kid!—drove the car.

Parentheses are used when the information enclosed is more of an aside to the reader than closely related to the main sentence:

John (I wish I could remember his last name) drove the car.

Double quotation marks enclose words quoted from a speaker, or a text:

"John," he said, "drove the car."
On page five, he wrote: "John drove the car."

Single quotation marks enclose quoted material within quoted material:

"I watched as he wrote, 'John drove the car,' in his report," he told the inspector.

Brackets are used to enclose remarks by the writer that are not a part of the main text:

John drove the car. [Once this was known, the mystery was solved, and the inspector closed the case.]

The examples above illustrate three basic uses of punctuation: *terminating*, *separating*, and *enclosing, to set off*. These three functions represent the majority of applications for punctuation in the English language, and offer a framework for mastering its use.

Notice that in each case, the basic sentence, "John drove the car," remained the same. Introductory elements and parenthetical information were added to increase the amount of information presented, and to clarify the meaning. Each time something was added to the original sentence, it was set off by punctuation marks. Each example illustrates the original premise that punctuation shows the reader what words to read together, where to pause for emphasis or importance, when to separate closely-related thoughts, and where one statement ends and another begins. Understanding these simple basics is the key to understanding punctuation. Learn to apply the principles of *terminating*, *separating*, and *enclosing*, and you have learned how to punctuate.

We want to make it clear at this point, that there is a difference between punctuation and grammar. Grammar is the study of the classification of words, their inflections, and their functions and relationships in sentences. Punctuation is the practice of inserting standardized marks in sentences to clarify meaning and separate structural units. Knowing how to punctuate will not by itself make you a better writer; but it will make what you write more understandable.

Because punctuation and grammar go hand-in-hand, however, a mastery of punctuation will increase your awareness of grammatical sentence structure. In time, your writing will improve to the extent that your subconscious mind has absorbed the principles of grammar from your early education and from your reading. You can accelerate this process by studying additional texts.

Punctuation marks are listed in alphabetical order in this handbook to allow quick reference. We encourage you to browse through the text to pick up general information, as well as use it as a reference manual. By applying the basic framework concept described in this chapter, you can rapidly assimilate the most common principles of punctuation use. A solid mastery of punctuation should follow soon after.

Please note as you read through the text, that the main purpose of this handbook is to present as complete and clear a presentation of the principles of punctuation to as wide an audience as possible. With this in mind, the authors have made a conscious effort to use as few technical words or expressions associated with the study of grammar as possible. Technical words or expressions that are used, are defined in a glossary following the main text. Lesser-known terms are defined both in the text immediately following their use, and in the glossary. To help clarify some rules of punctuation, portions of example sentences are underlined to highlight the area under discussion.

APOSTROPHE   '

The apostrophe is used to show possession, to form plurals, and to indicate the omission of letters or numbers.

I. USE AN APOSTROPHE TO INDICATE POSSESSION

A. Add an apostrophe and an "s" to singular nouns and proper nouns not ending in "s" to form the possessive:

Sam's chair	President Reagan's strategy
the cat's collar	his mother's husband
a ship's captain	the car's windshield

B. Singular nouns and proper names ending in "s," "ss," or an "s" sound form the possessive by adding an apostrophe and an "s":

Dickens's *Great Expectations*	the waitress's pen
the boss's office	Mars's beard
the gas's odor	Yeats's poetry
Porfirio Diaz's regime	the bus's door

(1.) The names "Jesus" and "Moses" are traditional exceptions. The possessive case is formed by adding only an apostrophe.

Jesus' parables	Moses' law

(2.) Greek or hellenized names of more than one syllable ending in "s" or with an "s" or "eez" sound take only and apostrophe to form the possessive.

Archimedes' inventions	Parmenides' philosophy
Dionysius' torture	Theocritus' poems
Orestes' life	Xerxes' reign

(3.) Traditionally, certain nouns that end with "s" or "ce" and are followed by a word beginning with "s" take only an apostrophe to form the possessive.

for goodness' sake   for appearance' sake

for conscience' sake   for rightousness' sake

C. Add an apostrophe and an "s" to plural nouns not ending in "s" to form the possessive:

the deer's favorite drinking spot   the men's club

the children's toys   the alumni's dinner

D. Plural nouns and plural proper names ending in "s" use only an apostrophe to form the possessive:

the puppies' food   the Smiths' apple trees

the Joneses' party   the four dentists' chairs

a teachers' meeting   the two churches' rummage sale

E. Compound nouns use an apostrophe and an "s" on the last word of the compound to form the possessive:

my mother-in-law's books   the man-of-war's guns

his brother-in-law's business   the president-elect's files

the mothers-in-law's books   *[plural compound]*

F. To show joint ownership, the last noun is possessive and takes an apostrophe:

his grandmother and grandfather's trip to China

Mr. Kefauver and Ms. Townsend's bar

Muriel and Dan's dog

the Katzes and the Rosses' beach house

G. To show separate ownership, each noun is possessive and takes an apostrophe:

Eva's and Scott's exam

the hamsters' and rabbits' food

Wilson's or Harding's or Hoover's presidency

the professors' and the students' and the administration's grievances

H. Indefinite pronouns use an apostrophe and an "s" to form the possessive:

one's car   someone else's cup   each other's

everybody's responsibility   no one's mistake

I. Certain general expressions of possession use an apostrophe:

cow's milk   traveler's check

writer's cramp   confectioner's sugar

(1.) An apostrophe is used with some expressions even when actual ownership is not indicated.

a stone's throw   two weeks' worth

wit's end   a day's work

J. A double possessive uses both "of" and an apostrophe and an "s":

that hobby of Guy's   an appointment of my mother's

a daughter of Jim's   these books of the Wheelers'

[Plural: the books belong to all of the Wheeler family.]

K. A gerund (verb ending in "ing" and used as a noun) is generally preceded by a noun or pronoun in the possessive:

Albert's coming to New York surprised his lawyer.

They were all worried about Judy's drinking.

Someone's whispering upset the seance.

We objected to the tower's swaying.

L. When writing geographic names, the titles of books, the names of business firms, organizations, and institutions, use of the . apostrophe to indicate possession should follow the original form designated by custom or usage:

Boys' Clubs of America   Harpers Ferry

Authors League of America   Kings Canyon, California

Lion's Gate Bridge   *Jane Fonda's Workout Book*

Weight Watchers Fast and Fabulous Cookbook

II. USE AN APOSTROPHE AND AN "S" TO FORM PLURALS

A. Of small letters:

There are four "i's" in Mississippi.

Remember to cross your "t's."

All "p's" over by the window; "q's" line up here by the door.

B. Of abbreviations with periods, and capital letters that would be confusing with only an "s":

There are nine M.D.'s in this building.

How many Ph.D.'s?

Look under the "I's," the "M's," and the "U's."
[Without apostrophes, the sentence would read: Look under the "Is," the "Ms," and the "Us."]

C. The plural of words used as words is usually formed by adding an "s" or "es." Both an apostrophe and an "s" are used if the "s" ending alone would cause confusion:

You have too many "ands" in that sentence.

You have too many "as's" in that sentence.
[Without the apostrophe, this sentence would read: "too many 'ass'."]

How may "I do's" do we have?

[Without the apostrophe, this sentence would read: "how many 'I dos'."]

III. USE AN APOSTROPHE TO INDICATE OMISSIONS

A. An apostrophe is used to form a contraction by marking where one or more letters have been omitted:

shouldn't (should not)	I'll (I will)
could've (could have)	she'd (she would)
isn't (is not)	they're (they are)
there's (there is)	you're (you are)

B. Use an apostrophe to show where numbers have been omitted:

the crash of '29   (1929)

the class of '85   (1985)

Richard Nixon was reelected in '72.   (1972)

She was born in '21.   (1921)

IV. DO NOT USE APOSTROPHES

A. To form the possessive of personal pronouns:

I — my, mine	we — our, ours
you — your, yours	they — their, theirs
she — her, hers	it — its
he — his	who — whose

B. To form the possessive in expressions where one noun modifies another:

The state capitol in Salem.   *[wrong: The state's capitol in Salem.]*

They put him in the Oregon State Penitentiary *[wrong: They put him in Oregon State's Penitentiary.]*

He pulled a quarterback sneak.   *[wrong: He pulled a quarterback's sneak.]*

C. To form the plural of numbers:

1930s (not 1930's)	8-½s (not 8-½'s)
747s (not 747's)	sixes, tens, fourteens

The veterans were in their fifties and sixties.

D. To form the plural of most terms containing all capital letters, or single capital letters, used as words:

Two CPAs share a suite.

We saw six UFOs last year.

This school still teaches the three Rs.

ASTERISK   *

The asterisk is a reference symbol used after a word, figure, or sentence that directs the reader's attention to additional information in a note at the bottom of the page. When used in a table, the asterisk note is placed at the bottom of the table instead of the bottom of the page.

I. USE AN ASTERISK

A. To mark a place in the text that directs the reader to related information that may be incidental, or may disrupt the narrative if included in the body of the text. The asterisk alerts the reader to go to the bottom of the page where a note containing the related information is usually placed. The note is marked by a matching asterisk.

B. As a reference symbol when noting specific parts of tables, particularly if the table consists of figures, equations, or formulas. Use of the asterisk (and other symbols) avoids mistaking the notes for parts of the equations or formulas.

(1.) Symbols used as reference marks are placed in a superior position from (one-half space above) the line of text, or information in a table.

(2.) Do not use more than three asterisks for notes (***) on a single page or table. Use additional symbols or letters as needed, but do not use a combination of asterisks and other symbols, numbers, or letters (*ab).

BRACE   { }

A brace is a mark used to show that a relationship exists between one group of lines, equations, or statistics and another. The point of the brace is directed toward the logical flow of information, or toward the fewer number of lines, whichever is most appropriate.

I.   USE A BRACE

A. To show the connection between one group of lines and another:

Kent
New Castle } Counties of Delaware
Sussex

Henry Knox
Timothy Pickering } Secretaries of War under George
James McHenry   Washington

1 kilometer { 0.621 mile
             { 3.2815 feet

BRACKETS   [ ]

Brackets are used in pairs to enclose the author's comments about the text.

I. USE BRACKETS TO ENCLOSE

A. Author's interpolations, comments, or translations:

One comment about the Masterson papers [most authorities agree on this] is that they contain unusual insights to life in a seventeenth century manorhouse.

He announced that he had just heard from the stationmaster and more beer was on the way [cheers and thumping of mugs on the table].

For his tombstone, they ordered the Latin inscription requiescat in pace [may he rest in peace].

B. Notes indicating omissions, corrections, or descriptive information:

They [the South American countries] will have to get their financial houses in order before the world banking community will feel comfortable dealing with them again.

With a shaking hand, the old man wrote, "I grew up in Ronok [Roanoke] Virginny [Virginia]."

According to Jamison, they arrived on July 10, 1936 [1938] and moved into the big house.

C. Notes indicating the reproduction of errors found in source material:

"The tenth of May we arrived at the Canaries, and the tenth of June in this present yeere [sic], we were fallen with the Islands of the West Indies. . . .

— Arthur Barlow in a
report to Sir Walter Raleigh

II. WHEN BRACKETED MATTER TAKES UP MORE THAN ONE PARAGRAPH, START EACH PARAGRAPH WITH A BRACKET; PLACE THE CLOSING BRACKET AT THE END OF THE LAST PARAGRAPH ONLY

COLON :

The colon is used as a break in a sentence to emphasize what follows. Its effect is more formal than that of a semicolon. Rather than indicating a pause, the colon signals the reader to go ahead with focused attention on what comes immediately after.

I. USE A COLON TO SEPARATE

A. When introducing an independent statement, a formal extract from a text, or a speech in a dialogue:

The question to be debated was: Should the student body benefit from profits made by the University book store?

In his well-known book, *Critical Path*, Buckminster Fuller had this to say about copper: "Copper is the most plentiful of the most efficient electric-power-production and conduction metals."

Tammy: I'm too scared to go in there.
Roger: Come on, there's nothing in there that can harm you.

B. When setting off separate clauses in compound sentences when the second clause amplifies, explains, or illustrates the first:

John didn't like the cafeteria food: he felt it was too salty.

Monday was terrible: I overslept, was late to class, and got my feet wet because I forgot my galoshes.

It was a beautiful painting: a sailboat silhouetted on an orange, red, and silver sea in front of a huge setting sun.

C. When introducing a list or a series:

The Commission's study focused on three areas: the downtown core area; the Burnside renewal area; and the waterfront.

The mayor announced three objectives:
1. Lower the city budget.
2. Improve residential area police patrols.
3. Clean up the waterfront.

(1.) Periods are used after entries in a vertical list only when at least one of the entries is a complete sentence. When a list completes an introductory sentence, no final period is used unless the listed items are separated by semicolons or commas.

(2.) Use a colon with "as follows" or "the following" when items in the list or series follow immediately after.

The areas focused on were as follows:
1. The downtown core area
2. The Burnside renewal area
3. The waterfront

(3.) But do not use a colon with "as follows" or "the following" when the introductory statement is complete, and is followed by one or more sentences:

The Commission focused on unused land, business, and residential property, with emphasis on the following.

1. Underused commercial property in the downtown core area was identified.

2. Historically important buildings in the Burnside renewal area were tagged for special attention.

3. City-owned land along the waterfront was evaluated for park development.

(4.) Use a colon with "namely," "for instance," "for example," or "that is" only when the series consists of one or more complete sentences.

The Commission's study covered three downtown areas, namely, the downtown core, Burnside, and the waterfront.   *[no colon]*

The Commission's study covered three areas, namely:
The area between Burnside and Jefferson Avenue and
from Second to Ninth Street was designated as area
one. From Burnside Avenue north to Lovejoy Avenue was
designated as area two. From the waterfront to Second
Street was designated as area three.   *[colon used]*

(5.) Do not use a colon when the list or series introduced
is a complement or object of the introductory statement.

The Commission's focus areas are (1) the downtown
core, (2) the Burnside renewal area, and (3) the
waterfront.

*[Items (1), (2), and (3) are complements of
"focus areas."]*

The Commission is planning to investigate
   1. the downtown core;
   2. the Burnside renewal area;
   3. the waterfront.

*[Items 1., 2., and 3. are direct objects of the
introductory clause.]*

D. Formal salutations from a body of text:

My Dear Sir:

Ladies and Gentlemen:

To Whom It May Concern:

E. The parts of Biblical and other citations:

Mark 1:39

II Corinthians 9:5

The Historian 46:4

F. When dividing titles from subtitles:

*Editing Your Newsletter: A Guide to Writing, Design,
and Production*

The Peter Principle: How to Make Things Go Right

G. When indicating proportions:

Mix water and vinegar 30:1

His chances of success are 10:1 against.

H. When dividing hours and minutes in clock time:

10:21 p.m.   6:15 a.m.

II. USE OF COLONS WITH OTHER PUNCTUATION MARKS

A. Always place colons outside quotation marks or parentheses.

B. When a quotation taken from a text ends with a colon, drop the colon and add an ellipsis.

COMMA ,

For the English language, the comma is like salt on food; it brings out the flavor. It is used in more places than any other punctuation mark, and is therefore considered to be complex. This is not true. The comma follows the simple principles of separating and enclosing parts of a sentence to clarify its meaning.

Commas separate amplifying, explanatory, or digressive information from the beginning and end of sentences. They are used before and after the same type of information when it is in the middle to set it off or highlight it from the rest of the sentence. Commas are also used to separate items in a list, so it can be identified as a list.

It's as simple as that. Keep these three uses in mind and you will rapidly master the use of commas.

I. USE COMMAS TO SEPARATE

A. Elements in a series. Place a comma between all words, phrases, clauses, letters, or figures in a series of three or more, including before a conjunction preceding the last item:

Marty kept books on <u>physics</u>, <u>history</u>, <u>poetry</u>, <u>and computers</u> on his shelf at home.

She returned home, <u>fed the cat</u>, <u>did the laundry</u>, <u>then cooked dinner</u>.

Did you choose <u>a</u>, <u>b</u>, <u>c</u>, <u>or d</u>?

His locker combination was <u>20</u>, <u>8</u>, <u>17</u>.

Note: Some authorities advocate omitting the comma before the conjunction preceding the last item in a series. The authors disagree with this practice, since the writer must make a judgement each time the rule is applied as to whether or not the resulting sentence can be misunderstood. Nothing is gained by omitting the final comma in a list, while clarity can be lost in some cases through misreading.

(1.) When a conjunction is used between the last two elements in a series, place a comma before the conjunction. A conjunction is a linking word that ties together clauses, phrases, or words.

The boys asked for a baseball, a bat, <u>and</u> four gloves.

(2.) Do not use commas when the elements in a series are all joined by conjunctions.

The orchestra played compositions by Mozart <u>and</u> Brahms <u>and</u> Chopin.

(3.) Do not use a comma between the last item in a series and an item being described.

He wore his old, faded, <u>stained   jeans</u> to work on his car.

(4.) Do not use a comma between items in a series that are employed as closely related pairs or sets.

The establishment offered comfort, solitude, a well-stocked library, and <u>bed and breakfast</u>.

The menu listed <u>eggs and bacon</u>, <u>eggs and ham</u>, and <u>eggs and hash</u>.

(5.) When one or more of the elements in a series contain commas, use semicolons instead of commas to separate the elements.

They travelled through <u>Denver, Colorado</u>; <u>Ogden, Utah</u>; and <u>Pasadena, California</u>.

Some of the members picked <u>fruit, cotton, and vegetables</u>; <u>others worked in banks, bookstores, and restaurants</u>; <u>still others were employed as doctors, lawyers, and stockbrokers</u>.

B. Chapter and page references:

Jason's quote is in <u>Chapter 12</u>, <u>page 237</u>.

C. Parts of an address when the address is joined in a line:

The book was sent to <u>4891 Elm St.</u>, <u>Portland</u>,
<u>Oregon 97865</u>.   *[Do not use a comma before the Zip Code.]*

D. Parts of a date:

I left for Europe on <u>Wednesday</u>, <u>June 15</u>, <u>1990</u>.

The meeting was scheduled for <u>November 1</u>, <u>1986</u>, but was actually held two days later.

(1.) No comma is used between the month and year when the day of the month is absent.

The book was published in <u>March 1967</u>.

(2.) No commas are used when the day of the month is written first (a style commonly used by the military and in Europe).

<u>8 April 1924</u>   <u>27 June 1764</u>

(3.) No commas are used between dates and holidays, seasons, or the abbreviations A.D. and B.C.

The last time they came was <u>Christmas 1936</u>.

The class was scheduled for <u>spring 1987</u>.

The 774th year of the Roman Empire is equivalent to <u>29 A.D.</u> on our calendar.

E. Numbers of more than three figures signifying quantity:

<u>6,045</u>   <u>$78,900.00</u>   <u>4,580,991</u>

F. Inverted proper names:

White, Stanley   Clark, Alvin T.

G. Names of places:

San Diego, California   Dublin, Ireland

They wrote to him through the express office,
Trafalgar Square, London, England.

H. An informal salutation from the body of a letter:

Dear Joan,   Dear Mom,   Dear Aunt Gail,

I. The complimentary close of a letter from the signature:

Sincerely yours,   Truly yours,

Affectionately,   Always,

J. Words or figures that otherwise might cause the reader confusion (try reading the following examples without the commas):

Instead of a few, thousands came.

Instead of 40, 70 were sent.

During 1956, 460 athletes competed for the award.

Toward Marsha, Martin was very cool.

The way it was, was okay with them.

II. USE COMMAS WITHIN A SENTENCE TO SET OFF OR EMPHASIZE

The use of commas to set off, emphasize, or enclose phrases or
clauses is frequently controlled by whether the phrase or clause is
nonrestrictive or restrictive.

(1.) If the phrase is not essential to the meaning of the
sentence, it is nonrestrictive, and set off by commas.

Bill Dixon, who spoke to the group, represented the
State Energy Commission.

The Senate, by a narrow margin, passed the bill.

(2.) If the phrase is necessary to, or restricts the meaning of the sentence, it is restrictive, and not set off by commas.

The man who spoke to the group represented the State Energy Commission.

The Senate passed the bill by a narrow margin.

A. Clauses joined by a coordinating conjunction in a compound sentence. The most common coordinating conjunctions are *and*, *but*, *for*, *nor*, *or*, *so*, *still*, and *yet*:

Sara wanted a new dress for the dance, but she didn't have enough money.

The desert is beautiful, yet it is dangerous to the unwary.

(1.) Some authorities allow elimination of the comma when the connected clauses are short (three to five words).

Edna washed the dishes and John dried.

George held the horse's head and Sue mounted.

She went in but he hesitated.

B. An introductory modifying phrase, or adverbial clause from an independent clause that follows it:

By setting aside money earned during the summer, Laura was able to pay her tuition.

Moving quickly and quietly, Henry wrestled the boxes onto the truck.

C. An ending modifying phrase or adverbial clause from an independent clause that precedes it:

Roger sailed the boat upstream, careful of the channel buoys.

Sally first drove the car around the block, slowly and cautiously.

D. Direct quotations from the rest of the sentence (always place commas inside quotation marks):

When associates complained to Lincoln that General Grant was a heavy drinker, he said, "Can you tell me what kind of whiskey? I should like to send a barrel to some of my other generals."

> — Ida M. Tarbell,
> *The Life of Abraham Lincoln*

"I should like," said Lincoln, "to send a barrel to some of my other generals."

(1.) Omit the separating comma if you use only part of a quotation, or if you introduce it with "that."

When told General Grant was a heavy whiskey drinker, Lincoln asked for the brand, so [that] he could "send a barrel to some of my other generals."

Lincoln asked the brand of General Grant's whiskey, that he might "send a barrel to some of my other generals."

(2.) Do not use commas to separate indirect quotations.

Lincoln said he would send a barrel of General Grant's whiskey to his other generals if he could find out what brand he drank.

E. Adages, maxims or other special expressions from the rest of the sentence (always place commas inside quotation marks):

"Who first coined that old saying, 'Blood is thicker than water?' " asked Jim.

Only one aphorism, You cannot help loving who loves you, has remained in my mind.

F. Tag questions from preceding independent clauses:

You've just returned from the store, haven't you?

She put the book on the shelf, didn't she?

You are sure, aren't you?

G. Contrasted elements or expressions in a sentence:

He lives in apartment <u>A</u>, <u>not B</u>.

Pat turned <u>35</u> last year, <u>not 29</u>.

He plays <u>golf</u>, <u>never tennis</u>.

She parks <u>in the garage</u>, <u>seldom out on the street</u>.

H. Two or more adjectives modifying the same noun:

Polly wore an <u>old</u>, <u>threadbare</u>, <u>brown</u> sweater.

(1.) When consecutive adjectives modify equally, no comma is used. This is especially true for adjectives that refer to age (young, old, new), size, color, or location. Two simple tests are to mentally place "and" between the adjectives, or to switch the sequence of adjectives. In either case, if the resulting sentence seems awkward, the commas may be left out. If the resulting sentence appears to read correctly, use commas.

They accepted his <u>revised</u> <u>draft</u> <u>manuscript</u>.

The <u>small</u> <u>white</u> <u>knob</u> on the stove.

It was one of those <u>old</u> <u>one-street</u> <u>frontier</u> <u>mining</u> towns.

I. The person speaking, or spoken to, in dialogue (always place commas inside quotation marks):

"I don't think," <u>said Peter</u>, "I'll ever understand statistics."

"Go to the kitchen, <u>Nancy</u>, and help Tom with the vegetables."

(1.) Note that in dialogue, where appropriate, a question or an exclamation mark replaces the second comma.

"Are you back again<u>?</u>" asked George.

"The potatoes are boiling over<u>!</u>" shouted Theron.

J. Initials or personal titles after proper names:

Eva Kubinsky, <u>D.D.S.</u>, is on the board of directors.

Professor Alfred Miller, <u>Ph.D.</u>, made the introductions.

Jerry Anderson, <u>Sr.</u>, started the business in 1904.

Dennis Noble, <u>chairman</u>, criticised the new incumbent.

III. USE COMMAS (BEFORE AND AFTER) WITHIN A SENTENCE TO SET OFF

A. Parenthetical words, phrases, or clauses that amplify, explain, or offer a digressive statement without changing the meaning of the sentence (nonrestrictive phrases):

The senator, <u>however</u>, refused to comply.

Rodney, <u>his heart beating rapidly</u>, donned his parachute.

The Portland Building, <u>which was controversial when it was first built</u>, is now a valued addition to the city.

B. Absolute phrases: a phrase within a sentence with an informal relationship, but no clear grammatical relationship, to the rest of the sentence.

He saluted, <u>a nostalgic lump forming in his throat,</u> as the flag passed by.

C. Words in apposition (adjacent nouns, pronouns, or groups of words where one of the expressions restates, amplifies, explains, or further identifies the other):

<u>My wife, Josephine</u>, bought a goat last week.

<u>We, the undersigned</u>, agree to support Roosevelt for President.

<u>His company, the shoe factory in Brockton,</u> showed increased profits this year.

(1.) When an appositive is restrictive, it is not set off by commas.

The <u>sailor</u> <u>who was the first to volunteer</u> was designated the leader.

<u>Steinbeck's book</u> "<u>The Grapes of Wrath</u>" described Midwest dustbowl conditions in the 1930's.

<u>The quotation</u> "<u>The only thing we have to fear is</u> <u>fear itself</u>" is from Franklin D. Roosevelt's first inaugural address.

D. Vocatives (nouns, pronouns, and other terms used in direct address). Vocatives may also appear at the beginning or the end of sentences, and are set off by commas:

Let me assure you, <u>Bob</u>, your job is secure.

I promise you, <u>fellow Democrats</u>, I will represent you to the best of my ability.

Take your seats, <u>ladies and gentlemen</u>, the play is about to begin.

E. "Of" phrases:

John Maxwell, <u>of Taylor, Bass, and Young,</u> represents our firm in London.

Captain Kangaroo, <u>of television fame</u>, spoke to our communications class.

(1.) When a place name is generally accepted as a part of a person's name, it is not separated by commas.

<u>Montgomery of El Alamein</u>   <u>Jesus of Nazareth</u>

IV. USE COMMAS TO INDICATE OMISSION

A. Of a word or words, understood through the context of the sentence:

Helen was elected president; Cheryl, [<u>was</u> <u>elected</u>] vice president; and Valerie, [<u>was</u> <u>elected</u>] treasurer.

Last semester, the assignment was ten pages; this
semester, [the assignment was]fifteen pages!

V. DO NOT USE COMMAS:

A. Before the first item in a series.

B. After the last item in a series.

C. To separate a subject from its verb.

F. Between two independent clauses where a stronger mark
(semicolon or period) is required.

G. With restrictive words, phrases, or clauses.

H. Together with a dash or parentheses.

I. Before an ampersand (&).

J. Between the name or number of an organized unit.

   Teamsters Local 233   American Legion Post 24

DASH   --

The dash is used to indicate a sudden interruption or sharp break in thought, or to add an air of surprise or emotional tone. It can always be replaced by some other punctuation mark, and should be used only where strong emphasis or stylistic effect is desired.

In typed manuscripts, a dash is formed with two hyphens with no space separating it from the words before and after. In typeset copy, it is optional whether or not to place spaces before and after the dash, and is frequently dependent on the typesetting system being used.

I.   USE DASHES TO SEPARATE OR SET OFF

A. Nonrestrictive modifying phrases or clauses:

No one in the fraternity—not even David—dared to oppose the Dean's ruling.

The Muses—nine sister goddesses in Hellenic mythology—were a source of inspiration to the ancient Greeks.

B. Nonrestrictive appositives (adjacent nouns, pronouns, or groups of words where one of the two expressions restates, amplifies, explains, or further identifies the other). Appositives may also occur in the middle of a sentence:

She could forgive him everything but this—the theft of her grandmother's pearls.

Steven was motivated by three things—wealth, power, and prestige—in his race up the corporate ladder.

C. The summary of a thought, a series of thoughts, or a list of items from that which it summarizes:

Food, clothing, shelter—these are considered basic to survival.

The egg, that staple of a million breakfasts; that common element in thousands of baking recipes; the royal ingredient in a mixed orange drink, or a morning-after hangover remedy; the basis of the

multi-billion dollar chicken industry—is one of
America's chief sources of cholesterol.

II. USE DASHES TO ENCLOSE

A. Parenthetical elements that cause a sharp break or interrupt thought:

I've sent Eddie and Guy—those boys can certainly
eat—to the store for chips, dip, and soda.

(1.) When a modifying phrase or clause set off by dashes
calls for a question mark or exclamation point, the appropriate punctuation is placed in front of the second
dash.

Jeff and I—do you know Jeff?—are going to the
opera on Saturday.

B. Parenthetical elements you wish to emphasize:

The blankets—soft, warm, and colorful—were
made of wool.

C. Parenthetical elements used for stylistic effect:

He was irritated beyond belief—irritated by the
incessant hum of the transformer.   *[reiteration]*

He was relieved—oh was he relieved!—when his
financial aid check arrived.   *[dramatization]*

III. USE DASHES TO TERMINATE

A. An expression, the meaning of which is completed by two or
more parallel elements (items of equal importance expressed in
the same grammatical form) that follow:

The committee recommended that material for
recycling—
    1. be placed at curbside;
    2. be collected once a week;
    3. be transported to the county recycling
       center.

The girls said their good health was the result of—
    frequent exercise;
    a high fibre diet;
    adequate sleep.

(1.) Do not use a dash when enumerated elements are used in a continuous sentence structure.

a. In a compound sentence with more than two elements:

The committee recommended that material for recycling: (1) be placed at curbside, (2) be collected once a week, (3) be transported to the county recycling center.

b. In a compound sentence with only two elements:

The committee recommended that material for recycling (1) be placed at curbside and (2) be collected once a week.

c. In a sentence containing a list:

The girls gave three reasons for their good health: (1) frequent exercise, (2) a high fibre diet, and (3) adequate sleep.

B. An unfinished word or sentence:

"I don't mean to be—"

"The word 'emphasize'—"

"The word 'emp'—"

(1.) Use a comma following a dash to separate unfinshed quotations from the speaker.

"I don't care—," began Henry, as the noise from the passing train cut him off.

C. In-line subheadings:

Key Outline— The desired area is . . . .

START EARLY— Begin thinking about . . . .

D. Run-in questions and answers in testimony:

Q. <u>Was he with you</u>? — A. <u>No</u>.

E. Dates when indicating an indefinite span of time:

George Potter (1951—)

The American industrial age (1880—) shaped the country's cultural perspectives.

IV. USE DASHES TO INDICATE OMISSION

A. Of letters or words in a sentence:

<u>Marie D—</u> was the key witness in the drug dealing case.

"That's a <u>h—</u> of a way for you to act!"
[See hyphens for a similar use in text.]

V. MISCELLANEOUS USES OF DASHES

A. To indicate halting or interrupted speech:

"It was—well—you know—it was bad. There was blood everywhere, and—my God—I couldn't see where the door was, and Barb was—she was screaming, and—God, it was terrible."

B. In place of a colon, where preceded by a question mark or an exclamation mark:

<u>What do you think of this?</u>— "House for sale, $200,000."

C. To precede a credit line or a run-in credit or signature:

How do I love thee? Let me count the ways.

—Elizabeth Barrett Browning
"Sonnets From the Portuguese XLII"

Give and it shall be given unto you. . . .

—Luke 6:38

D. In place of commas or parentheses, if clarification is improved (where emphasis is not otherwise desired):

The school's top decision makers—the chancellor, the president, and the vice president for finance—represented the university during the negotiations.

Three of the four sisters—Mary, Nancy, and Joan—took jobs with the gas company.

VI. DO NOT USE DASHES

A. Immediately after a comma, colon, semicolon, or period.

ELLIPSIS   . . .

The ellipsis (plural ellipses) is used almost exclusively to indicate the omission of text from quoted material. Ellipses are formed by typing three periods, with letterspaces between them. The ellipsis is always separated by a letterspace from words or other punctuation marks preceding or following it. When ellipses represent words omitted from a direct quotation, they are placed within the quotation marks.

Quoted material employing ellipses to indicate deleted material should always retain the basic meaning intended by the original author. It should also retain a sense of grammatical correctness and express a complete thought.

I.   USE ELLIPSES TO INDICATE THE OMISSION OF TEXT FROM QUOTED MATERIAL

Original sample text

When the depression struck, businessmen took the view that the various phases of the business cycle were inevitable and that, in time, prosperity would return. Some said the economy was sound, and that the only thing wrong was the people's lack of confidence.

No one could truly ignore the depression. It penetrated every aspect of life in the United States. A year after the crash, 6 million men walked the streets looking for jobs that did not exist. In 1931, unemployment in the nation rose to 9 million, and in 1932 climbed to about 15 million. Thousands of banks failed, prices dropped, foreign trade shrank, and business failures increased.

By the summer of 1932, steel plants were operating at twelve per cent of capacity. Many factories had shut down completely. People lost their savings; they could not make mortgage payments, so they lost their homes; charity soup kitchens opened in the cities, and long bread lines formed; the jobless slept where they could—on park benches or in the doorways of public buildings; many suffered from cold, starvation and malnutrition.

—Current, DeConde, and Dante
United States History

Shortened sample text, using ellipses

When the depression struck, businessmen took the view that . . . in time, prosperity would return. . . .

No one could truly ignore the depression. . . . A year after the crash, 6 million men walked the streets looking for jobs . . . . In 1931, unemployment in the nation rose to 9 million, and in 1932 climbed to about 15 million. Thousands of banks failed, . . . and business failures increased.

. . . Many factories had shut down completely. People lost their savings; . . . charity soup kitchens opened in the cities; . . . many suffered from cold, starvation and malnutrition.

A. When text is omitted from the middle of a sentence, insert the ellipsis only:

When the depression struck, businessmen took the view that . . . in time, prosperity would return.

B. When text is omitted from the end of a sentence, insert an ellipsis in the position of the missing words, and follow it with the original punctuation of the sentence:

A year after the crash, 6 million men walked the streets looking for jobs . . . .
[The last dot is the period.]

NOTE: Some authorities advocate placing the punctuation before the ellipsis when text is deleted from the end of a sentence. The writers of this handbook feel such placement would confuse readers. This potential for confusion is eliminated, it is felt, when the ellipsis is consistently placed in the position of the omitted text, and punctuation precedes or follows it as in the original sentence.

C. When text is omitted following the end of a sentence, or between sentences (including between paragraphs), follow the original punctuation mark with an ellipsis:

No one could truly ignore the depression. . . . A
year after the crash, 6 million men walked the
streets looking for jobs . . . .

[In the first sentence, the first dot is the period ending the sentence. In the second sentence, text has been omitted from the end of the sentence, so the last dot is the period.]

D. When an incomplete sentence follows a punctuation mark preceded or followed by an ellipsis, and is the beginning of a complete thought, capitalizing the first letter is optional:

No one could truly ignore the depression. . . . men
walked the streets looking for jobs . . . .

or—

No one could truly ignore the depression. . . . Men
walked the streets looking for jobs . . . .

or—

No one could truly ignore the depression. . . .
[M]en walked the streets looking for jobs . . . .

E. When text is omitted from the end of a paragraph, end the last sentence with the original punctuation, then add an ellipsis:

When the depression struck, businessmen took the view
that . . . in time, prosperity would return. . . .

[The first dot is the period ending the sentence, and is not separated by a space.]

F. When text is omitted from the first part of a paragraph, whether whole sentences or the beginning of an opening sentence, retain the original indentation and insert an ellipsis in place of the deleted text:

. . . Many factories had shut down completely.
People lost their savings; . . . many suffered from
cold, starvation and malnutrition.

G. When one or more paragraphs are omitted when using widely spaced portions of a quotation, insert a single ellipsis in place of the deleted material:

When the depression struck, . . . 6 million men
walked the street looking for jobs. . . .

H. When appropriate, retain original punctuation before or following the ellipsis representing deleted text:

People lost their savings; . . . charity soup
kitchens opened in the cities; . . . many suffered
from cold, starvation and malnutrition.

In the early days . . . , property was readily
available.

The list was clear, but ridiculous . . . : raisins,
snails, copper flasks, and bed curtains.

"Money and politics, . . . !" she shouted.

I. When a direct quote is grammatically incomplete, use an ellipsis only, with no punctuation unless an exclamation point or question mark is called for:

"I wonder if . . ." Susan began.

"I resent the implication that . . . !" the old lady
screamed, as he shut the door on her.

"Do you need a . . . ?" Tom started to ask.

[Used in this manner, the ellipses infers that the speaker intended to continue, as opposed to the sharp interruption indicated by a dash used for the same purpose.]

J. When one or more lines of verse are omitted, indicate the deletion with a row of spaced periods approximately the same length as the last line quoted.

Original sample text

All day the waves assailed the rock,
I heard no church-bell chime,
The sea-beat scorns the minister clock
And breaks the glass of Time.

                    —Emerson, "Nahant"

Shortened example text, using ellipses

All day the waves assailed the rock,
. . . .
The sea-beat scorns the minister clock
And breaks the glass of Time.

II. ELLIPSES MAY BE USED (INFREQUENTLY AND WITH DISCRETION) IN NARRATIVE PROSE

A. To indicate an implied expansion of thought:

She wants me to go, but . . .

B. To indicate the passage of time:

The night grew cold . . . the moon rose . . . stars appeared . . . still we waited.

III. DO NOT USE ELLIPSES

A. Before or after a partial quotation used in a complete sentence:

They wrote "6 million men walked the streets looking for jobs," and government statistics support their statement.

B. Before a quotation set apart from the main text, and beginning with an incomplete sentence that completes the last sentence in the main text:

After the stock market crash the depression struck, and

businessmen took the view that the various phases were inevitable and that, in time, prosperity would return.

C. Following a quotation set apart from the main text that ends with a complete sentence, unless it is considered necessary for clarity. See III B (immediately above) for the example.

D. To indicate missing words or letters in the original copy (see hyphens).

EXCLAMATION POINT   !

The exclamation point is a mark of terminal punctuation that indicates or expresses strong emotion or emphasis. Use exclamation points sparingly, and do not use more than one at a time, or its emphatic force will be weakened.

I.   USE AN EXCLAMATION POINT WITH A WORD OR SENTENCE

A. To show strong feeling or emphasis (may occur in a declarative sentence):

Help!

Turn off the light!

She loves me!

How right you are!

(1.) The exclamation point should be placed inside quotation marks when it is part of the quotation.

[Note the omission of the comma in the following sentences.]

"You fool!" shouted the artist. "You've ruined the painting!"

"Ouch!" cried Tommy. "That hurts!"

B. To indicate a forceful command or request:

Stop! Come back with my car!

Go to your room now!

Get that dog away from the table!

"Please give me something to eat!" the starving man cried out.

(1.) The exclamation point may occur in an interrogative sentence.

[Note the omission of a question mark in the following sentences.]

"Where are you going!" shouted Glen.

Who is yelling, "give me liberty or give me death!"

HYPHEN -

Hyphens are primarily employed to improve reading comprehension by connecting parts of compound words or phrases. Common usage also supports a wide range of other applications.

I. USE HYPHENS TO JOIN THE PARTS OF COMPOUND WORDS OR PHRASES

Compound words may consist of: (1) two or more distinct words written as one (footnote, bookstore); (2) two separate words, which, when joined by a hyphen, express a thought more than, or different from, the words used individually (penny-wise, break-in); (3) or a root word joined to a stressed prefix (ex-boyfriend, pro-government).

Compound phrases may consist of: (1) commonly employed prepositional phrase compounds containing three or more words (mother-in-law, man-of-war, government-in-exile); (2) improvised descriptive compounds (lighter-than-air, first-come-first-served).

The use of hyphenated compounds constantly changes in English language usage. Many combinations that began as two-word descriptions have evolved into single-word compounds through an interim step as a hyphenated compound. Base ball (a ball game played with bases that the player must run to and touch), for example, evolved first to base-ball, and is now written as baseball. Book store, which evolved into the single word, bookstore, is another example.

The only dependable way to determine if current practice calls for hyphenated or solid spelling of a compound word or phrase is to consult an unabridged (or at least a collegiate) dictionary. Most, but probably not all, of the noun forms and many of the adjective forms will be listed there. Note that all the dictionary entries are divided into syllables. Your dictionary's explanatory notes will tell you how to distinguish between the marks used to separate syllables and hyphens joining parts of a compound word.

A. Hyphenated noun-compounds consist of two proper nouns so closely associated that they constitute a single concept when used together, but are spelled individually and joined by a hyphen:

cure-all	place-name
blood-alcohol	scholar-poet
dog-ear	author-publisher
father-confessor	crop-year

B. Hyphenated adjective-compounds consist of two or more words that express a single thought, which in turn, precedes and modifies the meaning of a proper noun, or of a closely related single word and the noun it modifies:

cat-like	old-fashioned	great-uncle
orange-red	trade-mark	fellow-member
light-haired	high-ranking	off-the-record
law-abiding	half-baked	all-encompassing

(1.) When a compound adjective follows the noun it modifies, the hyphen is usually dropped:

His manner was old fashioned.

His contracts were always awarded to fellow members.

Their testimony was to be off the record.

Their plan was only half baked.

C. Hyphenated prefix-compounds connect a prefix to the noun it modifies:

ex-president	pre-Columbian
anti-Communist	co-author
de-water	trans-Pacific
pro-Ally	un-American
self-employed	mid-ocean

D. Hyphenated phrase compounds are three-or-more-word combinations expressing complex descriptive titles or thoughts:

stick-in-the-mud	one-man-one-vote
brother-in-law	18-year-old
hard-and-fast	know-it-all
grant-in-aid	what-you-see-is-what-you-get

II. MISCELLANEOUS USES OF HYPHENS

A. To divide words carried over from one of line text to the next:

The advantage of this process is the <u>achieve-ment</u> of multiple color effects.

(1.) Words carried over from one line of text to the next are always divided at a syllable break.

(2.) Never divide a word between two lines of text in a manner that leaves a single letter by itself on either of the lines.

(3.) Divide hyphenated words only at the hyphen:

self-employed	**not** self-employed
ex-manager	**not** ex-manager

B. To join single letter modifiers to nouns:

A-bomb	I-beam
U-turn	S-curve
V-neck	T-square

C. To join capitalized names when indicating relationship or distance:

The Washington-Moscow talks

The New York-Paris flight

D. To distinguish between the word used, and another, similar word:

co-respondent	(correspondent)
re-solve	(resolve)
co-op	(coop)
re-creation	(recreation)

E. To avoid doubling vowels or tripling consonants:

pre-eminent	shell-like
pre-empt	co-opted

F. To terminate the first part of a hyphenated compound when used with another related hyphenated compound:

a two- or three-wheeled bicycle

a first- or second-level decision

three-, four-, and five-year-old cheese

G. When writing compound numbers between twenty-one and ninety-nine.

H. Between numerator and denominator when writing fractions:

a three-fourths majority

one-tenth liter

but

twenty-two twenty-fifths

sixty-seven one-hundredths

(1.) Some authorities advocate elimination of the hyphen when the first two words in a numerical expression serve as a modifier for the second.

three fourths of a majority   *[modifies majority]*

one tenth of a liter   *[modifies liter]*

I. Between a numeral and a unit of measure:

5-inch	16-day
40-hour	12-foot
six-mile	three hundred-yard

J. As an equivilant of "up to and including" when used between numbers or dates:

Sept. 21-29	from 10-16 miles
6-8 cups	about 3-5 days
pages 212-218	pages 212-18

K. Between letters of a word to show spelling or construction:

She spells her last name T-o-m-p-k-i-n-s.

C-a-u-g-h-t and c-o-t are homonyms.

L. To represent deleted letters or illegible words in copy:

I'll be d---ed!" she exclaimed.

The mi---ng letters had faded from the page.

M. To suggest stuttering:

I d-don't know y-y-you v-very well.

III. DO NOT USE HYPHENS

A. With adverbs ending in "ly."

highly   tightly   slowly

B. In civil or military titles denoting a single office:

ambassador at large	notary public
major general	secretary general
sergeant at arms	under secretary

(1.) Use a hyphen for double titles.

secretary-treasurer   treasurer-manager

general manager-secretary

PARENTHESES   ( )

Parentheses are used in the same manner as commas and dashes to set off amplifying, explanatory, or digressive information contained in, or immediately following, a sentence. The choice of which of these three punctuation marks to use depends on the relationship of the information to the rest of the sentence. If the parenthetical material is closely intertwined with the rest of the sentence, use commas. If it is desired to forcefully emphasize the information, use dashes. When the parenthetical material is used as if it is a whispered aside to the reader, employ parentheses. Parentheses are most effective when used sparingly. Used too often, they can become tiresome and distracting.

I.   USE PARENTHESES

A. To enclose supplementary, parenthetic, or explanatory material which requires more highlighting than indicated by commas, and when the material does not change the meaning, or has only a slight bearing on the rest of the sentence:

It is difficult to imagine why any unexpected person would (or how any unexpected person could) have come around the calmly seated Elwell (whose chair, with its back to the wall, faced the fireplace), stood squarely in front of him and shot him between the eyes.*

Had he been old enough to serve in what, in those days, we all naively referred to as the Great War? (Oh, yes.)*

By the quaint but familiar device of moving that the salary of the First Lord of the Admiralty (Mr. Reginald McKenna) be reduced by one hundred pounds, the honorable member for Kingston (Mr. Cave) started the ball rolling.*

B. To enclose a quotation source or other matter when noted in text:

For Humphrey . . . is recognized among geneticists as a first-rate original scientist, whose work has been published by Johns Hopkins (*Working Dogs: An Attempt to Produce a Strain of German Shepherds Which combines Working Ability and Beauty of Conformation,* by Elliott Humphrey and Lucien Warner, with a foreword by Raymond Pearl, Baltimore, the Johns Hopkins Press, 1934), and a few years ago . . . .*

* All examples marked with an asterisk are from: Alexander Woollcott, *Long, Long Ago* (New York: Viking Press, 1943).

C. To enclose numbers or letters used to enumerate a series when the series is run into text:

It is not easy to think of any other American play with so good a chance of being acted a hundred years from now. Perhaps (1) *Our Town*, (2) *The Green Pastures*, (3) *The Wisdom Tooth*, or (4) *Heartbreak House*.*   *[Paraphrased from the original.]*

D. To enclose numbers confirming a number spelled out in the text:

This memorandum will serve to confirm our order of thirty-seven (37) dozen conference notebooks with our school seal engraved on the front.

Your expenses for the trip should not exceed five hundred dollars ($500.00).

E. To enclose question marks or exclamation points when you wish to emphasize doubt, irony, or amazement:

The doctor told Emily she would only (!) have to reduce her food intake to 1200 calories per day to lose two pounds a month.

They visited us September 16 (?), 1943.

F. To enclose reference directions:

The amortization table (see p. 70) clearly shows that the investment is sound.

The company based their defense on a section of the environmental laws (Article III) that allowed local storage of radioactive material pending final disposition.

II. FOR FORMAL PAPERS, USE BRACKETS AS SUBSTITUTE PARENTHESES WHEN THEY ARE USED INSIDE EXISTING PARENTHESES. FOR INFORMAL PAPERS, A SECOND SET (OR MORE) OF PARENTHESES MAY BE USED WITHIN PARENTHESES TO ENCLOSE MATERIAL

Formal

The vending machine sells a variety of foods (sandwiches, soft drinks, milk, fruit, [and sometimes canned soups]).

Informal

The cafeteria has hot food (hamburgers, hot dogs, soup (and once in a while, casserole dishes)).

III. PUNCTUATION USAGE WITH PARENTHESES

A. Material enclosed in parentheses within a sentence may contain commas, semicolons, and other appropriate internal punctuation marks as required, but it is not begun with a capital letter except in the case of formal names, titles, or personal pronouns requiring a capital, and is not ended with a period including when the material consists of a complete sentence:

[Oscar] Levant (who, by the way, makes a fleeting appearance in one of Dashiell Hammett's books, under the guise of Levi Oscant) could be heard muttering under his breath, "An evening with Gershwin is a Gershwin evening."*

I have since forgotten every experience except that we used to roar a song called "Lightly Row" at the top of our lungs, and that Miss Snooks (I am reasonably sure that was her name) once caught me in the ungallant act of thumbing my nose at a little girl . . . .*

B. Material enclosed in parentheses but not contained in a sentence begins with a capital letter and ends with a period, question mark, or exclamation point placed inside the parentheses:

To acknowledge these he stood, pen in hand, at the high schoolmaster's desk in his home on I Street. (He always held that the seated position encouraged verbosity.)*

C. When the material enclosed in parentheses is a question or an exclamation, the appropriate punctuation mark is used within the parentheses:

Although the honorable member for Leicester, Mr. Ramsay MacDonald, was so far out of key as to call the motion an attempt to blackmail the Treasury (cries of "Shame! Shame!"), the resulting debate went to the heart of the matter . . . .*

D. Punctuation marks belonging to the sentence containing the material enclosed in parentheses are placed outside the closing parentheses:

The new home was a penthouse in East Seventy-Second Street, New York City, a bachelor apartment of fourteen rooms (counting the trunk-room).*

E. No punctuation should be used in front of a beginning parenthesis unless it is being used to enclose a number or letter enumerating an item in a series that has been run into the text. Internal punctuation required for the sentence containing material enclosed by parentheses is usually placed after the closing parenthesis:

I could not completely respect any man unless, like Robert Louis Stevenson (or, for that matter, Jane Austen herself), he was just a little bit in love with Elizabeth Bennet of *Pride and Prejudice*.*

F. When material enclosed in parentheses requires more than one paragraph, start each paragraph with a parenthesis and place the closing parenthesis at the end of the last paragraph.

PERIOD .

The period is used primarily as a mark of terminal punctuation, indicating a complete stop at the end of a sentence. It is also employed in a wide range of secondary applications.

I. USE A PERIOD TO TERMINATE

A. Declarative sentences:

The certificate is hanging on the wall.

Helga's towel is still wet because she left it
wadded up on the beach after she went swimming.

(1.) Periods should always be placed within quotation marks.

Suzanne replied, "I believe educating students and controlling them are almost always mutually exclusive."

B. Indirect questions:

Lisa asked when we were coming home.

He wondered if they wanted automobile insurance, or a
life insurance policy.

C. Commands or polite requests:

Come quickly.

[Imperative sentence fragment.]

Will you please turn off the lights.

[A polite request, not a question.]

I expect to hear from you soon.

D. Sentence fragments:

When will you graduate? Next month.

How much money did you make last year? Not enough.

"What's new?"
"Plenty. Lost my job."
"Laid off?"
"Fired."
"What for?"
"Hitting the boss."

(1.) A sentence fragment is not a complete sentence with a subject and a predicate, but when a fragment expresses a complete thought, it should be punctuated as a complete sentence.

II. MISCELLANEOUS USES OF PERIODS

A. Use a period with some abbreviations and initials:

Mr. Albertson	M.D.
S. W. Wheeler Ave.	R. J. Wagner
Warren G. Harding	Yeates Co.
Tetco, Inc.	J. E. B. Stuart

[Personal initials are separated by a space.]

(1.) When a person becomes known, or is referred to, by his initials, no periods are used.

FDR   (Franklin Delano Roosevelt)

LBJ   (Lyndon Baines Johnson)

JFK   (John Fitzgerald Kennedy)

(2.) Some abbreviations, because they are recognized and used frequently, are written without periods.

PTA   (Parent-Teacher Association)

FBI   (Federal Bureau of Investigation)

UFO   (Unidentified Flying Object)

AFL-CIO   (American Federation of Labor-Congress of Industrial Organizations)

UPI   (United Press International)

(3.) Acronyms are pronounceable words formed by combining initial letters of other words, or the letters of the major parts of compound terms. Acronyms are almost always written without periods.

OPEC	(Organization of Petroleum Exporting Countries)
BASIC	(Beginners All-purpose Symbolic Instruction Code)
NATO	(North Atlantic Treaty Organization)
FORTRAN	(formula translation)
sonar	(sound navigation ranging)

(4.) An abbreviation at the end of a declarative sentence uses the final period of the abbreviation to end the sentence.

Myron is taking the train to Washington, D.C.

(5.) An abbreviation ending an exclamatory or interrogative sentence keeps the abbreviation period and adds a question mark or an exclamation point.

Will Myron take the train to Washington, D.C.?

It's 4:00 A.M.!

(6.) An abbreviation inside a sentence retains the abbreviation period, and is followed by any necessary punctuation.

He will leave tomorrow at 8:00 A.M.; I will leave tonight.

This is the meaning of D.V.M.: Doctor of Veterinary Medicine.

B. Use a period after numbers or letters in a vertical list or outline:

1. Orange
2. Blue
3. Mauve

A. Cotton
B. Wool
C. Linen

I. Holidays
  A. Christmas
    1. Church
    2. Trees
      a. Ornaments
II. Vacation Days
  B. Trips
    1. Beach
      a. Shells

(1.) If one or more of the items in a list are complete sentences, periods should follow each of the listed items.

A. Your prose should be clear.
B. Your prose should be succinct.
C. Your prose should be without affectation.

(2.) If the list is introduced by a sentence, a final period is used if the listed items are separated by commas or semicolons.

I was certain
  1. that Thomas did not own a gun;
  2. that Thomas had no motive for killing Fay;
  3. that Thomas had left the city before the murder.

(3.) Enumerating a list with letters or numbers is optional. The period is eliminated from the end of the list unless the items are separated by colons or commas.

The following kinds of tea are served regularly:

lapsang souchong
jasmine
mint
chamomile   *[No period at the end of the list.]*

C. Use the period as a decimal point:

$8.95   4.78 percent
6.8 meters $.10
22.25 sq. ft.   7.2753

D. Use a period to separate parts of literary works:

Hamlet II.iii.5   *[act, scene, line]*

Moby Dick XV.78   *[chapter, page]*

F. Use a period after a run-in sidehead:

Getting started. Read through the directions carefully, and then locate the tools you will need.

3. Vegetable-fruit group. Four or more servings of fruit and/or vegetables should be eaten daily.

III. DO NOT USE A PERIOD

A. After title lines denoting major parts of a text, or after column titles in a table.

B. After numbers used to indicate order or position:

1st, 2nd, 3rd, 4th, 60th

the 2nd Ohio Volunteer Infantry

C. After Roman numerals used to indicate order or position:

King Henry VIII   Pope John XXIII

D. After chemical symbols, though they are abbreviations:

Al (aluminum)   C (carbon)   NaCN (sodium cyanide)

QUESTION MARK   ?

The question mark is used to end a sentence that asks a direct question, indicate a series of questions within a sentence, and may be used as an editorial mark to express uncertainty.

I.   USE A QUESTION MARK

A. At the end of a sentence that asks a direct question:

Can you come here for dinner Thursday evening?

What is he doing in there?

Who will volunteer?

(1.) When a quoted sentence asks a question, the question mark goes inside the quotation marks. If the question does not apply to the quoted material, the question mark goes outside the quotation marks.

Emily asked, "Is he working now?"

When did she say, "I've come to sing, not to talk"?

(2.) When both the quoted sentence and the sentence it is contained in are questions, the question mark is placed inside the quotation marks.

Why was he shouting, "Who is at the door?"

(3.) The question mark is placed inside parentheses only if it is part of the parenthetical matter, and another mark of punctuation must be used to end the sentence (first example). If the question mark is not part of the parenthetical material, it goes outside the parentheses (second example).

Helmut toured the Robert Mondavi winery (or did he?).

What is your favorite kind of pie (I mean fruit pie, not cream pie)?

(4.) When both the sentence and the parenthetical material are questions, one question mark is used, and is placed outside the parentheses.

How will we ever explain the pigeons in the kitchen (and who would believe us)?

B. To indicate a question or a series of questions within a sentence:

What does she want from me? Mark wondered.

When will the war end? is the question of the day.

How do you like your steak? rare? medium? burned?

Who is your favorite? Nancy? Kathy? Liz?

Did you lose your violin? or was it stolen? or did you leave it in the car?

(1.) The first letter of questions within a sentence may be capitalized or not, at the writer's discretion, unless the questions begin with proper names, or other words that require capital letters.

(2.) When a parenthetical question falls in the middle of a sentence, the question mark goes inside the parentheses, or before the second dash.

I was at the library yesterday—have you been there lately?—and was amazed at the changes that have been made.

It was fortunate that Franklin drove by (wasn't he supposed to be with you?) and picked me up.

C. To indicate editorial doubt or uncertainty:

John Alden (1599?-1687) sailed on the "Mayflower" in 1620, and settled at the Plymouth colony.

The professor believed that both ginger(?) and cloves were used.

(1.) The question mark is usually enclosed in parentheses when used to express the writer's doubt. Authorities are mixed as to whether a space should be used between the parenthesis and the word or number that precedes it. We recommend no space.

II. DO NOT USE A QUESTION MARK

A. With indirect questions:

Bob wondered whether to buy a new mini van.

B. With polite requests disguised as questions:

May I have a copy of that bill.

[Does not require a response.]

QUOTATION MARKS   " "

Quotation marks are primarily used to enclose direct quotations—the exact words of a speaker or writer—in the text. Quotation marks also have other, conventional uses as a mark of punctuation: certain kinds of titles are enclosed in quotation marks; and quotation marks are used to call attention to terms or words that may be unfamiliar to the reader.

I.   USE QUOTATION MARKS

A. To enclose direct quotations in the text:

"How long will you be in Germany?" Peter asked.

Gary volunteered to answer questions about his "philosophy of the hungry"; no one in the audience responded.

Who shouted, "Everyone down on the floor"?

B. To call attention to words, letters, or numbers that the writer is defining, explaining, or using as special terms that may be unfamiliar to the reader. An underline may be used instead of quotation marks for this purpose. When typesetting, attention is usually attracted by setting the words, letters, or numbers in an italic typeface. The same style (quotation marks, underlining, or italic type) should be used consistently throughout the document:

"Cold type" is a term covering a number of nonmetallic typesetting methods.

A "prompt" is a message or a symbol that the system displays when it is ready for the next command.

These "slugs" of lead, each containing a line of text, are then assembled in a holding frame.

He is the only dog I ever knew who could pronounce the consonant "F."

C. To enclose certain titles:

You must read Stephen Crane's short story "The Blue Hotel."

"Annabel Lee" by Edgar Allan Poe.

They studied Chapter Two, "The German Revolution."

Television's "Hill Street Blues" has become a
success.

Cyndi Lauper sings "Girls Just Want To Have Fun."

The article in <u>Inc.</u> magazine was called "The Spirit
of Independence."

(1.) Titles of articles, chapters, short stories, essays, short
poems, TV and radio programs, songs, unpublished
dissertations and theses, and manuscripts in collections
are among those enclosed in quotation marks rather than
underlined (see underlining).

II.   PUNCTUATION USAGE WITH QUOTATION MARKS

A. An expression that introduces or explains a quotation is
followed by a comma. An expression that interrupts a quotation is set off by commas before and after it, unless a stronger
mark of punctuation is needed.

<u>Clifton exclaimed</u>, "I'll never leave!"

"We've just arrived in Germany," <u>remarked Clifton</u>,
"and I feel very much at home here."

B. Commas and periods always go inside the quotation marks.
Semicolons and colons always go outside the quotation marks.
A question mark or an exclamation point is placed inside the
quotation marks if it applies to the quoted material, otherwise
it goes outside the quotation marks.

C. Longer quotations that are not part of a conversation, and are
not set off from the text, are usually introduced by a colon:

Financial advisor Howard Ruff writes lucidly about gold contracts:
"Gold contracts have value under certain, carefully structured conditions. They will not come into general use, as government is not about
to hedge in the futures market against its obligations, nor is it about
to tie its fortunes to a fluctuating commodity."

—Howard Ruff, *Howard Ruff From A to Z*

D. A quotation within a quotation is enclosed in single quotation marks (' '):

Michael answered, "It was Thoreau who said, 'Nations are possessed with an insane ambition to perpetuate the memory of themselves by the amount of hammered stone they leave.' "

(1.) A question mark or an exclamation point goes inside the single quotation marks if it applies to the material inside the single quotation marks, but outside the single quotation marks if it applies to the entire question:

Tony said, "I went over to Buddy's dorm, and he asked, 'Where's the pizza?' "

Tony asked, "Why do they call it 'pizza for a lifetime'?"

E. If a quotation is more than one paragraph, quotation marks are put at the beginning of each paragraph, but at the end of only the last paragraph:

"Again the whippoorwill called. And on this second invitation another whippoorwill answered courteously. For nearly half an hour they carried on their spirited duet.

"My small raccoon sat listening intently, well aware of the exact direction from which each call was coming. Having had his afternoon nap, he was now ready to make a night of it."

—Sterling North, *Rascal*

F. When quoting poems or excerpts of poems that are set off from the text, no quotation marks are used:

The fog comes
on little cat feet.
It sits looking
over harbor and city
on silent haunches
and then moves on.

—Carl Sandburg, "Fog"

G. When quoting poetry in the text, quotation marks are put at the beginning and end of the quote, and lines of the poem are separated by virgules:

> "The fog comes / on little cat feet. / It sits
> looking / over harbor and city / on silent haunches /
> and then moves on."

H. Dialogue is always enclosed in quotation marks, and generally a separate paragraph is used for each change of speaker:

> "And they carry the women to the island," said Joe; "they don't kill the women."
>
> "No," assented Tom, "they don't kill the women—they're too noble. And the women's always beautiful, too."
>
> "And don't they wear the bulliest clothes! Oh, no! All gold and silver and di'monds," said Joe with enthusiasm.
>
> "Who?" said Huck.
>
> —Mark Twain, *The Adventures of Tom Sawyer*

III. DO NOT USE QUOTATION MARKS

A. With quotations set off from the text:

> Charley likes to get up early, and he likes me to get up early too. And why shouldn't he? Right after his breakfast he goes back to sleep. Over the years he has developed a number of innocent-appearing ways to get me up. He can shake himself and his collar loud enough to wake the dead. If that doesn't work he gets a sneezing fit. But perhaps his most irritating method is to sit quietly beside the bed and stare into my face with a sweet and forgiving look on his face; I come out of a deep sleep with the feeling of being looked at. But I have learned to keep my eyes tight shut. If I even blink he sneezes and stretches, and that night's sleep is over for me.
>
> —John Steinbeck, *Travels with Charley*

(1.) Usually any quotation longer than four lines is set off from the rest of the text as a block quotation. The entire passage is indented and single spaced. Setting the passage off from the rest of the text indicates to the reader that it is a quotation.

(2.) A quotation within a block quotation is enclosed in double quotation marks:

> It would be pleasant to be able to say of my travels with Charley, "I went out to find the truth about my country and I found it." And then it would be such a simple matter to set down my findings and lean back comfortably with a fine sense of having discovered truths and taught them to my readers.
>
> —John Steinbeck, *Travels with Charley*

B. With indirect quotations:

Kate Daniels, the senior editor, said that she expects to buy more material next year.

Craig answered no to all the questions except the last; he had received one traffic ticket.

(1.) Yes and no should not be enclosed in quotation marks except in dialogue and direct quotations.

C. With indirect questions:

Why is everyone crying, Morton wondered.

Then he asked if I would shut the door and take a seat with the other candidates.

SEMICOLON ;

The semicolon would be more accurately named if it were called a "semiperiod." It is used almost exclusively to join independent clauses or statements sharing a close relationship that would, except for that relationship, otherwise be written as separate sentences. The semicolon is also used as a substitute for commas to improve clarity in some complex sentence structures. The semicolon indicates a sharp break in continuity stronger than a comma, but just short of the full stop called for by a period.

I. **USE A SEMICOLON BETWEEN TWO PARTS OF A COMPOUND SENTENCE NOT SEPARATED BY A CONJUNCTION**

A. Between independent or coordinate clauses:

The population of West Linn is 12,386; in the past year the city has grown by 800.

She felt reluctant to go on the plane; he was excited by the trip.

B. Between separate statements too closely related in context to be written as separate sentences:

Yes; you were right.

No; they shipped only half.

Wait; I'll go with you.

C. Before conjunctive adverbs or other transitional expressions. Some common conjunctive adverbs are: *then, however, thus, hence, indeed, besides,* and *therefore.* Frequently used transitional expressions are: *for example, i.e., in addition, in fact, in the meantime, however,* and *on the other hand.*

He was proud of his achievement; however, it did not come without hard work.

She passed all of her finals; in addition, she earned the highest grade point average in her class.

D. Between contrasting statements:

It is true in peace; it is true in war.

The walls are light brown; the ceiling is cream-colored.

He eats ice cream; I eat spinach.

II. USE A SEMICOLON BETWEEN CLAUSES IN A COMPOUND SENTENCE, INCLUDING THOSE JOINED BY COORDINATING CONJUNCTIONS, WHEN ONE OR MORE OF THE CLAUSES CONTAINS COMMAS

A. When clauses in a compound sentence are not joined by a coordinating conjunction:

The committee was to consider wages, hours, and job descriptions; its decisions would be used by the administration as guidelines.

By agreement, the two groups would equally fund the project; it would be managed by a joint committee, with two delegates representing each group; a professional manager would be hired, and exercise an equal vote with the representatives.

B. When clauses in a compound sentence are joined by a coordinating conjunction. The eight most used coordinating conjunctions are *and*, *but*, *for*, *not*, *or*, *so*, *still*, and *yet*.

The girls, who were all good athletes, wanted to play on the football team; and they wanted an equal voice in the team discussions.

The swamp, two miles wide by four miles long, was just outside the town; yet no one, not even old Harry Townsend, had ever been to its center.

III. USE A SEMICOLON BETWEEN WORDS OR GROUPS OF WORDS IN A SERIES WHEN ONE OR MORE OF THE SERIES ELEMENTS CONTAINS COMMAS

The class included Jennifer, age 5; John, age 4; Marilyn, age 7; Doris, age 5; and Wendy, age 6.

They went to Denver, Colorado; San Francisco, California; and Tucson, Arizona.

IV. ALWAYS PLACE SEMICOLONS OUTSIDE OF QUOTATION MARKS OR PARENTHESES

Davy had read the chapter entitled "Soldier Boys"; he assumed the rest of the class had read it, too.

The new books are in (I didn't think they would ever come); will you pick one up for me if I give you the money?

V. DO NOT USE A SEMICOLON

A. Between an independent clause and a dependent clause:

They bought a new car which they used to drive to Michigan for her graduation.

[No semicolon after car.]

B. Before a modifying phrase beginning with a participle. Participles are adjectives derived from verbs. Present tense participle verbs end in "ing" (crying, running). Past tense participle verbs most often end in "ed," "t," "en," or "n" (ordered, went, held, taken, sewn).

The boat was long, <u>extending</u> a full 50 feet beyond the dock.

[A comma, not a semicolon after "long."]

The leaves are gone, <u>blown</u> from their branches by the high winds.

[A comma, not a semicolon after "gone."]

UNDERLINE

In typed or written manuscripts, a single line under the text is used to indicate titles, names, and foreign or individual words the writer wishes to emphasize, that would call for an italic typeface if set in type.

I.   UNDERLINE THE TITLES OF BOOKS, PERIODICALS, PAMPHLETS, PLAYS, MOVIES, LONG POEMS, MUSICAL COMPOSITIONS, WORKS OF ART, AND THE NAMES OF SHIPS, TRAINS, AIRCRAFT, AND SPACECRAFT WHEN USED IN TEXT

He spent three days of his vacation reading Steinbeck's <u>East of Eden</u>.

They discontinued publication of <u>Popular Computing</u> last month.

As far as I know, he has the last remaining copy of The Public Speakers Society's 1925 pamphlet, <u>One Hundred Short Introductory Remarks For Speakers</u>.

Last week we went to see the play <u>The Fantasticks</u> at the community college.

<u>Terms of Endearment</u> won the Academy Award for best picture in 1983.

The second week's assignment in English 101 is to read Milton's <u>Paradise Lost</u>.

The second opera of the season was <u>The Magic Flute</u> by Mozart.

Gainsborough's painting <u>Blue Boy</u> is displayed at the Huntington Library in San Marino, California.

I served on the Navy Destroyer USS <u>James E. Keyes</u>.

The Southern Pacific's train <u>El Capitan</u> begins its journey in Los Angeles.

The B-29 Superfortress <u>Enola Gay</u> dropped the world's first atomic bomb on Hiroshima.

The spaceshuttle <u>Columbia</u> made its first landings on the dry lake bed at Edwards Air Force Base in California.

(1.) In typset text, these same examples would be set in italic type instead of underlined.

(2.) Descriptive or attributed titles of art work are not underlined.

Titian's portrait of the Duchess of Urbino, because of its lovely nude subject (the body of the Duke's favorite playmate with the head of the elderly Duchess) is popularly known as The Venus of Urbino.

II. UNDERLINE FOREIGN WORDS OR PHRASES NOT COMMONLY USED IN THE ENGLISH LANGUAGE

Foreign expressions in common use are usually found in the body of collegiate dictionaries. Additional familiar foreign expressions are listed in the "Foreign Words and Phrases" section at the back of the dictionary.

In reply, he said, "audi alteram partem."
[hear the other side]

"What you have here is an enfant gate," he said.
[spoiled child]

They dined en famille.
[at home]

(1.) Quotations entirely in a foreign language are not underlined.

(2.) Foreign language titles preceding proper names are not underlined.

(3.) The proper names of persons, places, institutions, etc., written in a foreign language are not underlined.

III. UNDERLINE LETTERS, WORDS, OR NUMBERS WHEN THEY ARE USED IN A SENTENCE FOR OTHER THAN THEIR MEANING

The ph in physics is pronounced as if it
were an f.

The 33 on the sign looked like 88 from a distance.

(1.) These same letters, words, or numbers may be set off with quotation marks instead of underlining. In printed text, they are usually set with an italic typeface. The same style (underline, quotation marks, or italic type) should be used throughout the document.

IV. DO NOT UNDERLINE; INSTEAD ENCLOSE IN QUOTATION MARKS

A. The titles of short stories, essays, articles in periodicals, and manuscripts in collections.

B. The titles of chapters or other divisions of a book.

C. The titles of unpublished papers, theses, and dissertations.

(1.) For the purpose of this rule, published material will carry a publisher's imprint on the cover or title page; unpublished material will not.

D. Television and radio programs.

E. The titles of short poems and songs.

V. DO NOT UNDERLINE (AND DO NOT ENCLOSE IN QUOTATION MARKS)

A. The titles of series, or the names of editions.

B. The titles of diaries, manuscript collections, or memoranda.

C. The Bible, or titles of its books or parts, or other sacred texts.

D. Musical compositions identified by the musical form and the key, with or without an identifying number.

VIRGULE   /

A virgule (known also as a diagonal, slash bar, slant line, shilling mark, or solidus) is a mark of separation, and may be used to divide two alternatives, or to separate lines of poetry that have been run into the text. The virgule is also used in other, related ways as a mark of punctuation.

I. USE A VIRGULE

A. To separate choices or alternatives:

He may have candy and/or fruit.

Commonly used correlative conjunctions include either/or and neither/nor.

Are you taking French for a grade, or on the pass/fail system?

(1) When indicating alternatives, no spaces are used before or after the virgule.

B. To separate lines of poetry that have been run together and inserted into the text:

In "Gerontion," T.S. Eliot expressed familiar themes when he said, "Think now / She gives when our attention is distracted / And what she gives, gives with such supple confusions / That the giving famishes the craving. Gives too late / What's not believed in, or if still believed, / In memory only, reconsidered passion."

(1.) When marking the end of a line of poetry, use a space before and after the virgule.

C. To separate equations that are written in-line rather than set off from the text:

$E(X) = \dfrac{a+b}{2}$ *would be* $E(X) = a+b/2$

$\dfrac{39+48+54+67}{4} = 52$ *would be* $39+48+54+67/4 = 52$

(1.) The virgule may be used for writing all fractions, particularly those not found on the standard keyboard.

5/16   4/5   9/10   1 3/4

D. To indicate successive time periods:

winter 1985/86   1066/1067   fiscal year 1965/66

E. To designate month, day, and year (or day, month, and year) in informal writing:

10/1/81   for October 1, 1981   *[American style]*

1/10/81   for 1 October 1981   *[European style]*

F. As a symbol meaning "per" when used to indicate "for each":

35 gal/min   *[gallons per minute]*

50 bbl/day   *[barrels per day]*

12 boxes/carton   *[boxes per carton]*

A SELECTED GLOSSARY
OF TERMS USED IN
THE PUNCTUATION HANDBOOK

absolute phrase

a phrase within a sentence that adds meaning, but has no clear grammatical relationship; as when adding narrative or descriptive details:

He saluted the passing flag, his heart beating rapidly.

His task completed, George put away his tools.

acronym

a word formed from the initial letters or syllables of a compound title or word:

ZIP code (from Zone Improvement Plan code)

NASA (from National Aeronautics and Space Administration)

radar (from radio detecting and ranging)

adage

a short, pointed, frequently humorous statement used to illustrate a point.

adjective

a word that changes, limits, or otherwise defines or describes a noun or a pronoun.

adverb

a word that changes, limits, or otherwise defines a verb, an adjective, or another adverb.

adverbial clause

a group of words containing a subject and verb that does the work of an adverb, usually answering such questions as How? When? Where? Why? Under what circumstances?

Mary drove away because the people made her nervous.

If he doesn't watch out, he could get hurt.

appositive

a word or group of words that restates, amplifies, explains, or further identifies the noun or pronoun that precedes or follows it.

classification of words

in English, and in other languages, many words are classified into groups according to their use. Nouns, for example, serve primarily as the names of persons, places or things. Verbs express action, and adjectives are used to define or describe nouns and pronouns.

clause

a group of words with a subject and a verb, and used as part of a sentence. There are two kinds of clauses; independent and dependent.

An independent, or main clause, though a part of a sentence, is grammatically independent of it:

> George didn't know it yet, but his raise had
> been approved.

> He turned slowly around; he knew he couldn't
> draw his gun fast enough.

A dependent, or subordinate clause, depends on the rest of the sentence to complete its meaning:

> George, the man who fixed the furnace, didn't
> know it yet, but his raise had been approved.

> He turned slowly around, carefully raising his
> hands; he knew he couldn't draw his gun fast
> enough.

complement

a word or words that completes the meaning of the verb in a sentence, usually answering the question "who" or "what."

compound noun

words linked to form the name of a person, place, or thing, and used as a noun (see also compound phrase below).

father-in-law	ex-husband	government-in-exile
first-born	stay-at-home	John-boy

compound phrase

a descriptive phrase containing three or more words:

following John's example	with his knife
light as a feather	to be first in line

compound sentence

a sentence made up of two or more independent clauses, each of which expresses a complete thought, and can stand alone as a sentence. The clauses in a compound sentence are joined by a comma, a coordinating conjunction, or a semicolon.

compound word

two or more words written as one (baseball, bookstore); two separate words joined by a hyphen and expressing a thought more than, or different from, the words used individually (penny-wise, break-in); or a root word joined to a stressed prefix (ex-husband, pro-administration).

conjunctive adverb

an adverb used to join thoughts in a sentence. *Then, however, thus, hence, indeed, besides,* and *therefore* are some commonly used conjunctive adverbs.

conjunction

a linking word that ties together clauses, phrases, or words. *And, but, for, yet, or, nor, so,* and *yet* are examples of frequently used coordinating conjunctions.

consonant

any letter of the English alphabet except the vowels *a, e, i, o,* and *u.*

contraction

a word formed by shortening another word or combining two words and replacing missing sounds or letters with an apostrophe. *Can't* (from can not), *we're* (from we are), and *don't* (from do not) are examples of contractions.

coordinate clause

clauses of equal type and importance linked together in a sentence:

She felt reluctant to go on the plane;
she was excited by the trip.

coordinating conjunction

words used to connect words, phrases, clauses, and sentences. *And, but, for, or, nor, so,* and *yet* are the most frequently used coordinating conjunctions.

correlative conjunction

two conjunctive structures used to form a parallel construction:

George not only washed the dog, but also
cleaned out the garage.

They neither appreciated nor acknowledged
the gesture of recognition.

declarative sentence

a sentence that makes a statement (as opposed to a question).

dialogue

a conversation between two or more persons.

digressive statement

a statement not specifically associated with the subject of the sentence or text in which it appears.

gerund

a verb ending in "ing," and used as a noun:

Susan was driving last night.

homonym

words with the same pronunciation but different meanings.

imperative sentence

a sentence that gives a command or makes a request

<u>Open</u> the door.

Please <u>give</u> me the gun.

indefinite pronoun

a pronoun referring to one or more things or persons:

one	no one	some
all	few	something
everybody	other	any

independent clause

a group of words with a subject and a verb, and used as part of a sentence, but grammatically independent of it:

<u>George didn't know it yet</u>, but his raise had been approved.

He turned slowly around; <u>he knew he couldn't draw his gun fast enough</u>.

inflection

a change in the form of a word to indicate case (we—us), gender (hero—heroine), quantity (cat—cats), tense (is—was), person (I—we), and other distinctions used in the English language.

interpolation

an explanation or comment added by the author.

maxim

a general truth, fundamental principle, or rule of conduct.

modifier

a word or group of words that, when used with other words, makes their meaning more exact by restricting or limiting their definition.

nonrestrictive

a group of words with a subject and a verb, used as a part of a sentence, and dependent on the rest of the sentence to complete its meaning:

George, the man who fixed the furnace, didn't know it yet, but his raise had been approved.

He turned slowly around, carefully raising his hands; he knew he couldn't draw his gun fast enough.

noun

a word used as the name of a person, place, or thing.

object

that toward which the action in a sentence is directed:

John drove the car.

[Car is the object of drove, the verb.]

parallel word construction

elements in a sentence that are of equal importance and expressed in the same grammatical form:

Their good health was the result of frequent exercise, a high fibre diet, and adequate sleep.
[Parallel; each item is written in the same grammatical form.]

Their good health was the result of frequent exercise, a high fibre diet, and their habit of getting adequate sleep.
[Not parallel; the first two items are the same, but the third changes form and makes the sentence awkward.]

parenthetical

an amplifying or explanatory word, phrase, or clause inserted into a sentence, and usually set off by commas, dashes, or parentheses. An amplifying or explanatory sentence inserted into a text.

participle

an adjective derived from a verb. Present tense participle verbs end in "*ing*" (crying, running). Past tense participle verbs most often end in "*ed*," "*t*," "*en*," or "*n*" (ordered, went, held, taken, sewn).

past tense

action in the past.

personal pronoun

a pronoun denoting a person or persons:

I	he	she	you
it	we	they	

phrase

a group of words without subject or verb, used in a sentence to modify or explain its meaning.

predicate

the verb and associated words used in a sentence to complete a statement about the subject of the sentence:

John drove the car.

preposition

a word that connects a noun or pronoun with the main body of the sentence:

He stepped aboard the boat.

[Aboard is the preposition, boat, the noun, is the object of the preposition.]

prepositional phrase

a group of words that connect a noun or pronoun with the main body of the sentence:

They used the ladder in place of the ruined stairway.

["In place of" is the prepositional phrase, "stairway," the noun, is the object of the prepositional phrase.]

present tense

action in the present.

pronoun

a word used in place of a noun (he, she, it, they, etc.)

proper noun

a word or words naming a specific person, place or thing

George Stevens	Crystal Lake
Oregon	The Citadel

restrictive

a word or phrase that restricts the meaning of a sentence:

The man who spoke to them represented the Navy Department.

sentence

a group of words, usually including a subject and predicate, which makes a statement, or asks a question. A sentence may sometimes consist of one word, with subject or predicate implied in the context of its use or expression.

sentence fragment

an incomplete sentence, or a part of a sentence which has been separated and punctuated as a separate sentence.

sic

Latin for thus—used in text to indicate that a mistake was copied the same as it appeared in the original.

tense

the indication of time, past, present, or future.

transitional expression

an expression used to connect thoughts in a compound sentence. *In addition*, *in fact*, *i.e.*, *e.g.*, *in the mean time*, and *on the other hand*, are transitional expressions.

verb

a word or group of words used to express or assert something about a person, place or thing.

vocative

a word or expression indicating the person addressed:

Mother, I need you over here!

"Help me, Bobby, I'm slipping."

"You, on the ladder! Come down.

vowel

any of the letters *a*, *e*, *i*, *o*, or *u*.

INDEX